D1738836

Treatment of
the Severely Disturbed Adolescent

Treatment of the Severely Disturbed Adolescent

by Donald B. Rinsley, M.D.

NEW YORK • JASON ARONSON • LONDON

Contents

Foreword

Dr. Donald B. Rinsley is eminently suited to be the author of this book on the treatment of severely disturbed adolescents. His outstanding theoretical and clinical endeavors have long been devoted to adolescents, and to their treatment as viewed from a developmental and psychodynamic approach. The present work gains in thoroughness and usefulness by virtue of presenting a psychoanalytic object-relations understanding of troubled adolescents, their families, and their treatment. The clarity of thought that characterizes the writing makes it apparent that Dr. Rinsley is a creative theorist and clinician, as well as a uniquely gifted teacher.

Dr. Rinsley's treatment of seriously disturbed adolescent patients and their families reveals clearly the vital contributions that good early object relations make to normal ego development. The longitudinal defects in object relations that typify these adolescents, their failure to resolve infantile object-dependency through normal separation-individuation, and their consequent inability to achieve autonomy of the self become the foci for an intensive and carefuly articulated therapeutic program directed at structural ego defects and functional ego regression. This volume demonstrates, both theoretically and clinically, that the adolescent borderline patient has a full capacity for internalization once the abandonment depression has been worked through. Dr. Rinsley vividly illustrates how the borderline adolescent patient deals with whole-objects as if they were part-objects. He further demonstrates that the persistence of part-object relations, based on a reliance on splitting defenses, precludes the child's negotiation of the depressive position. There then ensues a failure to mourn; a persistence of that particular form of partially structured separation anxiety that Masterson has termed *abandonment depression*; and a consequent and ongoing vulnerability to real and fantasied separations and losses.

Utilizing well-recognized psychodynamic concepts in his approach to the theory and practice of residential treatment of adolescents, both borderline and psychotic, Dr. Rinsley proceeds from a consideration of resistance to an in-depth exploration and discussion of the use and application of the therapeutic milieu. Focusing on etiology of major adolescent psychopathology, he suggests correctives to be taken within the milieu, a process that he illustrates with a superb clinical example of the relation of theory to practice.

This book serves the difficult and immensely valuable function of presenting in operational terms Dr. Rinsley's work of some fifteen years in the area of residential treatment of the deeply disturbed adolescent, and thus allows us to conceptualize a combined developmental and object-relations point of view that offers new hope for successful outcome. Through the application of the principles of intensive psychotherapy within a hospital or residential setting, the psychopathology of developmental failure can give way to the achievement of separation-individuation.

The book is essential reading for anyone who hopes to broaden his own conceptual knowledge of, and therapeutic skill with, adolescent patients and their families.

J. Cotter Hirschberg, M.D.
William C. Menninger Distinguished
Professor of Psychiatry
Menninger School of Psychiatry

Preface

This book is on the treatment of the severely disturbed adolescent, in particular the adolescent who requires inpatient, residential, or hospital care. The theoretical formulations are based on psychoanalytic principles and countless hours spent in direct clinical work with patients and their families, as well as in the supervision of junior staff colleagues, residents in general psychiatry, Career Fellows in child psychiatry under the auspices of the Menninger School of Psychiatry, and other staff and trainee professionals and paraprofessionals who came to work in the Children's Section of Topeka State Hospital during my sixteen-year tenure there.

What follows reflects my thinking about, and point of view on, the treatment process with adolescents who suffer from major mental disorders, and with their families. It provides a basis for an in-depth understanding of the etiology, evolution, and nature of major adolescent psychopathology and of its course and natural history within the residential therapeutic context. With the exception of chapter 13, published here for the first time, the text comprises a series of papers which appeared in various books and journals between 1961 and 1975. In particular, the book reflects the progressive

progressive development and refinement of my diagnostic and therapeutic thinking as my clinical experience and grasp and application of psychodynamic principles proceeded apace, a fact which will be evident, for example, as the reader compares the diagnostic formulations in chapter 11 with those in chapter 12. A book so constructed must necessarily suffer from more than a modicum of repetitiousness, for which I offer the reader my apology. I am much less apologetic, however, for the fact that such a book provides its readers with as large a window into its author's more personal growth and development as into the complexities with which he has wrestled; the two can, after all, never really be separated.

The reader will be aware that some authorities differentiate *residential* from *inpatient* or *hospital* treatment, in part depending upon whether a given treatment facility is full-time or part-time and whether it operates in accordance with a "medical," "educational," "casework" or some other "model." In this book, these terms are used interchangeably.

Numerous colleagues have from time to time urged me to do a book about this work or to assemble my various writings into a single volume. I am very grateful to Dr. Jason Aronson for affording me the opportunity to do the latter and to my friend and colleague, Dr. Sherman C. Feinstein, for providing much of the initial impetus to gather the material together. A debt of gratitude is owed to Dr. Joseph D. Noshpitz, who organized and opened the Adolescent Unit of the Children's Section of the Topeka State Hospital in 1951 and 1952, and to his very able successors and my predecessors and teachers in the Unit, Drs. Antonio S. Fueyo and George P. Inge, III, who revealed to me a great deal about adolescents and residential treatment. To Dr. Karl A. Menninger goes acknowledgment for serving me as an ego ideal and inspiring me to pursue clinical research, and to my friend, colleague, and teacher, Dr. J. Cotter Hirschberg, for having been guide, counselor, and model child psychiatrist and psychoanalyst. To various of my coauthor colleagues in the Children's Section and elsewhere I express my deep appreciation. To my friend and colleague, Dr. James F. Masterson, I owe a signal debt of gratitude for his insightful, original thinking and writing concerning adolescence and adolescents and for the opportunities he has afforded me to work collaboratively with him.

Finally, others too numerous to mention but of no less significance have in various ways shared in and contributed to the work here presented. Most important have been those many professional and paraprofessional colleagues who served with me in the Children's Section and its Adolescent Unit over the years as we labored together to understand the seriously ill youngsters and disturbed families we were privileged to work with and guide toward regaining their mental health. It is to these colleagues that this book is gratefully dedicated.

Part I

Resistance
and the
Therapeutic Milieu

Verbal and Nonverbal Resistance

BY DONALD B. RINSLEY, M.D.
AND GEORGE P. INGE, III, M.D.

Psychiatrists increasingly are viewing the hospital milieu as a locus of all kinds of communications. This interest stems in part from the current surge of research and speculation in communication and information theory (Ruesch 1957, Ruesch and Bateson 1951, Spiegel 1959). Stanton and Schwartz (1954) described ways in which disturbed communication plays a role in events among personnel and patients. They believe that one of the most important functions of the ward psychiatrist is intuition, which implies the ability to understand the countless metaphorical communications transmitted within the milieu and to translate them into words and acts appropriate to the needs of all concerned. Similarly, Redl and Wineman (1951, 1952) described the problem of metaphorical communication between disturbed adolescents and members of an adult treatment team.

Chapter 1 represents an attempt to formulate some basic messages transmitted between the treatment staff and the patients in an intensive residential treatment service for adolescent patients. This study was undertaken in an effort to abstract a minimum family of messages consistent with meeting the psychological needs of the patients. This process leads immediately to such questions as the following: What needs seem continually to be expressed and reexpressed by the patients? How are these needs coded in metaphorical language and in (expressive) behavior? What are the needs inherent in the metaphors and how do members of the treatment team recognize, or decode, them? Finally, how can the treatment team transmit to the patients that the messages have been received and decoded, and how can such needs be met?

This approach does not differ significantly from efforts to understand what transpires in individual psychotherapy. However, team treatment of disturbed adolescents faces certain problems that seem particularly associated with the psychological difficulties presented by patients of this age group. Nevertheless, our goals are well recognized as an integral part of any dynamically and therapeutically oriented hospital milieu: to understand as much as possible of each patient's genetic-dynamic history, to apply this to efforts to understand each patient's needs both to resist and to utilize treatment and to assist the patient to recognize and deal effectively with each, and to do no harm. The last condition is of special importance in the milieu treatment of adolescent patients who suffer from severe disorganizing (psychotic) illness, in which those parts of the ego functioning effectively must be preserved and supported while new ways of living are being taught.

SOME DIFFICULTIES IN TREATING ADOLESCENT PATIENTS

One of the significant features of adolescent hospital patients, taken individually or as a group, is the peculiar dilemmas they pose for the adults who treat them. Thus, it is often said, "Adolescents are extremely difficult to work with." "Adolescents are exceptionally demanding." "Adolescents are so changeable, unpredictable, and destructive." What frustrates adults who deal even with "normal," nonhospitalized adolescents are their emotional lability and unpredictability, the protean nature of their defenses, their bipolar swings of mood and thinking, their proneness to act out, their querulousness, fluctuant hostility, and preoccupation with their bodies and sexual feelings.

The literature devoted to the psychotherapy of adolescent patients reveals a variety of treatment modes and modifications of technique that reflect the peculiar therapeutic problems encountered. For example, one reads that the therapist must reluctantly modify classical psychoanalytic technique; he must be ever prepared to be especially flexible; and he must know how to deal with an intense and variable transference. At times, one reads that psychotherapy and psychoanalysis of adolescents are particularly difficult of not "impossible" (Gitelson 1948, Spiegel 1951, Eissler 1958). Again, it is the relationship that really counts. Thus, psychotherapists have proposed ways of treating disturbed adolescents that have varied from abject authoritarianism to unrealistic overpermissiveness. It is not without basis, therefore, that Anna Freud (1946a, 1958) considers all adolescents, hospitalized or not, as suffering from a sort of "normal psychosis."

In mechanized Western culture, the period of adolescence proves unsettling for most people (Erikson 1950). After adolescence has passed, the mechanisms of repression and denial operate to efface the adult's memory of it. When some degree of stable identity has been achieved, the adult is wont to forget that period in his life when, caught in distracting psychophysical turmoils and groping with considerable mental pain for some sense of self, he saw himself stalled between his needs to regress to dependent childhood and simultaneously to progress to mature adulthood. Thus, one hears, "I simply can't understand adolescents!" or, "I'd resign if they ever assigned me to the adolescent ward."

On the other hand, many adults who work with adolescent patients often indicate a need to return to a kind of adolescence themselves. An ominous feature of this, especially for any consistent milieu program, lies in what Johnson (1949) and Johnson and Szurek (1952) first saw as the parents' need to stimulate their children to act out antisocially, to thereby obtain vicarious gratification for their own forbidden antisocialness, partly through identification with the alloplasticity of their children. Adolescent patients are prone to evoke strongly ambivalent attitudes from the adult team members, and unless these are consistently understood and dealt with, the therapeutic effort will founder.

THE ADOLESCENT POSITION

A basic problem facing any inpatient treatment team is the team's continuing need to *engage* the patient, or to get him into treatment, and to maintain that engagement. Thus, as soon as possible following the patient's admission to the hospital, enough of his initial resistances to hospitalization must be overcome so that he may begin to sense that the hospital structure can somehow help him. The term, *hospital structure,* refers to the multitude of team attitudes and physical features of the hospital that together can be molded to recognize and meet the patient's individual needs. Among other things, structure comprehends such elements as the attitudes of team members toward the patient's person and behavior, medications and other somatic therapeutic modalities, and the devices through which controls are applied — including privileges, restrictions, and seclusion rooms. In other words, structure is roughly equivalent with *consistent and dynamic milieu,* and each of the numerous tangible and intangible elements of that milieu represent modalities whereby treatment is addressed to the patient.

Those who deal with adolescent patients soon recognize that the latter come to the hospital with certain predictable *resistances,* which add special coloring to the initial problems of motivating them to engage with the treatment structure of the ward. These resistances can only be fully understood if the predicament of *most* adolescents in our culture is taken into account — namely, that of finding one's self mired between dependent childhood and mature adulthood. This predicament, in turn, shapes both the content of the metaphors in which the adolescent patient conveys his needs to the treatment team and the lability and intensity with which he conveys them. If we add to this the wide spectrum of labile defenses the adolescent oscillates among in his seemingly tireless efforts to resolve his predicament, we are indeed confronted with a difficult challenge.

What we call the *adolescent position* comprises a group of attitudes and behaviors that can be described as follows:

1. In most cases, the patient is unable to understand or to admit the real "why" of hospitalization, and that he could be mentally ill is denied with conviction. The word *sick* is abhorrent to adolescents, and they respond to it with hostility.

2. The treatment team is composed of *adults*. The adolescent may be convinced that adults cannot understand him.

3. Adolescents ill enough to be hospitalized have suffered serious prior traumas at the hands of adults, who most often have been their parents. A consistent feature of adolescent personality is the readiness with which the child infuses his early transference to treatment figures with a need to perceive them as parent figures.

4. Because of the mode in which he perceives adults, the adolescent strongly anticipates the recurrence of three major traumas: (1) The adult will retaliate punitively and "hurt" him; or (2) the adult will reject or abandon him; or (3) the adult will prove by his actions that he is not a perfect, blameless, omniscient, and omnipotent figure — qualities in which, despite protests to the contrary, the adolescent wants desperately to believe.[1]

5. To preclude the recurrence of these three traumas, the adolescent must attempt to neutralize efforts of the adult team members to engage him in a therapeutic process. He views the hospital structure as an adversary with which he is locked in combat and must defeat. The hospitalized adolescent's efforts to vanquish treatment structure, like his defenses in general, assume many forms.

THE ADOLESCENT'S EFFORTS
TO DEFEAT STRUCTURE

The essence of the adolescent patient's problem can be reduced to the question of how best to deal with adults. Among the devices used are the following:

Identification with the aggressor. Some adolescents usually attempt sporadically or consistently to cope with the structure by becoming "little adults." Thus, we observe the phenomena of "assistant doctor," "assistant nurse," "mother hen," and "big brother," wherein the child adequately guides, advises, or succors apparently less integrated peers and emerges with a pseudoadult facade. The meaning of such behavior is often clear enough; the child says, "I will maintain control by controlling others." Again, the child states, "You see how grown up I can be, and that ought to convince you that I do not need to be treated (to be changed)."

One thirteen-year-old girl persistently acted as a "big sister" for her peers on the ward—counseling, advising, and guiding them. When this defense was frequently interpreted to her, she reverted from a placid, pseudo-mature-appearing girl to one indulging in frequent temper outbursts, moderate assaultiveness to peers, and haughty insolence toward team members, leading to numerous short-lived episodes of seclusion. Concomitantly, she discussed some of her problems about boys with her ward physician, as well as her problems regarding whether she was really able to attract male peers and to be looked upon as a "woman" by them.

Leveling. Leveling is one of the more frequently used devices to defeat structure. The child tries to make a sibling or a peer of the various adult team members; often, this assumes the form of being "buddy-buddy" or a "pal." The message here is, "If I can prove that you are no better than I am, I can be assured that you have nothing to offer me, and I need not *engage.*

At several weekly ward meetings with his patients, a new ward physician was met with numerous requests to indulge in telling off-color jokes with the patients, who offered to trade him a joke for a joke.

A familiar variety of leveling comprises efforts by the patients to degrade, or *devalue,* the physician, nurse, or aid. Thus, one hears, "Oh, he can't help us—he's as crazy as we are." One severely negativistic, psychotic fourteen-year-old girl persistently and openly stated to the ward physician, "Oh, get out of here . . . you're crazy . . . you're stupid." This was met by persistent interpretations that she seemed desperately frightened that the adults who were offering her help in reality wanted to injure her. After some weeks, the verbal tirades decreased in frequency, and she became more comfortable and mildly friendly toward adults.

Several boys asked their ward physician, half seriously and half playfully, whether *he* had problems just as they were supposed to have. Implicit in this query resided not only a need to level the physician but also a need to fathom whether the physician was enough like them to permit a degree of identification with him. Both needs were simultaneously interpreted to them, evidently to their satisfaction at the moment.

Flirtatiousness and seductiveness. A more complex message is contained in the various kinds of flirtatious and seductive behavior adolescent patients often exhibit toward the adult team members. More often, it is the adolescent girls, who by usually transparent but occasionally rather subtle, pseudosophisticated maneuvers, try to vamp the male adults. Such behavior represents counterphobic sallies at dealing with sexual impulses that are frightening and bewildering to the child. Again, however, one often apprehends the message, "If you can be seduced by me, you are not perfect," or "I can frighten you," or "You will thereby prove that you want to use or manipulate me," hence, "I cannot trust you and you cannot help me." Girls generalize, "He's just like all men" (meaning, like my father, a seducer); boys generalize, "She's just like all women . . . easy makes . . . can't resist" (castration wishes and fears).

One attractive, fifteen-year-old girl with surface hysterical features initiated her relationship with a new ward physician via seductive glances and posturings at various times. She was given gentle but persistent interpretations amounting to, "I wonder why you have a need to make something sexual out of your contacts with me?" As she began to assimilate this, she began to talk more about her needs to control things and to display a behind-the-scenes-operator approach to her peers and various ward situations. Her behavior was, in turn, dealt with by interpretations and restrictions from privileges. In this case, a "sexual layer" covered more deeply situated power strivings; her erotic maneuverings served both to cover and to allow expression for an aggressive manipulativeness.

Oversubmissiveness. The occasional adolescent patient who shows what appears to be ready compliance and eagerness to use the structure has almost always discovered that one can beat the adults at their own game. If such maneuvers are not dealt with promptly, the child remains unchanged. Abetting such a state of affairs is the reluctance of various team members to disrupt such a welcome placidity, especially in view of the difficulties they often must face in dealing with the majority of more disruptive patients.

In such cases, it becomes of paramount importance to help the child with understanding the meaning of his compliance and the ways in which he uses it to scotomatize underlying problems as well as to lull team members. A danger, often discovered as one "moves in" on the child's compliance, is the child's first line of resistance, expressed by the message, "So, you want me to be bad, eh?" The obvious conclusion is, "Anyone who wants me to be bad cannot help me." We have noted this defense frequently in children with an obsessive-compulsive character pattern.[2]

One such child, a twelve-year-old "model" child, entered because of disturbing thoughts that various members of her family would be better off dead. On the ward, she was the epitome of the sweet, compliant little girl, beneath whose facade lurked mounting, inhibited, and potentially disruptive hostility. With persistent interpretations, in part directed at her compliance, she began to evolve into an overtly more manipulative girl with a near-genius for involving her peers in disruptive behavior without being discovered herself. Her behavior was, in turn, interpreted, and outlets for her aggression provided. As a result, her disturbing obsession with death abated considerably.

Subsequent therapeutic work on a more intensive level allowed her to become comfortable in expressing her anger at her parents for having "made me a 'goody-goody' girl" and her further anger that they "gave me a wrong steer," since despite her efforts to comply with their wishes, she had wound up in the hospital. Later work revealed death wishes directed at her mother for having failed to protect her against her oedipal wishes toward her father and for having used her as a "little adult," a substitute for the mother in the latter's relationship with the father.

Persistent avoidance. Some adolescent patients will make consistent efforts to absent themselves, in various ways, from contact with the structure. Such efforts vary from daydreaming and fantasy to self-seclusion and refusal to participate in any of the regular on-ward or off-ward activities. In our experience, persistent avoidance serves a regressive need; the message implied is often, "By absenting myself, I will provoke you to retaliate and to counterattack. This will prove that you hate me (and will hurt, damage, or kill me); hence, you cannot help me." Again, avoidance may imply that the child fears his own aggressive or destructive impulses. The manifestations of avoidance are legion, including such phenomena as convulsive seizures, negativism, and chronic sleepiness; the less common dissociative, fuguelike, and oneiroid states in part also express similar needs.

A special form of avoidance is persistent refusal to eat; unlike the common food fads and dieting of adolescents, persistent refusal to eat seems more common among recently admitted patients and should be taken as a sign of severe illness. Thus, the majority of patients who showed such behavior were either borderline or frankly schizophrenic children, some of whom were currently suffering from acute, circumscribed psychotic episodes, which later cleared.

A not infrequent phenomenon is either the patient's own requests for seclusion or behavior aimed to provoke it, whether conscious or not. Aside from the patient's need to provoke seclusion to prove that the adults will retaliate is the child's need to escape from the structure and to avoid showing himself, meaning his traditional defenses, to others. In some cases, such escape permits freer indulgence in fantasy of major degree or in frank hallucinations, which the child senses would disturb peers. One of the most untherapeutic uses of seclusion is to allow the patient to accomplish such avoidance; on closer examination, most cases of daily, long-term seclusion are usually found to be doing just that.[3]

Scapegoatism. Many adolescent patients are prone to denigrate or vilify some of their more seriously ill peers. In addition, a patient may manipulate a more disorganized peer into acting out or into engaging in unacceptable behavior, thus affording vicarious gratification to the instigator. One of the messages this kind of behavior transmits is, "If I can divert your attention and energies to other patients (to the *really* sick ones), you will not notice how sick *I* am." Persistent interpretations directed at this particular motive are often of great value in convincing the patient that one understands the problem and has not been deceived.

A not infrequent variety of scapegoatism, applied to one's self, is noted in abjectly silly, bizarre, or untoward actions of various kinds. Thus, one fourteen-year-old boy—diagnosed as psychoneurotic—gesticulated, walked, and often spoke in a childish, silly way. Several interpretations amounting to, "I guess you really *are* trying to convince me you are crazy," brought these inappropriate actions to a halt.

Outright rebelliousness. Adolescents who deal with their inner problems by acting out (alloplastic defenses) initiate numerous episodes of disorder on the ward. Tantrums, pugnacious negativism, assaultive and destructive outbursts, self-mutilations, wild, frenzied furores, and other techniques may be used chronically or in rapid sequence. One of the most consistent messages such behavior conveys is, "If my extreme outbursts can disorganize you, you cannot apply structure consistently; I will have distracted and hence defeated you."

Of course, interpretations directed at this message cannot be given during such episodes nor, for that matter, can any others that are verbal in nature. On the other hand, they may be given at opportune moments between outbursts, along with whatever other interpretations are appropriate for the particular child. During the outburst, gentle but firm physical control, medications, isolation of the patient from as many external stimuli as feasible, and even restraints to limbs offer the best interpretation that the adult team members do understand the child's needs.

Transference splitting. A favorite technique by which adolescent patients attempt to dilute the therapeutic structure is a process called *transference splitting.* Adult patients often use this technique to draw two or more members of the treatment team into a more intimately therapeutic relationship with the patient. In such cases, the patient will try to confide in the ward physician material more legitimately dealt with in his regularly scheduled psychotherapy hours, or material legitimately shared with the ward physician may be brought to the ward nurse, an aide, or another physician. Such maneuvers are often transparent but may frequently be so subtle as to obscure their essentially manipulative character.

Transference splitting finds a ready outlet in the confidences patients share with their wardmates — especially among adolescents, who proceed to take material to their peers rather than share it with any adult. Like any other effort to defeat structure, transference splitting is overdetermined; confidences so shared meet the child's needs for group belonging or for close peer relationships, but they also serve notice that the child is unable to share material with those best equipped to understand it and to assist the child in evaluating and dealing with it. It is amazing how important data regarding a patient's thinking, feelings or overt behavior will percolate through a ward population and yet be withheld from the ward physician or other members of the treatment team.

An important variety of transference splitting comprises the child's efforts to move the physician to grant visiting privileges with parents, close relatives, or former peers as quickly as possible following admission. Of course, the child feels abandoned or deserted by family and friends to a strange institution and strange custodians and is frightened by the unfamiliarity of his situation. However, an often neglected aspect of the child's need to quickly visit with relatives and former peers is precisely his efforts to keep transference spread thinly enough to preclude engaging with the hospital structure. Hence, we routinely interdict such visiting privileges for at least two weeks after admission and make efforts to ensure that they begin concomitant with or following the inception of casework with the parents. The child's perception that the hospital and his parents comprise a team dedicated to helping him, which are in basic agreement with each other, constitutes one of the most vital factors in the inception of his treatment. If the child can make this observation soon after admission, the time required for residential treatment is often shortened considerably.

An aspect of transference splitting that often brooks ominously for the integrity of the adult treatment team is the subtle ways in which the patient will often try to play off different adult team members against each other. Aides or nurses may evoke and find themselves dealing with material that should be shared with the ward physician, or the latter may find himself suppressing data the aides and nurses should have. The child is often exquisitely sensitive to interprofessional frictions, and to the problems inherent in a team composed of members of different levels of psychiatric competency; he will often manipulate the situation in order to prevent a consistent body of data from reaching at least one responsible focus. The message here is, "If I can spread myself thinly among you, none of you can gather enough data by which to plan and execute a consistent approach to me."

Finally, a prime focus for transference splitting among adolescents is found in the often intense if fleeting boy-girl relationships that develop among patients living on different wards of a mixed unit. In these often profoundly moving and disturbing relationships, important confidences are shared and needs for experiences are explored which may never come into possession of adult personnel. Dealing with these relationships requires the utmost in delicacy and tact, lest the participants either feel that the adults are rending them apart or that the adults are unable to put a stop to the relationships out of fear that they will alienate the children.

Somatization. Neurasthenic complaints and hypochondriacal self-preoccupation are common enough among nonhospitalized adolescents. It is therefore not surprising that some hospitalized adolescents regularly seek out members of the treatment team with a variety of physical complaints. Aside from the deeper symbolic significance of the symptoms, the child may bring such complaints in an effort to deflect attention from his or her psychological problems, as if to say, "If I can succeed in attracting and holding your attention to my body, you will pay less or no attention to the sick ways by which I try to cope with things."

Peer-age caricaturing. A not uncommon effort to vanquish treatment structure is observed in a complex of behavior we have chosen to call *peer-age caricaturing*; another way of phrasing this would be to say that the adolescent "out-typifies" himself. Such behavior involves acute or chronic efforts to exaggerate overtly the kinds of behavior traditionally associated by adults with members of the adolescent age group. Thus, the child may try to emulate the histrionic behavior of the various teenage television or movie idols; he or she may affect to appear inordinately if happily helter-skelter, emotionally labile, playfully seductive; he may moon over stories in magazines of the *True Confessions* type. In his efforts to appear overly typical, he says, "You see how typically teenage I am. My behavior is really appropriate if a bit exaggerated for my age, and I am not sick, hence, you do not need to treat me."

Clique formation. Hospitalized adolescents' efforts to neutralize the treatment structure find frequent expression in their well-known propensity for clique formation. Employed as a resistance, the small, exclusive subgroup is often used to preclude staff-patient interaction and communication, hence to divert transference away from staff and toward peers as well as to exert and express territorial needs; in some instances, the clique serves as a nidus for group rebellion or uproar-creation on the ward. Again, clique formation may find expression in the 1:1 or dyadic pairing of two wardmates, who proceed to "confide in" each other to the exclusion of communicating important material that might other-wise be shared with staff members.

"Craziness" and "pseudostupidity." Expressed in a variety of symptomatic actions, these devices aim to arrest or paralyze staff attention to the adolescent's disturbing inner experiences. They bear the message, "I am too crazy (stupid) to bother about, so why don't you leave me alone (*or* let me out of here)?" As in the case of *persistent avoidance,* the adolescent's exhibiting or flaunting of "odd," bizarre, "dumb," or "retarded" behavior may serve to pro-voke or ward off attack or assault, or to warn away and hence protect staff from the adolescent's self-perceived "dangerousness."

"Intellectual" pursuits. These include literary, graphic artistic, and scientific pursuits and projects in which the adolescent attempts to engage on his own, or together with one or more ward-mates, essentially apart from staff involvement. Often such pur-suits are basically autistic in nature, and their content can reveal a great deal concerning the adolescent's inner experiences.

> An intellectually, superior, paranoid fourteen-year-old boy had requested quadrille-ruled graph paper on which to draw "blueprints" of deep-space vehicles, in which he would have indulged for hours on end had he been permitted. Instead his drawing was directed to his assigned OT class, where the occupational therapist worked with him on both the overt content and the interpretive significance of his drawings; the latter had to do with the boy's extensive autistic pseudo-community which centered on his self-concept as a deep space dweller on distant planets. [Ekstein 1966]

Elopement. In one sense, actual elopement from the hospital constitutes the child's most drastic method of neutralizing the treatment structure. Running away from home is a common symp-tom in many of our patients' prior histories and often served as one of the reasons for hospitalization referral. In fact, running away tended to occur when the supervising adults showed the child that they were either unable to grasp or meet the child's needs; the elopement itself often followed in the wake of progressively intolerable aggressive needs which, for one reason or another, the child could not express openly toward appropriate or displaced objects. Oftentimes, the child eloped to solve the problem of whether the hospital or the parents "really love me the most"; that is, which would exert the greater effort to hold onto him and to help him despite himself. Again, elopement often served to prove to the child that he or she could "make a go of it alone" and was really not dependent upon the team and parent substitutes.

Elopement from the hospital, as from the child's parental or other home, occurs in a setting in which one or more of the patient's basic messages is either not apprehended or not acted upon by members of the treatment team. In many instances, the elopement provides a means by which burgeoning aggressive and erotic impulses could gain access to motility; having thus dissipated them, the child would return to the hospital, voluntarily or not, and would be either contrite and guilt-ridden or boastful and haughty over the success of the extramural adventure.

BEHAVIOR OF ADOLESCENTS AS UNDERSTOOD THROUGH THEIR BASIC METAPHORS

Our central thesis is that despite the variety of verbal and expressive-motor vehicles by which the child transmits his basic metaphorical messages to the adult team members, the variety of such messages is exceedingly small. Without attempting a detailed, dynamic analysis of the origins or the multifold symbolic meanings each basic message comprises, we may list and briefly discuss each as follows:

"I am bad." It is safe to say that we have never observed a hospitalized adolescent who sooner or later and in various ways did not communicate his feelings that he was "bad." The "badness" is a function of the hostile stringencies of a punitive albeit inconsistent superego and implies guilt; it further implies a perception of one's potential or actual transgressions and implies a depressive position in which the "bad object" is incorporated into the ego—the "double introjection" of Rado (1928). Thus, depression among

these patients is part of a function of this self-view. As a corollary, much of the adolescent's alloplasticity represents an effort to prove to the punitively perceived adults and to the superego that he is indeed as "bad" as they believe he is, and he must show them.

To the adolescent, "I am bad" has many different meanings. Thus, it may mean "I feel bad (depressed; hopeless; 'no good')," "I have hurt others (or, my parents)," "I am responsible for my parents' divorce (or for my mother's, father's, siblings' death)," "I can hurt (kill, injure) you (adults)," or "I can destroy you (property)." As noted, an especially important aspect of the "I am bad" message concerns the child's fancied or actual perceptions of the adult team members' wishes that he act out. The team members' wishes become potent stimuli and reinforce the child's chronic belief that acting out of control is really what the adults, or parents, have always desired of him anyway.

Thus, the meaning of much of the observed breakdown of the child's inner controls becomes clear enough. In doing what he senses the adult wants him to do, he identifies himself with the adult's "bad self."[4]

"I am about to lose control." When the adolescent perceives an imminent breakdown of his devices to hold aggressive or erotic drives in check, he becomes anxious. If the treatment team fails to perceive and then act on his plight, various kinds of panic will often ensue. Difficulties in inhibiting fresh instinctual charges of unneutralized aggression and eroticism constitute one of the major problems of hospitalized adolescents, and the failure of the treatment structure to respond to the child's metaphor that transmits a threatening loss of control abets the progress of the breakdown.

Thus, a fourteen-year-old girl signaled loss of control at least twenty-four hours prior to an outburst by complaining that "nobody can do me any good." Another preceded panicky rage attacks on furniture and peers by showing increasingly erotically seductive behavior toward male team members. A third girl signaled by open masturbation. A thirteen-year-old boy signaled that he was about to attack and severely beat a peer by playfully slapping adult team members on the back repeatedly during the week prior to his assault on the peer.

"I am afraid you will abandon me." The fear of abandonment is perhaps basic to all the other fears expressed by the child and is usually associated with other fears and messages that amount to the same thing. Thus, the child may express in metaphor or directly—especially in the case of psychotic children—to the adult team members such messages as "I am afraid you will hurt me." In such instances, fear of injury (castration), seduction, retaliation, or one's own potential destructiveness symbolize fear of abandonment and masquerade more basic fears that the adult will allow the child to starve and perish. The struggles of adolescents for a stable self-identity partly represent and are somewhat dependent on the depth of their psychopathology and struggles against the loss of boundaries. Thus, some authors conceptualize adolescence as a struggle against disintegration. For example, the fear of abandonment or death may express itself in a fear that the adult will not understand the child.

Although our formulation of the child's fear of abandonment may seem reductionistic, we prefer, for the purposes of this discussion, to state it as follows:

Fear of "lack of understanding" by the adult.
Fear of retaliation by the adult.
Fear of lack of control by the adult.
Fear that the adult will condone "being bad."
Fear of one's own instinctual demands.
Fear of one's dependency, which places the child in the vulnerable position of helplessness if abandoned.

CONCLUSION

Our efforts to understand the metaphorical messages of hospitalized adolescents have led us to perceive their struggles as the inevitable conflict of generations between them and the adult figures who represent and articulate treatment structure. On the one hand, the child tries to defeat structure; but on the other hand, he is terrified lest he succeed. Many behavioral incidents on an adolescent ward can be understood if we remember that the behavior itself often results either from the child's perception of his imminent success in defeating structure or of his having already defeated it.

As we see it, then, effective treatment comprises an adequate recognition of the child's efforts to defeat structure and appropriate ways to convey to the child that recognition has occurred. Just as the child expresses his needs in metaphor, the adult team feeds recognition of the needs back to him in metaphor. Operationally defined, the feedback from the adults comprises those myriad efforts by which structure is built and maintained. Thus, an injection of ataraxic medication, restriction from a recreational activity, a verbal interpretation, or a period of enforced seclusion constitute the feedback metaphor the child needs to perceive. By intricate communicative processes not fully understood, this structural, metaphoric feedback helps the child to inhibit and neutralize unsublimated aggressive and erotic impulses, thereby freeing energy to enable growth. The essence of treatment structure is, of course, consistency; and the degree to which the adult team members can agree on how to use structural metaphor in each individual case determines the degree to which they help the child to inhibit and neutralize impulses that constitute one of the foundations of his need to be hospitalized.

Notes

1. The persistence of the wish to find the adult, or parent, figures perfect and all-powerful, albeit ambivalently held, accounts for the well-known and often heroic efforts made by adolescents to *devalue* these figures. This phenomenon is, in turn, a function of their needs both to remain dependent upon and simultaneously to break free from adult controls. The problem of the child's ego ideal is especially important in the case of adolescents with antisocial character problems and those who show delinquency. See Johnson and Szurek (1952).

2. Buried within these messages lie several of the adolescent patient's major fears, such as, "You really want to rob me of my self-determination, and to make a conformist out of me." Again, "None of my ideas are any good, and you really want me to think just as you do." In our experience, handling these basic messages is best accomplished in individual psychotherapy and can usually be undertaken only after a significant relationship has developed between patient and therapist, generally only after many months of therapeutic work.

3. Often the need to provoke retaliation (aggression, counteraggression) subserves the need to be loved. Thus, "If you punish me, you must love me." It also subserves needs to be injured, violated, or attacked — which are, of course, sadomasochistic.

4. Regarding this identification, the acting out (1) implies that the child has incorporated the "bad self" of the adult; (2) may express the child's need to destroy the incorporated "bad self" by displacing aggression onto substitute objects; and (3) may express the need, therefore, to destroy part of the child's own self, either via displacement or through evoked punitive retribution from others. The original incorporation involved a parent figure at a stage before the child could make any kind of good-bad judgment and when the parent figure was perceived as a perfect, omniscient, or omnipotent object.

2

Parental Resistances

BY DONALD B. RINSLEY, M.D.
AND DONALD D. HALL, M.S.W.

In chapter 1, the behavior of adolescent psychiatric hospital patients was described in terms of the child's need to view hospital treatment structure as an adversary with whom he or she is locked in combat. Fourteen devices were listed as means by which patients consciously or otherwise seek to defeat the efforts of the treatment team to understand them and to help them accept the hospital as an ally in their struggle to find themselves and grow psychologically. These devices include both verbal and nonverbal behavior expressing resistance to the treatment milieu and comprise what can best be considered *resistance metaphors.* As an outgrowth of these considerations, we have postulated the following:

1. Resistance metaphors comprise much of the verbal and nonverbal behavior of adolescent patients during the initial phase of hospitalization, which is termed the *resistance phase.*

2. These resistance metaphors represent transference paradigms whereby patients repeat the varied maneuvers from their past that they employed to deal with conflicts surrounding dependence-independence in relation to parents or parental surrogates.

3. The basic task of the treatment team during the resistance phase of hospitalization comprises the recognition of the *basic*

messages conveyed by the resistance metaphors and their interpretation, by verbal and nonverbal means, to the patient.

4. When the patient has worked through his resistance metaphors, in part by means of these interpretations, he has completed one-half of the work necessary before he can come to accept the hospital's efforts to be of help to him, and hence be ready to enter the second or *definitive treatment* phase.

In chapter 2, the "other half" of the working through that is necessary for the patient's entrance into the definitive treatment phase of hospitalization is examined. This other half involves the role of the patient's parents or parental surrogates as these begin to sense, deal with, and work through their own feelings about their child's hospitalization (Peck, Rabinovitch, and Cramer 1949). Although much of what follows will be seen to apply as well to preadolescent children, the material here presented is derived from a two-and-a-half-year intensive study of the metaphorical communications among patients, parents or parental surrogates, and members of the treatment staff of an inpatient unit devoted to the treatment of psychiatrically ill adolescents.

ROLE OF PARENT FIGURES IN THE HOSPITAL COURSE OF ADOLESCENTS

The hospitalization of any individual who suffers from psychiatric disorder implies that that individual can no longer manage himself amid the manifold stresses of daily living. Among children, including adolescents, hospitalization means that, in most instances, either the parents or legal guardians, the community, or both have found themselves unable to meet the child's needs and hence have appealed to the inpatient facility for help. For both patient and parents, such a situation both leads to and results from deep-seated feelings of failure, frustration, anger, and guilt. In the patient's case, these and other related feelings are projected onto the treatment structure of the hospital and the ward; in the parents' case, they are projected onto the caseworker; in both cases, they are concomitant, so that the ward personnel find themselves dealing with verbal-behavioral metaphors having to do with the patient's feelings about hospitalization that are basically similar to metaphors emanating from the parents in the casework process (Shugart 1957, Linn 1959, p. 1834; Maxwell 1950).

As already noted, a very great part of the adolescent's early behavior in the hospital expresses metaphors that have to do with resistance to the treatment structure. From these metaphors arise similar metaphors that express the parents' resistance both to the fact of their child's hospitalization and to the incursions that they fantasize casework treatment will make into their own life adjustments.[1] Hence, before the patient can enter definitive treatment, the parents must have come to grips with and to a significant degree worked through their own resistances to the meaning and implications of their child's hospitalization. This, then, comprises the *other half* of the work necessary before the patient will submit to the hospital's therapeutic efforts, will begin to deal with his own resistances to treatment, and hence will begin to change (Hamilton 1950, pp. 275–315).

PARENTS' EFFORTS TO DEFEAT STRUCTURE

The efforts of parents and parental surrogates to defeat the structure of the social casework process, like the efforts of the adolescent to vanquish the hospital's therapeutic milieu, comprise a variety of resistance metaphors. Among the aims of the parents' efforts to defeat structure are the following: to deflect the caseworker's attention away from the parents' unhealthy interactions with the child and to preclude any significant degree of emotional involvement with the hospital, of which the casework process is viewed as an integral part. Although the variety and subtlety of these metaphors vary widely from parent to parent and from time to time for any given parent or parental pair, we have noted that the following metaphorical communications appear relatively early and tend to recur frequently in parents' interactions with the caseworker (Cohen, Charny, and Lembke 1960, Mandelbaum 1959).

"I am afraid to trust you with my child because you will see that I am a failure as a parent." Parents' concern that the hospital caseworker will view them as parental failures represents one of the earliest metaphors expressed in casework. In addition to the more conscious concern with inability to "bring up the child right" or to "provide good examples for the child," this metaphor often conveys more profound preconscious and unconscious preoccupations with self-concept, ego ideal, and conflicts centering on the genital-erotic sphere. On these levels, parental failure also implies concern over one's role as a sexual object. Hence the implications, "I am a failure as a sexual object" and, therefore, "I am a breeder of monsters."

More overtly, these messages usually appear as statements of how difficult were the mother's pregnancy and labor with the child (unconscious rejection of the phallus, the baby, and the feminine role by the mother); or, the opposite may be expressed, which implies a denial of these concerns. Again, parents may attempt to ascribe the child's psychological problems to the usual gamut of childhood accidents, especially head injuries, or to the sequelae of infectious exanthemata, deliria, and febrile or nonfebrile seizures. Or, the parents may attribute the child's difficulties to "justifiable neglect": "I (my husband) didn't pay enough attention to him because I (he) had to go to work," "because the other children took too much time," or "because I was sick so much." Thus, parents will attempt to deny their anxiety over having spawned and nurtured defective, damaged, or monstrous offspring, hence to ward off such judgments of them by the caseworker (Shugart 1957, Klineberg 1954, p. 16).

A particularly subtle way in which mothers of hospitalized adolescents seek to deal with their anxiety as monster breeders lies in *erotic transference,* including various seductive verbal and nonverbal maneuvers aimed at reassuring themselves that the male caseworker finds them sexually attractive, a defense not rarely used by fathers with female caseworkers as well. A rather frequent maneuver devoted to the same end is the parent's efforts to impress or regale the caseworker with his or her business, professional, intellectual, general housewifely competence, or such attributes as physical strength, athletic ability, and the like. Hence, the message becomes, "If I can impress you with my genuine abilities or accomplishments, you will not think so harshly of my failure as a parent."

"You will allow my child to express his 'badness' which in turn will expose my 'badness.'" Based upon a regressive identification with the child, this metaphor expresses the parents' anxiety that the identification will be exposed (Cohen, Charny, and Lembke 1961). In particular, the "badness" includes a welter of aggressive and erotic impulses that parents cannot accept in themselves, which they cannot consciously abide in their child but which they may have long stimulated the child to act out in their stead (Johnson 1949). It is a commonplace that parents express to the caseworker their fears that the child will become delinquent, "crazy," or physically abusive or destructive, or will act out sexually as a result of associating in the hospital with other disturbed adolescents and will be contaminated by peers already in residence on the ward. Hence, they readily project their own disowned needs onto the hospital, its personnel, and the caseworker.

Parents convey this metaphor in a variety of concerns about the hospital's potential "laxity": thus, they inquire whether their child will be permitted to curse and swear on the ward, whether he will be allowed smoking privileges, whether he may attend church services, etc.

Another device parents often use in this respect is to conceive of the hospital as some sort of school or training center that will teach the child the lessons he needs to behave properly and to learn skills. The implication of such a conception is, of course, denial of the hospital as a psychiatric treatment facility and hence denial that the child is "sick" and therefore "bad."

"You will punish me for my unacceptable wishes toward my child." Parents' fear of being upbraided, admonished, reviled, or punished by the caseworker often centers on their concern that the latter will uncover their unacceptable, guilt-ridden wishes toward the child. The lonely parent may attempt to make a sibling of the

child, thereby relinquishing controls over him and bewildering him; the parent may harbor erotic wishes toward the child directed at using the latter as a genital sexual object; or the parent may be displacing unacceptable aggressive and erotic impulses onto the child, and encourage him to act these out. Again, the parents may attempt to regress to and maintain a dependent relationship with the child, adultomorphize the child by reversing the parent-child relationship in an effort to obtain oral-narcissistic supplies from the child (Spitz and Wolf 1946). Whatever the specific universe of wishes may be, the parent expects punishment, hence rejection from the "knowing" caseworker.

In some cases, the parent will try to ward off anxiety over unacceptable wishes toward the child through counterphobic maneuvers which render the wishes almost too obvious to the caseworker. Thus, the mother of a seriously delinquent fourteen-year-old girl related nonchalantly how she and her daughter would often dress up as sisters, hang around a local bowling alley, and vie with each other for the attention of teenage boys.

Another metaphorical device for warding off detection and punishment of unacceptable wishes toward the child is used by parents who never seem able to tell the caseworker about themselves, as if to say, "If you know nothing about me, you cannot know about my unacceptable wishes toward my child."

Another warding-off maneuver parents sometimes use may be seen in their efforts to "level" the caseworker (and the hospital) by attempting to convey the impression that they are otherwise learned or knowledgeable in the matter of child-rearing. Thus, "We know as much as you do about taking care of children — let's discuss things as equals." This "leveling" maneuver also serves to deny parents' fear of being viewed as failures.

"You will carry out my unacceptable wishes toward my child." As noted before, parents often fear that their unacceptable aggressive and erotic impulses toward their child will be exposed in

casework. One defense against this becomes, therefore, a projection of the disowned impulses onto the hospital, its personnel, and the caseworker. One of the most important of these disowned impulses toward the child comprises the parents' need to punish and exact retribution from the child, to "pay back" the child for his delinquent or disorganized behavior that has visited so much pain and suffering on the parents. Soon after admission to the hospital, many adolescents utilize letters to and visits with parents to complain that the hospital treats them cruelly or brutally, that the ward is a chamber of horrors, that all manner of intrusions and indignities are visited on them by peers and by ward personnel, that they are "learning bad habits," or that they are exposed to unmentionable sexual and hostile performances by their associates. Such communications from the child readily induce guilty feelings in the parents, who proceed to respond in various ways. This guilt often assumes the form of overwhelming solicitousness toward the child, leading to efforts to placate the child via endless gifts, clothes, and items of food or candy. It may even extend, if allowed, to bringing gifts to the child's wardmates. In some instances, parents will earnestly try to meddle in the conduct of the child's ward affairs.

In addition to bringing numerous gifts of toiletries and food items to the child, the mother of a psychotic fifteen-year-old girl insisted that the patient be given their family Bible to read each day and angrily denounced the hospital as an atheistic prison with a "Godless" environment.

Some parents may bring sharp objects as gifts for the child or glass items easily filched by severely disturbed patients with which to cut or injure themselves, as if to say, *"Go ahead and hurt yourself."* Some parents bring gifts of cosmetics, including lipsticks, mascara, perfumes, and the like, with the implication being, *"Go ahead and be sexy"*; one psychotic mother of a severely disturbed boy sent him an unexpended thirty-two-caliber bullet through the mails. Another sent her son a cake, concealed within which was the proverbial file. Thus, the nature of the specific gift item has important communicative implications.

In some instances, parents will covertly or directly express their fear that the hospital will actually physically harm, even brutalize the child, implying that, "Now that you have him, you will hurt (or kill) him." Such an implication reflects their own inadmissable wishes (Peck, Rabinovitch, and Cramer 1949).

"You will take my child away, and that would destroy me." Basic to all the foregoing metaphors is the message that separation from the child means destruction for the parent, the child, or both. This fear may be expressed openly and directly by psychotic parents, who perceive themselves as fused or in symbiotic relation with the child, and in various unsubtle ways by infantile-narcissistic parents for whom separation from the child implies rejection, loneliness, stimulus- and affect-hunger, and damage to their identity. For these parents, hospitalization of the child is a real calamity, irrespective of the suffering the child has brought them. Inherent in this metaphor lies the message, "I need my child as he is; he must never change; he must never grow up and leave me" (Ribble 1943). There are a number of variations on the major theme of the parent's dread of separation from the child.

"Since my child and I are one and the same object, I cannot admit that the child is sick because I should have to see myself as sick also." Thus, parents' inability to acknowledge that their child is psychiatrically ill may bespeak regressive identification with the child. Expressed in a huge variety of ways both to the child and to the caseworker, the message admonishes the child to keep aloof from involvement with the treatment structure and thereby precludes the child's engagement with the hospital; thus, "If my child changes, I shall have to change. I am terrified of change because to change means to be destroyed."

"I cannot talk about my child without talking about myself." This message is implied in the almost total inability of some parents to discuss their relations with the child without displacing the casework process onto themselves and to their own problems. In some cases, the caseworker finds himself or herself in a seemingly never-ending battle to keep the parent from converting casework into psychotherapy with the parent to the exclusion of consideration of the child. Sometimes this message expresses the angry

feelings of a frustrated, depressed, oral-dependent parent, who implies, "You are giving my child all he needs, and I demand that you do the same for me. You must admit me, take care of me, and feed me too."

"I will keep showing you how crazy I am so you cannot 'get to' me and change me; hence, you will fail also to change my child." One of the functions of regressive, disorganized, or psychotic symptoms and behavior is to ward off, to confuse others who the individual fears would attempt to change (damage, kill) him. Thus, the parent with these symptoms both resists change in himself and attempts, magically, to influence the child likewise.

METAPHORS DEALING WITH FAMILY EQUILIBRIUM

Although every resistance metaphor the parent presents in casework concerns the parent's relationship with the child, there frequently occur metaphorical communications that allow the caseworker additional insight into the ways in which both parent and child interact within the family setting (Ackerman 1958, pp. 159–187; Mahler and Rabinovitch 1956). Some of these metaphors include the following:

"My child is my instrument of control over my spouse and you want to take it away from me." The variety of marital conflicts in which one or both parents use the child as a shield, club, barrier, or communication channel is legion, and hospitalization of the child may deprive parents of the major device by which they are able to contend with or communicate with each other. Thus, the child's illness is embedded in the "family neurosis" or "family psychosis," irrespective of how the situation arose. The parent who seeks use of the child as a sexual object thereby expresses his or her inability to use the spouse legitimately in this way, or adultomorphization of the child and use of the child as a dependency object signify inability to obtain narcissistic gratification from the spouse.[2] Again, a parent may imply to the spouse, "Your child is a failure (stupid, crazy, delinquent) because you are a

failure to me." This message is often expressed by a parent when he or she discusses the spouse's "poor family background" or hints or implies that the spouse is derived from poor or hereditarily tainted stock, "Look at his family. What else could I expect!" In many such cases, the parent will stimulate the child to act out aggressive, retaliatory, or frustrated sexual impulses that the parent harbors toward the spouse in order to draw the spouse's attention to them in one's self or to direct the spouse's attention away from them and onto the child's difficulties. The more basic message here often is, "My spouse neglects or mistreats me, and my child's problems represent my way of getting even."

Again, the casework transference may reveal the parent's efforts to use the child to manipulate the caseworker just as the parent used the child to manipulate the spouse. Thus, such statements or implications as, "My child hates (neglects, hurts, loves; makes too many demands on) me," may impute similar needs to the caseworker.

A particularly direct use of this metaphor could be discerned in the remark of the mother of a delinquent boy to a male caseworker, "What are you going to do about Ray. After all, he's a man just like you!"

"You will recognize how I compete with my child and will terminate the competition." In many cases, one or both parents maintain active if covert competition with the child for a variety of reasons, including the need to compete in expressing aggression, for love objects (regressive oedipal wishes in the parent) or for narcissistic supplies. The competing parent often identifies with the child as a peer and often battles for position, status, and a variety of supplies from the spouse. Thus, the competition often expresses the repetitive acting out of the parent's own unresolved rivalry with siblings from an earlier period. In these cases, the competing parent repeatedly defeats the child; wins the competition; sabotages the child's relationships with the other parent, siblings, and peers; and stunts the child's psychosexual growth and acquisition of stable object relations.

Hardly less disruptive and frustrating to the child is the converse situation in which the parent always manages to structure the competition so that the child inevitably wins it. In these cases, the ultimate denouement is the child's discovery that the victory is hollow indeed, that the sought-after fruits of victory are not forthcoming, and that the defeat of the adult leads only to anxiety and terror, or to more anger and hostility.

Mounting concern over loss of the competition finally induces some parents to seek professional help for a child nearing or in adolescence whose emotional disorder dates clearly back into preadolescence. Thus, parents' fear of the child's growing size and physical prowess and of the child's maturing capacity to act out aggressive and erotic impulses prompts them to seek assistance long after it was needed. Thus, the messages, (1) "I am afraid that my child will soon be big and strong enough to retaliate upon, hurt, or kill me," or (2) "My child will finally seduce me sexually or allow me to seduce him," or (3) "My child will finally seduce my husband (wife)," or (4) "My child will finally be able successfully to act out all the antisocial wishes I myself harbor."

The child whose parent inevitably allows him or her to win the competition likewise faces insurmountable problems post hoc. If the competition was for narcissistic supplies, the child finds that they were inadequate all along. If for possession of the parent of the opposite sex, the child soon realizes that he or she is not yet mature enough to claim the erotic prize without assuming the adult responsibilities that vouchsafe it. Thus, the child fought for nothing, and the battle was loaded from the beginning.

Finally, the child who has vanquished the parental adult is in a sorry state indeed, for he has dispatched the very figure he yet depends mightily upon for his gratification of so many of his needs. As a result, the fruits of his victory are rejection and psychological starvation.

Whether he wins or loses the competition, the child repeatedly discovers that the parent has brought adult strengths and stratagems to the fray. Thus, whether in victory or defeat, he always loses in the end. Whatever the situation, the child becomes anxious, frightened, angry, and frustrated.

"You will cure my child and return him to me and fail to realize that I have given up and do not want him back." For whatever reasons, some parents bring their child to the hospital as a final expression of their need permanently to banish the child from their midst. The child's hospitalization poses the major threat that the child will be cured and will be returned to them, an event to be prevented at all costs. For some parents whose child is seriously organically brain-damaged or destructive toward persons and property, hospitalization represents the endpoint of chronic struggles with anger, frustration, and guilt toward the child that have come seriously to threaten the integrity of the parents' marriage. In other cases, it may represent the result of herculean struggles among family members over their and the child's psychological problems, which the parents have come to conclude can only be resolved by permanent dispatch of the child.

Whatever the basis for such an attitude, parents will express it either by ongoing efforts to sabotage casework or by staying away from casework and the child for long periods. In some cases, parents never come to the hospital and thereby express their wish to deny even the fact of the child's existence. The strength of the denial is often proportional to the depth of the parents' concern with aggressive and destructive (death) wishes between them and the child; hence the message, "My child wants to destroy me. You will strengthen his ability to do this and will send him back to me and thereby get the job done."

Thus, in the case of a psychotic fourteen-year-old boy, the caseworker discovered, after several months of work, that the boy's parents, both professional people, had evolved a complex series of paranoid delusional elaborations in which the hospital was conceived to be in league with the boy's purported plan to return home "well" and to set about killing them. As a component of this, the parents had informed the caseworker that they (the parents) had made a mutual pact to determine which of them would die first.

LOYALTY PROBLEM

It is safe to say that the degree to which the adolescent child is able to use the hospital in the service of needs to acquire identity and to unsnarl pathological ways of living depends on the degree to which he or she has previously made successful beginnings toward these goals with parents or parental surrogates. In addition, the extent of the child's failure in these tasks prior to hospitalization will determine the form, content, intensity, and chronicity of his or her resistances to the treatment milieu and the metaphors by which he or she conveys them. In brief, the child asserts, "Adults have repeatedly failed me in the past, so why should I trust you now?"

Thus, one sees in the form and content of the child's initial or resistance phase of hospitalization a clear expression of the child's prior conflicts with adults. The "conflict of generations" that the child has hurled at adults in general and at parents in particular is now hurled at the hospital treatment team, and unless ways are found to render this resistance unnecessary for the child, he will not get well.

There are a number of messages which the parents may transmit to the hospitalized adolescent aimed at frustrating the child's groping efforts to use the treatment milieu and to work through his resistances to it. Thus, the parent may say, "You must not trust the hospital. You must not tell them about your disturbed relations with me." The following reasons may be given: (1) "They are just like me. They will not understand you any more than I have understood you, hence you will only be frustrated again." (2) "If you tell them how bad (sick) you are, they will hurt (damage, destroy) you." (3) "If you tell them about us, you will destroy me." (4) "I will retaliate and destroy you." (5) "I will abandon you." Thus, the basic communication from the parents admonishes the child that he must not trust or cooperate with the treatment milieu under pain of the worst calamity a child can experience — namely, rejection either by parents or hospital or both, thereby leaving him to perish. Because the child's relations with parents long antedate those he has with the hospital and because no matter how sick his relations with his parents have been, they are all he has had; the child is forced apart from the treatment milieu, and his resistances to it go on apace.[3]

The "other half" of the work required for successful hospital treatment of the adolescent comprises a significant degree of success in working through by parents or parental surrogates of the latter's own resistances to the child's hospitalization as these come to be expressed in casework. Only when this has largely been accomplished can parents allow themselves to permit the child to trust and use the hospital milieu as he or she has been unable to use *them*. When this occurs, the child enters the second or definitive treatment phase, at which point the treatment staff begins to observe the onset of more lasting alterations in the child's ways of dealing with himself in relation to inner and outer events and objects. The child is then able to resolve the problem of to whom to be loyal and to come to understand that to be loyal means loyal not to the parents *or* the hospital, but to *both* and to the self.

SOLUTIONS TO THE LOYALTY PROBLEM

In the final analysis, there are three basic solutions for the hospitalized adolescent's loyalty problem; they may be expressed as follows:

"My parents have given me permission to use the hospital." This ideal solution implies that the parents, with expert casework assistance, have begun to work through their resistances to the child's hospitalization, have begun to deal constructively with the meaning of the child's separation from them, have sensed their own needs to change and have actually begun to change, and have extended permission to the child to do likewise. In our experience, it has usually required a minimum of six to eight months for child and parents to reach this stage of therapeutic involvement with the hospital.

"My parents are too sick to allow me to use the hospital, but I will do so anyway." The hospitalized adolescent who is able to recognize and treat his situation in this way has already come a long distance toward getting well. To attain such involvement with

the treatment milieu, the child must possess a natively good intellectual endowment and be able to develop and use the "abstract attitude" (Goldstein 1939); he must have begun to transfer major object ties from parents to the hospital and its treatment team; he must have introjected some of the treatment figures' techniques of handling conflicts; and he must have been gratified by the introjection. In our experience, it has usually required a minimum of one to one and a half years for an otherwise well-endowed if psychiatrically disturbed adolescent to reach this stage without assistance from the parents.

The following excerpt from an interview with a fifteen-year-old formerly delinquent black girl is a case in point:

> Doctor: I guess you really do love your folks, eh?
> Patient: Yeah . . . they're kinda screwy . . . I don't understand them, but they mean well so I guess they're all right.
> Doctor: What are you going to do when you leave the hospital?
> Patient: Well, I guess I'll go home to my folks and try to make a go of it until I'm of age; then I'll get out of there and try to make it on my own.

"My parents are so sick and my relations with them so mutually destructive that I can use the hospital only if my separation from them is complete and permanent." A certain number of hospitalized adolescents come from families that harbor a stupendous degree of psychopathology; some come from homes unworthy of the name. The histories of such families are replete with the behavior of drunken, sadistic, grossly psychotic, and severely character disordered parents. Some of these may be recidivistic criminals, pimps, and prostitutes, given to bouts of murderous rage and open sexuality, including incest with their offspring. Again, the parents may be lackadaisical, apathetic individuals whose defective child-rearing involves less active destructiveness than chronic, passive neglect, which often places their children in a position where their frustration and ensuing hostility turn upon themselves.

In many such cases, the community has legally separated child from family, and many of these adolescents come to the hospital as court or state wards. It is no surprise, therefore, that a large number of these adolescents are already seriously disorganized personalities, and if the child is not yet legally separated from the family, the hospital is likely to recommend such action. Thus, the message, *"You can't go home again,"* becomes, of necessity, a cornerstone of treatment. It is among these adolescents that the hospital achieves its poorest success in assisting the child to overcome resistances to the treatment milieu. The child either mounts endlessly repetitive and often violent battles with the milieu; or the child may regress, despite the treatment team's every effort, to a protractedly dependent relationship with it. In the latter situation, the child "fuses with the hospital." In such cases, inpatient care becomes a matter of years as the treatment team labors to build meaningful object ties with a child, one of whose basic messages is, "I have never learned what parents are, so how can I use you as substitutes?"

Notes

1. It has long been recognized that for many troubled parents, the most acceptable way to seek help for themselves is to seek it, instead, for their child. The overt wish to have the child treated masks, in very many cases, the covert wish of parents to have themselves treated. Denial of their own problem underlies much of parents' resistance to casework.

2. Parents' inordinate efforts to use their children either as sexual or as oral-dependency objects imply grave disappointment in the spouse, for whatever reasons—including the spouse's loss through separation, divorce, or death. Hence, these efforts are often discerned among the widowed and divorced of both sexes.

3. In the case of psychotic, borderline, or infantile-narcissistic adolescents, early defects in object relations dwarf the loyalty problem. Here, the problem becomes the exceedingly difficult task of promoting those nuclear identifications with adult treatment figures from which it is hoped that the beginnings of object ties will crystallize. Hence, there is no loyalty problem in the sense implied in this discussion, since there are no genuine object relations even with the child's parents.

3

Approaches to Hospital Treatment

In 1900, the Swedish sociologist, Ellen Key, prophetically named the twentieth century the "century of the child" (Kanner 1961). As the psychiatrist sees it, the "century of the child" symbolizes a time of growing recognition that children may suffer from all kinds of psychiatric disturbance, of an evolving understanding of the psychopathology of children, and of efforts to heal its victims. In the United States, child psychiatry began in earnest with the child guidance movement, in an effort to deal with the problem of juvenile delinquency; and the child guidance movement drew its energies from psychoanalysis (Levy 1952, Healy and Bronner 1936, Healy, Bronner, and Bowers 1930, Friedlander 1947). Thus, from its earliest inception in this country, the evaluation, diagnosis, and therapy of preadolescent and adolescent children with mental illness developed from the womb of the outpatient clinic, nurtured on a diet of psychoanalytic theory. Whereas the basic tradition of adult psychiatric care (often meaning custody) stemmed from the large state hospitals (Bryan 1936, pp. 13–45), the psychiatric care of children was, for many years, largely in the hands of clinics and their staffs.

In the years following World War II, increasing recognition by the profession of severe intrapsychic and behavioral disorders among children has led to initially slow albeit accelerating growth in the number of full time, inpatient, *residential* (hospital) services devoted to the care of psychiatrically disturbed children (Reid and Hagan 1952, Beskind 1962). Often called "schools" or "treatment centers," the greatest proportion of these institutions are, in fact, psychiatric hospitals. And as yet, the larger part of "trained" psychiatric workers with children, in both inpatient and outpatient facilities, have received their training in outpatient settings. That this is both natural and understandable is obvious from even a superficial perusal of the history of child psychiatry in this country; that it may be an anachronism is now even more important to consider. For it follows that psychiatrists, psychologists, social workers, and other *team* personnel, trained as many are in outpatient clinical settings, often lack the necessary hospital experience to initiate and maintain good inpatient treatment services. In their understandable need to carry their clinic experience over into inpatient settings, they may often be guilty of attempting much that is either difficult or, at worst, impossible. The result is often a considerable waste of time, energy, and motion as clinic-trained workers learn the arduous lessons of adapting their prior clinic experience to the complex, multidisciplinary problems inherent in hospital structure, as well as recognizing and dealing effectively with hospital problems of which there are no real counterparts in clinic experience.

A second phenomenon, derived from the guidance clinic history of child psychiatry, has been the problem of translating psychoanalytic insights, originally derived from the retrospective analysis of adults, into a reasonable and productive body of understanding appropriate for the needs of the child. The truism that children are not merely little adults constitutes a basic awareness that has led psychodynamically trained workers into a complex of profound epistemological and psychotherapeutic problems from which their ensuing energetic efforts have not as yet fully extricated them. Children's responses to the psychotherapist's efforts are, in many ways, different from those of adults and from "ideal neurotic" adults at that. Hence, from the methodological ferment of child psychotherapeutics have come numerous modifications of classical therapeutic technique too numerous to detail here. One need only mention, in passing, the names of Melanie Klein (1932), Anna Freud (1928), and August Aichhorn (1935), who have wrestled with the technical problems of how to treat psychiatrically disturbed children, including adolescents (Lorand 1961).

A third problem for child psychiatry, which is part of a broader psychosocial context, is the extent to which training in the art and science of medicine should be prerequisite for child psychotherapists (or for *any* psychotherapist), at least for the individual who will supervise their work. If, as Thomas Szasz (1961) says, "mental illness is a myth," then the proper management of those who are "mentally ill" should not be restricted to those who are graduate physicians. The child guidance clinic has been in the van of movements that have tended to blur the distinction between medically trained and nonmedically trained therapists. Thus, although clinics have been organized, in part, as treatment facilities and treatment implies some sort of illness to be treated, careful study of guidance clinic organization often reveals that no one in particular, including the psychiatrist, subscribes to the dicta that such clinics are medical facilities and that no therapy shall be done in them unless conducted or supervised by a duly licensed physician (Felix 1961).

We therefore have a diffusion of roles: the psychiatrist is not necessarily responsible for a full case study. In some settings, psychologists, social workers, and, in some cases, even school teachers and recreational and occupational therapists practice therapy, not rarely of an intensive dynamic kind. The psychiatrist is sometimes considered a kind of psychologist, but he may be seen as lacking in competence with the refined procedures of diagnostic projective, and thematic testing, or he may be viewed primarily as a "medical man" who does the requisite physical and neurological examinations and must be called upon to dispense medications when needed. The psychiatrist may also be perceived as a kind of caseworker without deeper and more formal training and interest in the broader familial, group, and social problems of the patient and the latter's relatives.

The obfuscation of professional roles to which guidance clinics tend seems to have been intimately a part of their development, both historically and professionally. A not invalid argument in its favor holds that children, psychologically disturbed or not, see *all* adults as equal, cannot appreciate professional differences of role, and are liable to be confused by these. Although one suspects that this argument has tended to be overworked and that in very many instances it underestimates children's capacities for shrewd observations of adults, it ignores the professional worker's own needs to view himself in a stable and meaningful role. It further ignores the adult worker's need to come to grips with the well-known *regressive pull* that children exert upon him. Unless recognized and dealt with, this regressive pull often impels the worker to preadult forms of behavior as part of his own transference and countertransference response to his young charges. If this has not proved an insuperable burden in the guidance clinic, it can court therapeutic disaster if carried over into an intensive inpatient milieu. Therein, unless each staff member has a well-delineated role, a degree of internecine confusion comes to afflict the staff — which, in my experience, is able to throw the treatment structure into a state bordering on chaos (Schwartz 1957). This does not mean, of course, that roles need be highly rigid; without some degree of overlap, the therapeutic edifice resembles a skyscraper designed without the ability to yaw or lean in the wind, and a slight breeze may then easily disintegrate it.

A fourth problem arising from the increasing emphasis upon child psychiatry is related to structure. Often derived from a well-meaning misapplication of August Aichhorn's theories of how to treat delinquent children, this problem witnesses therapeutic personnel addressing themselves to the child with what amounts to an "anything goes" attitude. The cult of overpermissiveness, practiced by badly misguided parents whose "sophisticated" intellectual approach to their children usually masquerades their profound rejection of them, holds that restricting, circumscribing, confining, curtailing, and "locking up" disturbed children is naturally "punitive" and hence untherapeutic. In some cases, this attitude is extended to patients in individual or group psychotherapy but nowhere else in an otherwise closely structured hospital environment, thus, "No, you can't smash up the ward, but you can do anything you like in here." Although a laissez-faire approach may be better (if at all) suited to the needs of certain adult, otherwise well-motivated patients, it often constitutes an abysmal error when offered to hospitalized children (as well as to many hospitalized adults), whose normal needs for external controls are exceeded by profound difficulties with readily mobilized erotic and aggressive impulses. The latter, in turn, comprise part of the roots of their disturbance and the basis for their hospitalization to begin with.[1] To court or permit direct expression invites them to do the very thing that terrifies them most. It speaks ill for a treatment milieu that, logically enough, locks doors and applies external controls at point X, whereas at point Y it allows the child destructively to act out. Lurking behind uncritical, inconsistent, or pervasive over-permissiveness is often the misguided notion that controls imposed on *any* child, sick or not, will somehow block his capacity to express himself and his problems. Instead, such an attitude can be viewed as a reaction to more deeply lying retributive, punitive, and sadistic impulses directed toward the child.

An interesting facet of the previous discussion may be noted in the official names accorded inpatient psychiatric facilities for disturbed children. Thus, we have the "training center," the "treatment center," the "training school," or, simply, the "school"; or, in some instances, the "institute," the "foundation," the "guidance center," or anything but the "hospital." One suspects that these terms represent far more than a mere linear outgrowth from the pedagogical background of the child guidance movement, with such figures to conjure with as Itard, Seguin, Pestalozzi, and Binet. It partly represents a genuine reluctance on the part of adults with "tender" feelings for "disturbed" children to lump them together with the "crazy" adults who inhabit the large state mental hospitals. Thus, the attempt to deny that children can and do suffer "mental illness" of a degree at least as profound as that suffered by adults blurs further the role status of treatment personnel by eliminating from the titles of treatment institutions the very word that would mark these institutions as hospitals for the sick. If this is the case, then who can object if a psychologist or a social caseworker or a schoolteacher assumes the role of the physician?

TREATMENT MILIEUS—
THERAPEUTIC AND OTHERWISE

We might briefly consider a concept of psychiatric hospital milieu that could fairly be labeled the "open door policy."[2] Simply put, this view holds that in very many cases (if not in all) it is both therapeutically wrong and morally derelict to lock patients behind closed ward doors, even as it is medically and socially unenlightened to apply physical restraints to patients against their will. These concepts descended to us, in part, from the pioneering work of John Conolly (1856). There is much to be said for this view, and much to be said against it. So much of the discussion will depend upon the kind of patient; his social origins and environment; the nature, depth, and chronicity of his illness; the actual therapeutic structure into which he comes; and myriad other factors that could lead this discussion into sterile dogmatism. There are, however, certain elemental concepts in need of consideration.

PHILOSOPHIES OF HOSPITAL TREATMENT

At the outset, we recognize at least three basic philosophies of psychiatric hospital treatment. The first of these we may dismiss, perhaps at our peril, as "nontherapeutic"—that is, it is a philosophy committed to keeping, segregating, isolating, and custodializing socially obnoxious or dangerous behavior. Its institutional manifestations vary from overt neglect and brutalization of inmates, against which our honored forebears—Pinel, Chiarugi, and Miss Dix—struggled, to "humane care," wherein no solid efforts are made to promote inner change or growth and the patients undergo, with varying velocities, a process of social stagnation and psychological petrification.

The other two philosophies are, at root, "therapeutic" and differ on the question of what constitutes "adequate therapeutic change" and over how long a period of time and by what means it may be brought about.

The first of the therapeutic philosophies might be called the "patch and dismiss" school. It stresses how quickly patients are dismissed back to the community; it takes pride in its high dismissal rate and boasts of short periods of inpatient stay; it views the hospital as a poor substitute for the patient's own home or communal living; it plunges the hospital's psychiatric, psychological, casework, and adjunctive therapeutic services into the task of getting the patient out as quickly as can expediently be accomplished; it looks with suspicion upon prolonged inpatient care, referring to it by such terms as "institutionalization," "infantilization," "prolonged regression," and the like; it seeks a quick return of its patients to extramural life because protracted inpatient care costs too much money and likewise deprives the community of the presumed productivity of hospitalized patients; and it holds that any major, extended, structural reorganization of the patient's personality should be the proper task of the outpatient clinic, once the patient is discharged from inpatient care and living extramurally. This approach is a philosophy both "progressive" and "enlightened," in reaction to the brutal, neglectful, often lifelong incarceration of the mentally ill which made the Bedlams, snake-pits, lunatic asylums, and crazy houses what they were and, in so many cases, still are. As a result, it profoundly alters few people, "cures" almost nobody, and is exquisitely unsuited to the psychological rehabilitation of those who, paradoxically, comprise the majority of its patients — those with chronic, disorganizing, "psychotic" illnesses, characterological deformations, addictions, and "organic cerebral disorders." And, in increasing numbers, such patients are psychiatrically ill children. For all these and most impressively the last, it is little else than what some would call humane custody. Because open doors, loose treatment structure, and quick dismissal neglect many of the profound difficulties hospitalized children so often have with impulse control, such treatment betrays their trust in the adults they look to for these controls and metaphorically invites the patients to further allo-plasticity, a seduction toward self-destruction. This is very largely why children, particularly adolescents, are often so annoying and disruptive if circumstances force their hospitalization on "adult" wards. Like adult character neurotics, they sense the betrayal and proceed to act out uproariously in futile efforts to obtain the controls they so desperately need; or, like many adults, some of them settle into a state of hospital living aptly called "becoming good patients" — which means giving staff personnel what the latter want by covering up symptoms and dissimulating. There is no cure amidst such an environment.

The third philosophy of hospital treatment, and the second of our so-called therapeutic approaches thereto, represents our own view of psychiatric hospital treatment. It assumes that the hospital's primary commitment is to induce and maintain healthy change (or personality realignment, structural, characterological, or defensive rebuilding, or whatever one chooses to name it) within the patient; it further assumes that such change should have taken place to a significant extent intramurally; and finally, that such change, to be genuine, must be lasting. As a corollary, the institutional staff and administration are barely if at all concerned with how long such change requires in any given case: It may require six months, a year, or five years — the result is what counts. As will be apparent, such a philosophy not only does not assume that the hospital is but a poor substitute for the patient's own home but also is fully committed to the fact that, in many cases, the hospital is the better of the two. Thus, the hospital comprises a vast thera-peutic edifice, within which the patient will proceed to mount resistances in his compulsion to repeat within the hospital those maladaptive ways of dealing with himself and others that he employed outside it. The early, basic task of the staff thus becomes to recognize and deal with those resistances, to interpret them verbally and nonverbally to the patient, to help in their reso-lution, and hence to direct the patient toward the next stage of hospitalization in which basic, lasting inner change begins to set in.[3] The entire process of what is popularly termed *milieu* therapy therefore becomes nothing more than a complex extension, with many suitable modifications, of the same kinds of processes that occur in individual psychotherapy.[4]

Both implicit and explicit within such a frame of reference is recognition of the need for treatment, not only of the patient but also of his family, as the social workers have labored to teach us. Thus, concomitant psychotherapeutic casework is in most instances absolutely essential if the goal of major rebuilding of disordered personalities is to be accomplished. This means, in turn, that the social work staff of such a treatment institution must be trained in dynamic process—an uncommon talent of a large number of contemporary caseworkers, whose graduate training seems oriented toward producing social engineers rather than process-trained therapists (Szasz 1961, pp. 52–72).

If this philosophy is to succeed in its avowed purpose of doing more than a "patch and dismiss" job for hospitalized patients, an essential component of the therapeutic approach must be the staff's profound conviction that anything less will not do. Moreover, the hospital must be prepared to assume the greatest part, if not all, of the responsibility for the care of its patients. Total responsibility for care thus infantilizes patients only where it remains unresponsive to their needs, where it fails to comprehend the metaphorical parts of their communications, or where it neglects to undertake the arduous process of dealing with their resistances to change. Thus, infantilization means changelessness, and it is certainly understandable, even among so-called progressive institutions, why the emphasis is on speedy discharge, where the treatment personnel have settled for proximate therapeutic goals. This usually means that they have satisfied themselves with dissimulation, avoidance, and evasion by "good" patients who cover up symptoms. It is simply too hard to do more—to do more requires a staff characterized by excellent training and dedication. Why make such demands when rapid discharge statistics are so pleasing to boards of directors and to state legislatures? Hence the goal is, "Get the patient out when he looks good"—or, in institutional jargon, "Maximum Hospital Benefit."

One suspects that psychiatric hospital people have remained ignorant of why such large numbers of patients never "really get well", because the "treatment" has been basically inadequate from its inception. Thus, the "failure" of the various "talking" and "relationship" therapies proceeds from a cause so striking because it is so often overlooked. It is evident, in keeping with dynamic and process concepts of how inner personality reorganization comes about, that the patient will not really change unless he has to. This means either that he has enough ego strength to impose upon himself the condition that he will bring to the treatment staff the conflicts that beset him, or else that, lacking this strength, the therapeutic milieu will force him to it by precluding his capacity either to act out his problems elsewhere or to conceal them.[5]

Thus, the major task of the hospital and ward structure is to provide minimal, if any, opportunity for the patient to escape facing the manifold of disturbed, painful ideas, feelings, and behaviors he brings to and externalizes within it. That this is basic follows from the evident fact that psychiatric patients would ordinarily not be in the hospital were they able to handle the many stresses of life outside it. Thus, should the hospital defect in its responsibility to provide an intensive, basically interpretive treatment milieu, it frustrates the fundamental needs of those who cannot otherwise get well. Under such circumstances, the "good" patient departs only to continue to suffer, to burden himself and society with the products of his illness, to seek readmission at a later time, or to find his way to another institution where the whole sorry business is repeated (Main 1946).

Finally, we have the preadolescent and adolescent children, who need external controls for normal psychosexual development, especially when anxiety short-circuits their already inadequate ability to interpose symbols between need and act. For these patients, the "patch and dismiss" approach is doubly inadequate. Their capacity to dissimulate, to cover up, to do what is demanded of them, and to be "good patients" is smaller than that of the adult. Hence, sensing the failure of the treatment milieu to recognize, confront, and translate into appropriate verbal and nonverbal interpretations the basic needs they transmit to it, children respond with mounting anger and bitterness by remaining disturbed and by plunging the ward into repetitive turmoils to provoke the controls they demand. Or they will elope and disappear, either on their own or with the contrivance of parents or other relatives, who have perceived that the hospital is likewise unprepared to help them with their own problems — both with and apart from their child, from the context of which the child's hospitalization has developed.

CONCLUSION

Several generalizations can be distilled as a foundation for the philosophy of psychiatric hospital treatment set forth in chapter 3:

1. The psychiatric hospital is not merely a "harbor," "haven," or "refuge" for its patients (Main 1946). If this is all it is, it is profoundly neglecting its therapeutic responsibilities, which extend throughout the entire period of its patients' residence.

2. The hospital is usually the best home the patient currently has and perhaps has ever had. Treatment personnel need to assume this and make no excuses to themselves, to relatives, or to others for believing it. This implies that the treatment staff must assume full and complete responsibility for the care of its patients. They may and usually must take family members into concomitant (casework) treatment, but they cannot share responsibility for treating the patient with these. To do so splits transference and hobbles the therapeutic effort.

3. The various members of the diagnostic and therapeutic team should enjoy adequately defined professional roles. With very rare and unusual exceptions, one cannot have everyone doing some or much of everyone else's job; the result is a "vegetable soup milieu" that blurs personnel's self-image and dilutes and diffuses their treatment efforts. I have seen this in a number of children's residential treatment institutions, and I regard it, in part, as an expression of the treatment staff's failure to work through their need to

regress with their patients, based, in turn, upon the staff's own unresolved infantile conflicts. I do not think that the "vegetable soup milieu" reflects the best efforts of the treatment staff to healthily regress with their patients in order to promote the latters' treatment.

4. The initial phase of the patient's hospitalization comprises the period of resistance to the treatment milieu. During this phase, which may last for many months, the main task of the treatment team is to recognize the nature and depth of the patient's resistances to them and to interpret these in appropriate verbal and non-verbal ways to him. Thus, this phase may be crudely compared to the opening game of chess, during which both sides proceed to "develop their pieces," to "get things out in the open" (chapters 1 and 2). In my experience, many "progressive" institutions never get past this phase with the patient. This happens either because the patient dissimulates and is quickly dismissed, or because the patient lacks the capacity to dissimulate, proceeds to "deteriorate," and therefore becomes "chronic."

5. The ensuing phase of the patient's hospitalization comprises the period of inner change. Much less is, unfortunately, known about this — hence its comparison with the middle game of chess. In actual fact, it is the phase that may require the most difficult and protracted work of the treatment team. Although it may be ably assisted by appropriate individual, group, or adjunctive therapies, the core of the work accomplished in this period is done on the ward. This is often not understood, and patients may be discharged to outpatient treatment before comprehensive inner change begins to occur — which may be before the patient has dealt to a significant extent with his resistances to change and has come to view the hospital and its staff as his allies, not his adversaries.

6. In fewer individual cases than is commonly realized can the difficult work required of both patient and treatment staff be accomplished in an open setting, certainly during the initial and, often, part of the second phases of hospitalization. The opportunities for the patient in such a setting to split and dilute his resistances and to avoid and evade the treatment structure are too great. The *locus minoris resistentiae* thus available disorganizes the

treatment team and its efforts; the patient remains, therefore, essentially unchanged.[6]

Notes

1. It is certainly not intended to condemn permissiveness willy-nilly. Many psychiatrically disturbed children and adults require proper "doses" of permissiveness, but these should be dispensed by an otherwise well-structured milieu. Thus, the patient may need to know if the treatment figures will condemn and suppress action as such out of need to keep him infantile; or the patient may need to undergo varying periods of regression to infantile, action-oriented behavior in order to comfortably reexperience childish ego states as a necessary precondition for later growth toward more adult forms of response. Again, it may be necessary to allow both direct and displaced instinctual mobilizations for patients who are pathologically overinhibited. For such patients, it is important that they perceive that more or less direct expression of aggressive impulses will not destroy or provoke rejection from the treatment figures, their wardmates, or themselves — a cornerstone of early hospital management of depressed and certain obsessional and compulsive individuals.

2. This discussion does not primarily concern such planned "open-type" programs as the day hospital, pioneered by Cameron (1951) and his group, wherein considerable "active treatment" may be accomplished during the periods of patients' actual residence in the hospital. I conclude, however, that the "open" or "semiopen" nature of the milieu limits the extent and depth of more profound changes in patients' personalities by affording them means whereby they may and do evade coming to grips with their resistances to the treatment structure (vide infra).

3. One way of viewing the early approach to institutional treatment used at the Menninger Hospital aimed at unconscious needs would conceptualize it at least in part as an effort to recognize and assist the patient to externalize preconsciously and unconsciously motivated maladaptive adjustive techniques (Menninger 1936b, 1937). In my view, the Menningers' valuable methodology serves, in part, to come to grips with the patient's early expressed resistances to the hospital treatment structure.

4. Maxwell Jones's confirmation (1953, pp. 69–84) of Simmel's prior observation (1929) that hospitalized patients avoid transference by submerging it in accounts of daily hospital activities represents, in one major sense, a more

restricted formulation of our conclusion that transference behaviors, both verbal and nonverbal, represent resistances both to treatment figures and to the hospital as a larger symbol and are thus invariably a part of both the early and, usually, later phases of the patient's intramural adjustments.

5. The truism that in a vast number of cases the therapeutic agent, individual or group must "motivate" the patient for treatment is not well appreciated by many "dynamically trained" psychiatric workers. This appears to be one reason for the criticism that many psychiatrists devote their therapeutic efforts to a minority of less disturbed ("neurotic") patients to the exclusion of the larger number of those who need treatment far more pressingly. In many such cases, such selection of patients serves defensive purposes in the psychiatrist: The demand that the patient be motivated begs the therapeutic question for the majority of hospitalized psychiatric patients and serves as a self-satisfying rationalization for the therapist's not doing more to engage the patient in treatment and to maintain that engagement.

6. In an interesting recent paper, Ryan (1962) discovers (to the apparent surprise of some) that a large percentage of hospital inpatients found their closed ward psychiatric experience of value to them. This comes, of course, as no surprise to those who utilize closed ward structure in the manner set forth in this paper. Rather, the surprise is for those with the reactive bias that a closed ward is a kind of prison; it is easy to conclude, with such a view, that closed ward = back ward, an equality which is yet, alas, too often the case.

4

Reflections on the Behavior of Hospitalized Adolescents

The decision to hospitalize an individual with evident psychological distress is ordinarily taken in view of either or both of two significant and interrelated kinds of psychological encumbrance. The first of these, usually termed *autoplastic,* has to do with inner or subjective suffering, is always experienced in significant measure idiosyncratically, and is generally communicated in terms of the second kind of encumbrance, *alloplastic.* Alloplastic encumbrance has to do with the social or environmental effects of the former and represents the varying degree to which inner experiences are translated into *action,* or are expressed through *inhibition of action*; in either case, "somebody else" has usually noticed that "something is wrong." Irrespective of the relative importance of alloplastic and autoplastic symptoms in the case of any particular patient, his removal to a hospital signifies a major disruption of both intrapersonal and interpersonal functions. As Ernst Simmel (1929) noted almost fifty years ago, patients suffering from the "lesser" degrees of psychological dysfunction — the so-called psychoneurotics — do not ordinarily find their way into a hospital. Rather, the overwhelming majority of psychiatric hospital patients suffer from what are generally diagnosed as psychoses, character neuroses, or any of the variety of impairments of central nervous system function. Again, amongst these cases are found the borderline, addictive, infantile-narcissistic, emotionally unstable, impulsive, and perverse individuals, some of whom constitute potential threats to themselves and to others.

These patients are usually regarded as, if not frankly psychotic, at least suffering from borderline or "as-if" conditions, which means from a wide range of pregenital fixations that engender a multiplicity of protean and often kaleidoscopic symptoms, whether autoplastic or alloplastic. It is likewise clear that many of these patients fare poorly when efforts are made to treat them in an outpatient setting. They fail to keep appointments, or they may abscond entirely. If forced by threats of legal action to attend "therapy," they so contaminate the treatment process with split-off and displaced hostility as to render it impotent; they split and diffuse the notoriously labile transference they develop toward the therapist and act out either within or outside therapeutic hours, hence bringing little analyzable material into the sessions. This admitted majority of the more seriously ill population experience such disruptive difficulties and induce such consternation in their would-be therapists in part because they are notably infantile. They harbor grandiose fantasies directed toward bending the world, including the therapist, in a magical fashion to meet their regressive needs and to impose upon them a firm structure against which they feel themselves called upon to rebel. Underlying their grandiosity are deep-seated feelings of identitylessness, impotency, failure to master, emptiness of "good objects," absence of self-esteem, and despair.

Careful genetic-dynamic study of patients who do poorly in outpatient treatment and whose illness renders them candidates for inpatient care discloses a variety of characteristics ordinarily considered hallmarks of the *weak ego*. Thus, one observes failure of normal repression; persistence of primitive mechanisms of defense, with reliance upon projection, introjection, regression, and denial; impairment of the ego's synthetic function, with disruption of self-environment relations and dissemblement of perceptual, cognitive-ideational, affective, and motoric functions;

predominance of anxiety of the instinctual type; lack of "basic trust"; impairment of object relations; failure of sublimation of raw instinctual impulses; persistence of primary process thinking with reliance upon transitivism, infantile-megalomanic ideation, magic in gesture and word, and scotomatization and negative hallucination; and major problems with preoedipal and sexual identity.

These characteristics and their behavioral manifestations — impaired tolerance for frustration, lessened capacity for sustained attention and concentration, and proneness to externalize — render those individuals who consistently demonstrate them unattractive candidates for the dynamically trained therapist; indeed, the latter are wont to deem them "unmotivated," "unanalyzable," or at worst, "untreatable." Thus, whether the patient actively seeks hospitalization as in the minority of such cases or he is brought to it involuntarily as in the majority, he finds himself inside the hospital. What, then, is his fate?

Let us now assume that the patient has entered any of the large number of "humane" or "progressive" mental hospitals that are dedicated to the ideals of moral treatment as set forth by Pinel and his successors and developed and practiced during the first half of the nineteenth century in the United States. In many contemporary institutions, the concept of humane or moral treatment has evolved into the ideal of expedient discharge, which means that the patient may expect to remain hospitalized for the shortest possible time consistent with symptomatic remission (chapter 3). This remission is, in most cases, a result of the operation of several interrelated factors:

1. The patient has been spirited away from the exigencies of the extramural world within which his illness developed. In particular, he is removed from the disturbed family setting regularly found to have contributed to his ongoing psychopathology. Away from the pathogenic family and wider social environments amidst which his difficulties were initially spawned and subsequently maintained, the patient's anxiety proceeds to fall away, and he begins to feel rather more comfortable.

2. The hospital serves as a transference object (maternal) that "takes him in." The patient then proceeds to regress as he perceives

that he will be housed, fed, and in various ways ministered to—all of which evidences that his anaclitic needs may be gratified.

3. The hospital is a compulsively styled institution. Thus, the payment the patient must make for the narcissistic supplies he receives is conformity to its rules of acceptable conduct. His conformity, in turn, offers him repeated opportunities to expiate his guilt, which is a cornerstone of his illness, and to further cede to the hospital structure and its officers a measure of his infantile megalomania, a process that has its normal inception during the second year of life. There is ample reason to believe that these factors—removal from external stresses, regression, expiation through behavioral conformity, and partial projection of infantile-grandiose wishes onto the hospital—comprise signal aspects of the frequent symptomatic remissions observed in patients within a few weeks to months following their admission to the hospital.

Translated into more pragmatic terms, the patient "admits" that he "needs help"; he seeks forgiveness for his "transgressions" (symptomatic behavior); finally, he causes no major difficulties to others, whether peers or staff. Thus, he becomes what the sociologists call a "good patient"; he "goes along" with the milieu, and he dissimulates. Some would say he "plays the game" (Berne 1964a, Szasz 1961). But irrespective of the semantics of what he does, the patient, if successful, is rewarded with speedy discharge to his home and his job. But this very process, the variety of techniques by which the patient effects a short-term adaptation to hospital life, serves precisely to bring his more definitive treatment to a halt, if indeed it had ever begun in the first place (chapter 3). The price of his efforts is, in the end, rejection, and with this bitter pill he returns to the outside basically unchanged.

Let us next consider the patient whose immediate and not infrequently extended postadmission behavior is the opposite of that just described. His demeanor is quickly labeled with a variety of pejorative terms: resistive, passive-aggressive, obstreperous, recalcitrant, negativistic, disruptive, manipulative, provocative, staff splitting, acting out, psychologically dishonest, assaultive, combative, destructive, seductive, and so on. The patient signals his dissatisfaction by a wide spectrum of distracting, abient behavior; thus, he may attempt to level staff figures, be flirtatious or seductive, attempt persistently to avoid contact with others, scapegoat peers and staff members, engage in transference splitting, rebel outright against institutional rules and schedules, or elope from the hospital. His modus operandi seems to convey a wish to divide and confuse, to outwit and defeat the staff, to "keep them off base," or to escape from them entirely (chapter 1). His behavior may paradoxically bring about the same end result that accrues to the more compliant, submissive patient who has "adapted" so well to the hospital milieu; that is, he is prematurely gotten rid of. In both cases, the patient has separated from the hospital long before the staff could penetrate into the dense thicket of thoughts, affects, wishes, and fantasies that lie beneath the overt behavior that has concealed them.

It is not unreasonable to assume that superficially different congeries of behavior that bring about essentially the same result serve the same aims. These aims are well known to the psychoanalyst, and in fact represent resistances. The resistances serve, in turn, to divert the staff's attention from, and hence conceal, the wide range of conscious and unconscious experiences arrayed behind the patient's obvious, conscious acts. Thus, one quickly discovers the further apparent paradox of the patient who, once resident in a therapeutic institution presumably devoted to changing him toward a healthier modus vivendi, proceeds at once to a complex of active, passive, verbal, nonverbal, conscious, and unconscious efforts to resist, counteract, and ultimately to negate the hospital's potential impact on his painfully disordered way of living (chapters 1 and 2).

The case of the second, obstreperous patient deserves further consideration. If he perceives no immediate possibility of egress from the hospital, he proceeds to what seems to be efforts to outwit or actually destroy it. He sequesters himself; he forms cliques to marshal the disruptive strength of allies; he may attempt to destroy the ward and its equipment; and he may assault staff members and even attempt to riot against the perceived authority figures. Thus, so long as he remains and so behaves, he likely finds himself transferred to ever more secure surroundings and may wind up in seclusion or isolation. Unlike the compliant patient, the obstreperous patient refuses to expiate. Closer analysis of the motivation underlying his disruptiveness discloses several important findings. First, like the compliant patient, he too desires acceptance, except that instead of earning it by comformity, he demands it willy-nilly. Second, he cannot cede his infantile omnipotence to the hospital because to do so would vest in the latter a power that he perceives as being great enough to destroy him; hence, he challenges the hospital to wrest it from him if it dare. Third, compliant conformity, which ordinarily evokes the approval of the hospital-transference object, likewise poses the possibility of intimacy. Intimacy, in turn, threatens regression and the ensuing threat of symbiotic fusion, which massively threatens, in turn, what little, precarious identity the patient still has.

THE ADOLESCENT'S MOTIVATION
FOR TREATMENT

The usual "dynamic" view of psychiatric treatment, particularly psychoanalysis and psychotherapy, holds that therapy is a "contract" between two consenting and presumably competent individuals (Menninger 1958). Under the "terms" of the contract, the patient will speak as freely as he can about any and all aspects of his life, and the therapist will do his best to understand and help the patient. Aside from the considerable preconscious and unconscious distortions that transference and countertransference impose upon communication between the two participants, each must assume that the other possesses sufficient "basic trust" to be at least consciously honest. The contract further implies that the patient will accede to the therapist's rules of structure; that is, he will meet the therapist for a certain period of time at a specific location and under procedural stipulations required by the therapist, and he will pay the therapist's fees.

One need hardly restate that the behavior of the average, as well as the psychiatrically ill, adolescent does not often conform to the ideal of patient behavior according to the contract model view, nor does that of the adult psychotic, character disorder (psychopath), borderline, and brain-damaged patient. The contract model may reasonably be said to apply to a minority of individuals with more serious forms of psychopathology, including those who require inpatient care. If the stipulation that the patient will assume the supine or "couch" position in treatment and will observe the "basic rule" of psychoanalysis is imposed on the contract model, this minority shrinks even further.

The usual rationalization offered by therapists devoted to the more rigid technical orthodoxies asserts that such patients, including adolescents, are "unanalyzable" because their egos are "not strong enough" to bear the weight of expressive therapeutic work (Benedek 1952, A. Freud 1946). This transparently defensive generality is both factually incorrect and patently unfair to the adolescent who, quite to the contrary, *is* in most cases readily "analyzable," provided that the realities of his inner life are taken into account. It cannot be denied that some of the usual explanations for the adolescent's reluctance toward orthodox or vis-à-vis analytic work are relevant — such as his fear of the "dependent posture" during therapeutic hours, the threat of eruption of instinctual urges into the ego, the apprehension lest the therapist permit him to act out, and the nascent fear of fusion with reactivation of symbiotic and pre-symbiotic needs among others. But to cite these well-recognized phenomena to explain the adolescent's presumed lack of motivation simply begs the question. On the contrary, adolescents are notably curious about themselves and their world and are strongly motivated for the help they perceive psychotherapy can offer them; but they must couch their needs in indirect, oblique metaphors and behavioral maneuvers to avoid both stigma of childish dependency and their anxious concern that their infantile-grandiose pretensions will somehow be acted out.

There are several reasons, therefore, why therapeutic processes with adolescents augur poorly if the therapist attempts adherence to technical or methodological rigidities. Adolescents *are* prone to act out both during and outside therapeutic hours, in an effort to deintensify transferential and other feelings that arouse so much anxiety in them. Thus, the powerful if labile impact of the adolescent's transference finds expression in his efforts to *devalue* the adult therapist, to deny dependency upon the therapist, and to deny the omnipotent wishes which the adolescent projects onto him. Thus, as experienced therapists of adolescents readily attest, the patient is afraid of being made to "look silly" and is afraid that the therapist will overstimulate or even seduce him, will commit aggressions upon him, will not actively control him when impulses strain the limits of verbal communication, will attempt to "remake" him into a diminutive image of himself, will require that he act out ("Do bad things") for him (Johnson 1949, Johnson and Szurek 1952), will urge him to "grow up too fast," or will unduly criticize and even ridicule him.

A second and more important reason emerges from the peculiarities of the adolescent's interim position between childish dependency upon parent surrogates and the longed-for yet feared autonomy of adulthood. At a time when the latency defenses are giving way under pressure from instinct, with consequent threat to the integrity of the ego, the adolescent transposes his feelings of physical strength, of erotic vigor, and of heightened need of motility into a need to have an impact on others. The adolescent's long prior history of dependency on adult authorities has left behind accumulated resentments and frustrations that now threaten to erupt with new strength. If to this is added the naive yet amazingly shrewd capacity of children to observe adults and divine their intent, what may be called the "paranoid stance" of the adolescent emerges. There is no doubt that even "normal" adolescents are not a little overalert toward adults and suspicious of the latter's motives. The adolescent is thus especially prone to grasp, preconsciously or otherwise, the many rigidities, self-gratifying and socially "lubricating" intellectual dishonesties and concessions of principle and the multiplicity of petty insincerities and self-deceptions that adults otherwise employ to "get along." A further impetus for the adolescent's paranoid stance is given as a result of the far greater and more numerous traumas, seductions, rejections, and parental and social ambivalences the child destined for significant psychopathology has experienced. The sick adolescent thus brings into therapy the paradox of even greater dependency upon and more profound suspicion of the adult therapist, onto whom he projects the welter of traumas previously experienced at the hands of earlier adult figures.

As shown (chapters 1–3, 5 and 6) elimination of the adolescent's resistance behavior is essential for reconstructive psychiatric treatment within the residential milieu. To recapitulate, there are two major deterrents to achieving this goal: (1) a milieu that provides inadequate external controls and thereby allows the patient to evade engagement with the milieu and its therapeutic figures by acting out and (2) a relatively inflexible therapeutic orthodoxy, which fails to stay abreast of the adolescent's multiple, labile shifts of ideation, affect, and action and hence never really engages with him.

It is recognized, of course, that underlying such phenomena described by the terms *engagement* and *motivation* is the process of identification. As Aichhorn (1935) originally taught us, the foundation of psychiatric treatment of the adolescent, if not for all other patients as well, lies in the patient's ability to identify himself with the therapist, to "take him in." Identification means the internalization of object-representations within the ego and their assimilation to self-representations (Jacobson 1964, Kernberg 1966). In addition, it means that instinctual aims are displaced or inhibited, that a certain degree of defusion of instinct occurs, and that the resultant defused instinctual energies are available, in neutralized form, for sublimations (Hartmann 1955). Finally, identification implies that certain already present *internal objects* become *externalized.* Thus, in object-relations terms, internalization of the "good" objects accompanies externalization of the "bad" objects that comprise a major part of the core of the patient's psychopathology (chapter 5). Once this has occurred, the patient has departed from the *resistance phase* of treatment, and has entered upon the complex psychological work of the *definitive phase* of treatment.

THE ADOLESCENT IN RESIDENTIAL TREATMENT

Incomplete as they are, the foregoing considerations lead directly to a view of residential treatment structure for adolescents based not only on the generally accepted characteristics of the adolescent peer group but also on the characteristics of the seriously ill adolescent who actually needs inpatient psychiatric care. Inasmuch as he is yet a child, the adolescent must have appropriate educational, recreational, and occupational thera- peutic experiences prescribed for him commensurate with his degree of engagement with the residential setting and with his level of psychological development. Furthermore, the adults with whom the adolescent interacts in the hospital should be highly motivated, properly trained, and devoid of significant psycho- pathology themselves. In view of these two considerations, the adolescent should live on a ward with other patients of his age group and not with adult patients, as unfortunately is so often the case in many private and state hospitals. Residence on adult wards simply catalyzes the sick adolescent's proneness to psychological misuse of adults by affording them access to adult figures who, like their parents, cannot but fail the adolescent in the latter's search for meaningful identificatory objects, and who wittingly or otherwise lend themselves to the adolescent's defensive trans- ferential behavior toward staff members. In brief, continued daily exposure to sick adults merely extends the adolescent's exposure to the very kind of individuals who played such important roles in the etiology of his psychopathology long before admission to the hospital.

"Therapeutic community," pseudodemocratic, and basically permissive milieus—within which scant attention is paid to the staff's differences in experience and professional training and in which "anybody can do treatment provided he is well motivated"— are of little or no value in the reconstructive psychiatric treatment of the adolescent. Such milieus actually represent situations in which staff figures with blurred, muddled, or poorly developed and professional identities proceed to externalize these identities and displace them onto the patients. Efforts to identify one's self with such adult figures only deepens the adolescent's own struggles with his identity.

Finally, the open or semiopen ward finds no rational place in the residential treatment of the adolescent as long as he remains in the resistance phase of his treatment. Such a ward symbolizes the opposite of what the seriously disturbed adolescent, with his impaired object relations and proneness to action, requires — that is, absence of firm security, of dependable external control of his motility, and the adults' misplaced and premature expectation that he will conduct himself with "propriety" and "responsibility," since the lack of these qualities was what brought him to the hospital in the first place.

Part II

Toward a Theory
of Treatment

5

An Object-Relations View

The origins of what is now called *milieu* treatment of the mentally ill are buried in antiquity, and the earliest references to it date from ancient times (Zilboorg 1941). Concerning the so-called modern era of milieu treatment, Bockoven (1963) writes

> The great step to moral treatment was taken almost simultaneously by a French physician and an English Quaker in the last decade of the eighteenth century. Philippe Pinel transformed a madhouse into a hospital, and William Tuke built a *retreat* for the mentally ill. Similar reforms were wrought in Italy, Germany, and America by Chiarugi, Reil, and Rush. . . .

The pioneering work of these "moral therapists" and the efforts of those who have followed in their footsteps have yielded a vast and often controversial literature devoted to every conceivable aspect of the hospital treatment of the mentally ill. And, as in every other area of psychiatry, psychoanalytic ideas have made major contributions to our understanding of what is now called the *therapeutic milieu* and to understanding of the vast complex of verbal and nonverbal communications among the patients and treatment figures who live and labor together within it. That these psychoanalytic ideas have enriched and deepened our understanding of individual psychopathology and psychiatric treatment needs no restatement here. But if the problems of the practice, significance, dynamics, and effects of the individual psychotherapy are great and difficult, those associated with the multi-disciplinary treatment team on a mental hospital ward loom in staggering proportions (Stanton and Schwartz 1954).

One aspect of the problem of understanding how milieu or any other kind of treatment effects temporary or lasting inner psychological change in the patient is the matter of role. It is now generally accepted that the various *roles* with which the patient invests the therapist have intimately to do with the spectrum of overdetermined, perseverated (compulsively repeated) emotional and cognitive experiences, which both therapist and patient bring to and externalize within the therapeutic relationship. In psychoanalytic language, the problem of role becomes, in certain ways, the problem of transference. Thus, if one grants the complexities of individual psychotherapeutic transference, consider the transferential vicissitudes of the patient who has daily to deal with a ward team composed of psychiatrist, nurse, and aides and with a more extended hospital environment including clinical psychologist, social workers, and adjunctive therapists of various kinds as well. As the patient interacts within such a social milieu, the transference proceeds to assume added dimensions. Similarly, the *therapeutic countertransference,* difficult at best within the person of the treatment figure in the individual therapeutic situation, assumes within the ward the additional dimensions and subtleties that have to do with how the various team figures interact, in turn, with each other.

From an orthogenetic standpoint, psychiatric treatment, either individually or in a group, may be viewed from at least two interrelated vantage points. One is that any therapy represents a learning situation, in which the patient participates emotionally and intellectually, in varying degrees, in learning new forms of behavior as well as unlearning old, maladaptive or inadequate ones

(Hilgard 1956, pp. 290–327; Dollard and Miller 1950, Cameron 1947, Misbach 1948). A second is that psychotherapy shares much in common with puericulture and, of course, pedagogy; hence, for optimal therapy as for optimal learning, the therapist or teacher must have certain personal qualities with which the patient or student, as the case may be, may identity himself with him and proceed to internalize. (See also A. Freud [1935], Pearson [1954], Fenichel [1945], and Aichhorn [1935].) Among these, of course, are a highly developed and consistent self-image and self-concept, sincerity, sustained interest, emotional warmth, knowledge appropriate to his task, and freedom from disabling psychopathology. Thus, if these comprise in part the qualities that make the "good" parent, who promotes his child's psychosexual growth, they are also the very qualities that characterize the "good" teacher and the "good" psychotherapist.

Ernst Simmel (1929) made the first important effort to set forth the application of psychoanalytic principles to the treatment of patients in a sanatorium (hospital). Simmel drew the important conclusion that patients who needed hospital care were as incapable of orientation in reality as the psychotic. In other words, they harbored more or less severe ego defects that were well known to preclude their treatment with orthodox psychoanalytic technique. Simmel made reference, under this rubric, to such diverse cases as the major psychoses; the infantile, impulse-ridden, and inadequate characters; the addicts; and the organically based disorders. He spoke of the hospital as "a prosthesis, a crutch" for the patient, to render the latter's analytic work fruitful. Federn (1952) later spoke of providing libido from external sources for an ego suffering from impaired or inadequate narcissistic self-investment.

A second and crucially important advance in our understanding of the psychiatric treatment of these narcissistic patients was the repeated observation that such patients manifest the most profound if labile transferences and that they demand of those who would treat them the utmost degree of those personal characteristics previously described if their treatment is to have lasting effect. It is now generally understood why this is so. In part through the work of Melanie Klein (1932) and Fairbairn (1954, pp. 3–179), we have come to appreciate the fact that the object relations of these psychosexually primitive patients transpire at a preoedipal level and most often at a preponderantly oral level, just as they do among young children; hence, the therapeutic effort — whether individual, group, or milieu — must address itself to the enormous and vexing problem of the vicissitudes of the patient's internalized objects. In such cases, the ultimate resistance to treatment emerges from the patient's fear that he will, by whatever means, destroy or be destroyed by the treatment figure, as well as from the latter's corresponding fear of the patient as a manifestation of his regressive countertransference.

The similarities among child-rearing, pedagogy, and psychiatric treatment become understandable if one considers the similarities among the subjects' respective transferences. The paradigm is, of course, the relationship of the growing child to his parents. The child's *parentification* of his teachers is well known. And, especially in the case of the seriously ill psychiatric patient, the so-called parental transference to his treatment figure constitutes a basic manifold of responses, in terms of which a knowledge of his therapeutic needs must be founded. Thus, such a patient is "like a child" because he has, for whatever reasons, a preoedipal ego.[1]

Simmel and his successors understood that just as the individual psychoanalyst or psychotherapist must be a consistent and hence meaningful and significant transference object for the patient, so must be that group of treatment figures named the treatment team in the milieu of the ward. Just as the child's search for identity will be blighted by inconsistent or ambivalent handling, the seriously ill preadult or adult patient's treatment will also founder should the treatment team deal similarly with him. Thus, the enormous amount of work the team must perform to reach mutual agreement about how to deal with the patient's resistances and to meet his psychological needs does more than to disseminate important information about him. Disciplined collaboration also helps the various team members to recognize and deal with the *regressive pull* that the patient exerts upon them, thereby tending to force them into a variety of primitive, identificatory behaviors that preclude their *engagement* with the patient.

THE TREATABILITY OR ANALYZABILITY
OF THE ADOLESCENT

Adolescents, we are told, are usually "unanalyzable" (Lorand 1961). Their "unanalyzability" remains either a puzzle or else is accounted for by a variety of ego-psychological assumptions of limited significance unless the patient's environment is taken into consideration. One can rarely if ever perform psychotherapy or psychoanalysis of adolescents if one attempts to fit his efforts into the procrustean bed of some sort of orthodox technique. The same holds true for preadolescent children. Neither patient, preadolescent nor adolescent, is motivated to conform to the various rules that the therapist seeks to impose on the therapeutic process as conditions for engaging in it. The same holds true for the vast majority of psychiatric hospital patients, both for psychotic patients and for the various kinds of narcissistic or preoedipal patients. It holds true, in fact, for a far larger number of psychiatric patients than is reflected in the voluminous literature devoted to their treatment.

The adolescent readily and quickly proceeds to violate the therapist's fantasy of the "good" patient, who is presumably motivated to comply with the therapist's therapeutic structure (that is, rules, regulations, and spatio-temporal arrangements) and who, directly or otherwise, "admits to" being ill or that he "hurts" and will hence do whatever the therapist requires of him in order to "get well." When some writers assert that all adolescents suffer from a sort of "normal psychopathology" (Benedek 1952) or from an "as-if" (A. Freud 1946a) or borderline condition, they invoke the protean, labile vicissitudes of the adolescent ego to account for the fact that the patient does not view the fact or prospect of psychotherapy as do the therapists. This is no doubt partly valid, but it begs the question to attribute the adolescent's recalcitrance to inherent ego weakness as such and thus fails to explain anything. It is almost as if these writers tacitly or otherwise expect that adolescents will behave toward the prospect of dynamic psychotherapy as if they were highly motivated adults. Motivated for help they are; adults they are not. Thus, to expect that the child will act like an adult is to expect that the child will behave in ways inappropriate to the realities of his inner life. If the child violates the therapist's preconceptions of what psychotherapy ought to be like, it is the easier to find fault with the child (or with the child's ego) than to examine one's presuppositions.

The difficulties that dynamically oriented therapists experience with adolescent patients deserve a more comprehensive examination than they have usually received. An important consideration is that many therapists have attempted a psychotherapeutic process with adolescents on an outpatient basis, only to fail.[2] Another is that some have tried such a process without concomitant psychotherapy or casework treatment for the parental figures and have also failed. In the former instances, outpatient treatment metaphorically emphasizes a presumed adult therapeutic structure and a more mature motivation, which the child lacks. Hence, the child's difficulties with motility are never successfully translated into usable symbolic material, and they are carried elsewhere than in therapy. The situation that excludes concomitant therapy for the parents so grossly ignores the complex of parental motivations favoring the child's illness as expression for the parents' own difficulties as to preclude both parent and child from coming to grips with them. As a result, the child is denied parental permission to use therapy effectively and never resolves the loyalty problem, which eventually expresses the child's need to pit his parents against the therapist (chapter 2).

Thus, the reluctance of many therapists to undertake reconstructive psychiatric treatment of adolescents resembles their reluctance to undertake it with psychotic, character neurotic, and organically brain-injured patients. In each case, the vast majority of the patients are unable to conform to the therapist's a priori conditions for the structural aspects of the therapy.

I do not wish to argue the point that the adolescents pose some of the more difficult therapeutic problems that the psychiatrist must face, or that many of them need inpatient care in order to accomplish in therapy what their more "ideally" motivated adult relatives may, in a more permissive atmosphere, be expected to carry off. But it is, paradoxically, in the inpatient setting that the therapist's ambivalent motivations reappear in full measure and in ways that proceed to neutralize the superior therapeutic facilities such a setting ought to provide. The clash between the "moral treatment" approach and the staff's need to provide safe, secure, carefully enforced custodial structure becomes evident in the bewildering melange of therapeutic concepts, techniques and types of overt behavior one often observes in inpatient facilities where preadolescent or adolescent children are in treatment. The staff's inner needs to provide the moral values of personal worth and dignity and to maintain some sort of spurious democracy within the hospital often lead adolescent patients to attempt to destroy the milieu through episodes of sexual and aggressive acting out or to evade and escape it with a variety of techniques, including running away (chapter 1). Efforts to enforce a rigid, punitive custodial structure are, in turn, met by the same and by competition between staff and patients to prove who can maintain control over the milieu.

This ambivalence finds further expression in two antipodal attitudes among the treatment staff. First, they may urge upon the patients the acquisition of prematurely adultlike forms of behavior by expecting from them ideas, feelings, and overt behavior suitable for adults—expectations that ignore the obvious fact that hospitalized adolescents have never learned to enjoy their childhoods, have never experienced the pleasures of healthy regression supported by a controlling love object, and hence will rebel endlessly against efforts to thrust upon them spurious adulthoods in conformity with the adults' wishes. Second, the staff members, because of their own unresolved sadistic wishes and infantile needs, may alternatively impose upon the patients a punitive, regressive, correctional regimen, which ignores the patients' profound needs for controlled experimentation with psychosexual growth, and endlessly embitters them by keeping them infantile.

Chapter 1 discussed the variety of ways in which adolescents attempt to vitiate the impact of an intensive inpatient milieu upon them. The view was set forth that the entire gamut of overt and covert types of behavior that adolescents show immediately upon and for varying periods following admission to the hospital largely serve as resistances to treatment. The fact of resistance is, of course, less impressive than the forms it assumes, which among members of this age group will vary from the wildest and most violent physical behavior to adroit dissimulation of symptoms with the ensuing appearance of apparent but spurious inner personality change. A dynamic, interpretive milieu comprises a behaviorally consistent group of treatment figures whose task is to understand the verbal and nonverbal communications that take place among themselves and the patients. Basic to this task is an understanding, in turn, of that preponderance of communications from the patient, which convey his resistance to the treatment figures — including the spectrum of means whereby he will attempt to escape, avoid, deflect, or otherwise neutralize their influence upon him. During this resistance phase, the treatment team must strive to block the patient's effective use of these resistances, which, one discovers, are directed toward preventing the patient from internalizing the milieu, including its staff figures and the external controls they impose upon him. Charney (1963), who made this point, also observed that as the patient proceeds, despite his resistances, to internalize the milieu, he begins concomitantly to reexternalize already present introjects. In this dual process, the adolescent undergoes the experience of massively and multiply shifting ego states, which terrifies him and in response to which he feels the need to retreat even farther from contact with the staff or else to act out to bring to a halt these intense depersonalizing and derealizing experiences. Thus, this basic, early *introject work,* which begins as the resistance phase comes to a close, requires the use of a carefully supervised closed ward that simultaneously promotes such work and precludes the effective use of resistance by which the patient attempts to nullify it. (The reason for selecting the term *introject work* will become more apparent later in this discussion.)

CONCOMITANT PSYCHIATRIC CASEWORK FOR PARENTS DURING THE RESISTANCE PHASE

As indicated in chapter 2, the resistance phase of the patient, toward the end of which the introject work begins in earnest, roughly coincides with a similar phase in the parents' related case-work process. In the period before, during, and for some time following the child's admission to the hospital, the parents have already begun the task of separation from him. This separation is complexly overdetermined. For some parents, it symbolizes the child's death or rebirth. It may mean a confirmation for the parent of the parent's failure as a sexual and biological object and a final admission that one has brought forth a monstrous offspring. It may contain the parent's terrifying, projected wish that the hospital will hurt, maim, or kill the "bad" child. It may imply that the child will gain strength from the hospital, only to return home to hurt, damage, or kill the parents. It always implies that the complex familial balances, in part determined and maintained by the child, have become to some extent undone, with the prospect of the eruption of uncontrolled aggressive and erotic needs among those still at home. It usually symbolizes the loss of an anaclitic dependency object or the interruption of a variety of diffusions and reversals of role among parents and child; hence, the parent will perceive in the child's separation the loss of a substitute sibling, a proxy spouse, or a symbolic parental figure.

Several consistent and predictable effects ensue from the separation of parent and child through hospitalization of the child. First, no matter how much difficulty the child may have caused at home, one or both parents proceed to reinternalize the separated child, to direct aggression against the introject, and to thereby suffer varying degrees of depression. Second, the parent is prone to behave in the manner of the prelatency and early latency child and to expect that the interactions between the child and the hospital structure will approximate those between parent and child in the home (Friedlander 1949). Thus, the parent comes to project onto the hospital in general and onto the caseworker in particular variations of aggressive and erotic fantasies that the parent has long harbored toward the child. As a result, the early casework transference assumes a profound meaning, reflecting the parent's manifold of fantasies, wishes, and needs directed toward the hospitalized child as well as toward other family members. Third, the parent may be expected to quickly resist the casework process.

The parent's unconscious or conscious wish to prevent change in the child syncretizes with the wish to prevent change in one's self, to "hang on" to past conditions and techniques of adjustment, to perseverate with what is known, however discomforting it may have been. Both the natural fact that the child has not yet effected separation and the pathological grounds for maintaining the child's failure to separate conspire to engender and maintain the parent's inference that whatever happens to the child also happens to one's self. As a result, the parent will in visits and correspondence subtly or otherwise proceed to exhort the child to resist change, to hold back, to remain disturbed, or to dissimulate, with the hope of neutralizing the real and fantasied effects of the treatment structure on him and hence on the parent as well.

THE PATHOLOGICAL PARENT-CHILD DYAD AND THE PROBLEM OF FUSION

To understand further the interdigitation of the child's residential treatment and the parents' casework therapy, it is necessary to understand that when the child is ill enough to require hospitalization, his problems, including those he shares with his family members, are basically preoedipal. This means that one applies to adolescent inpatients Simmel's view of adult hospital patients, which is that their fixations are, at root, narcissistic. It further means, in genetic-dynamic terms, that the psychological uses to which the family members put each other find expression in terms of the most basic problems of identity, separateness, mastery, and the control of impulses. It is, of course, in the hospitalized group of psychiatrically ill adolescents that is most often found the symptomatic expression of the family members' exceptionally regressive uses of each other. In such cases, the patient's ongoing struggle to attain a measure of independence of the parental objects is invariably discovered, and the struggle, by virtue of the very fixations from which it emerges, encompasses both aggressive and erotic instinctual needs.

The overwhelming orality and the angry anacliticism of these adolescents may be viewed in either of two ways: (1) The struggles over basic identity, prereflective self, fusion with, and engulfment of and by the object may be regressive from anal struggles over the use of language and motility to achieve mastery and control in the service of postoral separation; or (2) they may reflect primary fixations in the earlier oral stage with hardly any progress toward anality having been accomplished. Thus, irrespective of whether the adolescent is diagnosed as suffering from nuclear schizophrenia, symbiotic psychosis, infantile personality, antisocial reaction, atypicality, borderline condition, or whatever, the initial therapeutic work addresses itself to the complex of difficulties that center upon separation from the parent as paradigmatic for struggles of the most primitive kind. It must not be forgotten, of course, that the very act of parent-child separation, hospitalization in these cases, has the potential for enormously regressive effects on both parties.

It must be reemphasized that the common core of familial psychopathology of which the child's illness is in varying degrees a symbolic expression leads ineluctably to conflicts over the latter's separation by hospitalization, and these conflicts have similar dynamic significance for the parent and the child. Such separation may mean death, dissolution, starvation, loss of external controls for self-destruction, or liquidation of what little identity is already present—that is, if it means for the child a thanatic disruption of the parent-child fusion, it has similar meaning for the parent. The patient's basic message has long been, "I have never really begun to grow up." For whatever reasons, the parent has had to use the child as a thing, an endlessly infantile baby, or a parental object, proxy spouse, or sibling. Hence, separation of the two disrupts such uses of the child—which are, in turn, in the service of the same kinds of regressive, preambivalent, and ambivalent needs that the parent and the child share.[3]

There are essentially two forms of parent-child dyad, in both of which the primarily orally fixated adolescent is locked in a struggle with a similarly fixated parent: (1) Apart from each other, each member of the dyad appears to perish and (2) each *appears* essential for the other because the "combined energies" of both seem necessary for the existence of either. In the first of these two forms of the parent-child dyad, the opening or resistance phase in the adolescent's hospital treatment must be based upon a total or nearly total physical separation of the two for periods of up to several months in order to bring the mutually destructive interaction to a halt and to begin to demonstrate to both parent and the child that each may, in fact, exist without the other. The carefully structured milieu of the ward and the concomitant efforts of the caseworker then come into play. The separation is often terrifying to child and parent, whose near-agonies comprise the gamut of shifting and fluctuating ego states and lead, at times, to herculean mutual efforts to evade and escape the treatment structure or to batter it to bits as they strain to re-fuse. The treatment staff members are perceived as murderers, and the parent and the child may bring forth hallucinations, delusions, and a wide spectrum of primitive types of behavior — both as expressions of their disorganization and as defensive means by which to intimidate the treatment figures psychologically and to motivate them to terminate the separation. The therapeutic goal remains, of course, to promote internalization of the milieu through its treatment figures, including the parental internalization of the caseworker. With the giving up of each other's introjects, parents and child begin to internalize new ones. When this process has set in, face-to-face contact between the child and the parent is permitted, and the two may reexperience each other as better-separated objects.

The second form of parent-child dyad is at once more primitive, more difficult to treat, and prognostically more ominous. In these cases, both the mother and the child share a deeper, more univalent fusion. Their separation on the occasion of the child's hospitalization entails the usual fluctuating disruptions and resistances. But the major differences from the former cases reside precisely in their utter inability to reorganize without each other, to perform the terrifying mourning work, to begin to internalize new objects, and hence to be able to come together again with strengthened ego boundaries. It often requires several months of intensive work to recognize that neither partner to the fusion possesses sufficient "energy" without the other, not only to begin to work through the separation but also to barely exist at all psychologically. Both partners, after a variable period, proceed to settle into protracted detachment and despair, with episodes of feeble but ineffectual efforts to resist the treatment structure. Both the ward staff and the caseworker report that they cannot "lay hold of" or engage the patient or the parent, and interactions among them appear to be determined by the patient and parent's ongoing autism, detachment, chronic anacliticism, and prolonged depersonalization and derealization, which signify, in both, a sort of living death. In such cases, the mother must be reintroduced as quickly as possible by way of supervised visits with the patient and must become a more directly integral part of the patient's treatment than would otherwise be necessary or desirable.

In the majority of such cases of severely disturbed adolescents and their families, a relatively consistent postadmission hospital course has been observed. In most instances, the patient rather quickly proceeds to resist the ward treatment figures with a variety of techniques, as described in chapter 1. The resistance ensues from relatively severe disruptions of the patient's ego as this becomes geographically detached from the maternal figure or surrogate following admission to the hospital. In weeks or months following admission, the patient begins to enter a condition that symptomatically signifies the emergence of various degrees of depression. If the active therapeutic program has "caught on" with the patient before this, the depression is more introjective in form and more angry, hostile, and aggressive, signifying that externalization of prior introjects has begun and that introjection of the treatment figures and the structure of which they are part has also set in. Usually after several more weeks or months, this depression begins to lift, and the patient has become ready for reassociation with the parents, who have meanwhile undergone a series of related experiences with the caseworker. The patient has begun to acquire "new" introjects and has begun to perceive that the world of extrafamilial objects is significantly different from that of the family (Friedlander 1949). If these steps are successfully traversed, the patient emerges at this phase of treatment much like a latency child whose ever-widening expansion of perceptions betokens an emancipation from the family and a growing awareness that the objects in the latter are differentiable from the self and are "meaningful others." Thus, a major goal of inpatient treatment is to exert considerable push on the patient to use the treatment team and structure as substitutes for what would otherwise have been the usual extrafamilial school-age objects and to stimulate further the self-objectification, the emancipation from primary dependency upon the family, and the growth of secondary process, which should otherwise have begun during the child's first five years.

In the second form of parent-child dyad, although resistance may be filled with a variety of expressed aggressions, depression take on a more anaclitic quality, which persists despite every effort by the treatment team. Furthermore, this depression seems to merge with what will become a chronic state of depersonalization and estrangement, with the occurrence, in many instances, of perceptual distortions and autistic ideation. The treatment team cannot "lay hold of" the patient, nor can the caseworker "lay hold of" the parents. In some cases, reintroduction of the parent by means of visits seems to bring about some fluctuating improvement; but in many cases, it seems to have little if any effect upon the extended course of things, and the patient, despite heroic therapeutic efforts, lapses into chronicity.

As has been seen, the psychological experiences shared by the patient and his parents before, during, and for a variable period following admission have to do with resistance toward the exchange of introjects. After careful analysis, what became increasingly apparent was that toward the end of the resistance phase of treatment in some cases, the patient entered into a condition that could be characterized as "showing distance," attempting to remain "unengaged with," or "untouched by" the treatment staff. Finally, in some of the most profound cases of parent-child fusion, the patient appeared to be in an inexorable progression toward a state of anergic changelessness, despite every effort to bring it to a halt.

As these phenomena came under extended observation, it was realized that their prototypes had already been described, in the case of separation at an infantile age, by Bowlby (1951, 1960a, 1960b, 1961, 1962) and others. Bowlby originally pointed out that the separated infant traverses three stages if the separation from the succoring maternal figure is not made good: the stages of *protest, despair,* and *detachment.* Indeed, what appeared to be taking place among the adolescent patients seemed best understood in terms of Bowlby's stages of infantile mourning. The stage of protest appeared to accord well with the phase of active and passive and both verbal and nonverbal resistance by the hospitalized adolescent, whose struggles with introjects, self-identity, and how to cope with ever-threatening primary process material are compounded with a variety of the most primitive fixations ensuing from the unresolved fusion with the parental object. Their efforts to resist were next seen to be superseded by despair, assuming the form of profound depression that is manifested among adolescents through a variety of somatic and behavioral equivalents. Finally, those patients who were to pass over into protracted chronicity were seen to enter a condition characterized by Bowlby as detachment, with its progressive constriction of the ego and deepening inability to be influenced.

Although hospitalized adolescents are well known for the variety of active and passive resistances to treatment, the aims subserved by the resistances require further clarification. As noted (chapters 1 and 2) the twin fears of undergoing change and of abandonment lie at the root of these resistances. It is now easier to schematize the intrapsychic processes with which these fears and the resistances which serve them are interconnected.

The defenses of resistance to change, of fear of being manipulated by adult treatment figures, of abandonment, and of starvation are defenses against depression; and the depression reflects internalized aggression and the terror of emptiness of internal objects. Thus, if the resistances fail in their defensive aim, depression (Bowlby's *despair*) ensues as the patient proceeds to exchange—to internalize and reinternalize, to externalize and reexternalize—introjects, with the terrifying fluctuations of ego state accompanying these processes. I believe that the prototype of these processes among hospitalized adolescents is found in the generically similar processes common to infantile mourning.

Experienced clinicians may often be heard to say, in the case of a very sick patient irrespective of his age, "His depression is going to come out when the treatment begins to have its effect." The reasons for this valid statement are not at all obscure. The depression *must* appear, as well as the fears of emptiness and death to which it gives metaphoric expression, as long as the patient's resistances toward expressing them are blocked. Among adolescents in particular, the mixed, "impure" depression emerges, with its many symptomatic equivalents, shifting episodes of overactivity and underactivity, and appearance of signs of disorganization and bizarreness that herald the switching of internalized objects. If, during this critical phase, the introject work gets done and the patient has "taken in" the treatment figures and treatment structure, he has "made the break" from the immediate parental objects and has begun to widen his object relations, which means that he has started to resolve the fusion problem that lies at the foundation of his illness.

FACTORS THAT BLOCK OR PRECLUDE THE INTROJECT WORK

What follows here is an admittedly incomplete list and incomplete discussion of the factors which tend to preclude the patient's accomplishment of the introject work and hence to prevent his resolution of the problem of fusion:

1. One begins with what, out of ignorance, may be called "endogenous factors" in patients who seem to lack the wherewithal to accomplish the introject work despite the most favorable conditions otherwise conducive to it—that is, access to an intensive therapeutic milieu, reasonably healthy parents, and a productive casework process. The moderately to severely feebleminded patient comes to mind as a case in which the necessary intellectual resources are lacking and where the patient is unable to emerge from a protracted dependency on parental objects because little or

no prereflective (primarily narcissistic) and hence reflective (secondarily narcissistic) senses of self can develop (Rinsley 1962b). A careful study of these cases discloses that the patient harbors the same terrors of separation as well as the need to resolve them as would his better-endowed peers, except that any movement toward such resolution precipitates mounting anxiety. The latter overwhelms the ego and threatens gross disorganization, bringing the movement to a halt.

2. Something similar may be said about the so-called nuclear, or, in Fliess' words, autistic-pre-symbiotic adolescents. One seems to deal, in these cases, with innate difficulties that since earliest infancy have forestalled the formation of the anlagen of the mother-child relationship. It is as if these adolescents inhabit a world of massive and frequent shifts of ego state almost without end, just as they did throughout preadolescence. For them, it is never a problem of resolving a pathogenic fusion because there never was a meaningful symbiosis in the first place. They often resemble their somewhat healthier peers in the stage of introject work, except that such work never comes to a conclusion because the hobbled ego is unable to maintain prereflective integrity as it takes in and puts out objects.

3. Another block to the accomplishment of the introject work is the failure, for whatever reasons, of the parental objects to utilize psychotherapeutic casework. To begin with, the child may have long since had no real parents at all and may have existed amidst a congeries of magic-hallucinatory and delusional parental fantasy creations. Efforts to bring about their reexternalization threaten psychological disaster, and the patient clings desperately to them despite everything. Where natural, adoptive, or interested foster parents are present, their failure to utilize available dynamic casework almost always, in my experience, reflects the presence of significant preoedipal family difficulties in which the patient is deeply enmeshed (chapter 2). In the majority of these cases, parental failure to use casework expresses reluctance or failure to help the child in resolving the loyalty problem and thus to permit or encourage him to perform the introject work, which involves the exchange of parental introjects for those symbolized by the

treatment figures. Some adolescent patients are able to accomplish this without parental support, but the work is then prolonged and much more difficult, and the result more problematic.

4. An often overlooked block to the patient's introject work may lie in the treatment structure itself. Among the multiple forms it assumes are such insuperable difficulties as a paucity of dynamically trained caseworkers skilled in therapeutic process, inadequate numbers of therapeutic staff, and the like. Again, granted an adequate number of staff members, the ward and adjunctive therapeutic teams may prove unable to allow themselves to be used as meaningful substitute objects. A potent basis for this emerges as part of the staff's countertransference. The staff may never really engage with the patient because the latter's earlier resistances prove overwhelming; hence, they are never sufficiently understood or interpretively dealt with. Or the staff may recoil with mounting anxiety from the multiple regressive symptoms, which indicate that the patient has begun to enter the phase of depression (despair); they may view this as a turn for the worse, to be halted soon and at all costs; and if this occurs, the patient's mourning work ceases.[4]

5. A commonly observed block to the introject work finds expression in some sort of "enlightened" expectation that the very sick adolescent child can, at least initially, accomplish such work in the absence of a closed, carefully structured, and interpretive milieu. This means, in short, early providing the patient with an open or a semiopen hospital environment, and it is one of the most effective ways to ensure that the resistance and especially the introject work never really begin at all. As has been seen, both the resistance work and the introject work are difficult and painful for the patient and arduous and demanding for the treatment staff. The patient will attempt to avoid such work as often and in whatever ways he can, and the staff may follow a similar course. The patient's continued regressive use of the parents through premature or psychologically ill-advised visits, the granting of grounds passes, home visits, and the prescription of individual or group psychotherapy—especially of the willy-nilly permissive kind—before the resistance work has really gotten under way regularly provide the patient with escape routes through which he proceeds

to dilute and diffuse the work he must do and the pain attendant upon it if he is to begin to change. I believe that this is one very important reason why outpatient and "open" institutional treatment often fails with adolescents, as it so often does with character-disordered, infantile and psychotic adults — the very kinds of narcissistic patients to whom Simmel originally made reference. In these cases, resistance and introject work are so painful and difficult that the patient either absents himself from psychotherapeutic hours or else enters prolonged regressive (unproductive) periods as he shrinks from coming to grips with his narcissism.

DEPRESSION IN ADOLESCENTS

Although there is much psychodynamic literature devoted to the subject of depression in adults, there is much less devoted to the dynamics and phenomenology of depression among adolescents and still less devoted to these matters for hospitalized, seriously ill adolescents.[5] What follows is drawn from both intensive and extensive experience with this latter group. As a result, the conclusions are admittedly biased, but they nonetheless offer fascinating and instructive insights into depressive phenomena in general.

Adolescents are known to harbor and demonstrate wide and frequent affective fluctuations. In the midst of these notable swings of mood, depressive feelings are exceedingly common and more or less irregular cycles of depression and hyperphoria lend an almost manic-depressive color to the protean affective life of so many adolescents in our culture. Thus, if and when an adult has gained some measure of trust from an adolescent boy or girl, answers to such stock diagnostic questions as, "Do you sometimes (often) feel blue (down in the dumps, sad, worried)?" are often answered in the affirmative. Among hospitalized adolescents and under similar circumstances of trust, the answers are invariably, "Yes."

What becomes increasingly evident on more careful study and inquiry is that the subjective experiences that the adolescent (and, one might add, the adult as well) conveys with the term *depressed* or its vernacular equivalents pass far beyond the phenomena these terms usually comprehend. When most depressed people admit depression, they are conveying, in addition, a congeries of much more sweeping inner suffering; this suffering, in my experience, turns out to be various degrees of *depersonalization* and *estrangement (derealization)*. If *depressive* experiences are usually classified as *affective* disturbances, the invariably associated continuum of depersonalization-estrangement experiences reflect much more comprehensive alterations in ego state, self-perception, and perception of outside objects, in which the affective experiences are embedded but with which they are in no sense coterminous. It is, after all, easier to say that one feels "blue," "bad," or "down in the dumps" than to attempt to convey the much more subtle pre-reflective experiences of change of ego state for which there exists but a limited and specialized vocabulary. It is easier also if the examiner fails to examine carefully for ego state fluctuations and is content with answers that reflect affective experiences.

From the standpoint of object relations, it is known that later depression ensues in the wake of a disappointment in early life (Abraham 1927, pp. 248-279, 407-501). The prototype for this disappointment is the loss of the maternal object, with which the infant is in varying degrees fused. Hence, maternal object-loss during early life is a loss of part of the self, leaving, as it were, a greater or lesser "hole" in the child's anlage of primarily narcissistic self-representation. Such a hole or defect is, of course, an ego defect, and it is no wonder that such a defect, originating as it does when the mother-child boundaries are hazy, should lead to difficulties with the ego boundaries and with the ego states associated with them in later life.

But something more is required for an understanding of the basis for the "impure" depressions common among preadult individuals. One begins with the recognition that depersonalization and derealization experiences abound in the depressions one encounters in the young. But these experiences abound as well among the adult—more classical—cases of depressions. How can one account for the symptomatic differences between them? The answer is that the differences may be accounted for, in large part, in terms of the development of secondary narcissism. The growth of secondary narcissism implies the growth of self-as-object (Rinsley 1962b) and of the self as object of one's own and of others' intended perceptions, and such growth signals a move toward a more differentiated (adultlike) form of object relations. It is certainly true that the development of secondary narcissism may be perverted, warped, and pathologically accelerated and that it may serve economically exceptionally expensive, defensive purposes: Witness the latency child with a compulsion neurosis whose vivid, logical self-objectification so often rests metastably upon a foundation of preambivalent fixations and traumata. Nonetheless, secondary narcissism serves, by virtue of the very self-objectification that characterizes it, to strengthen the ego boundaries, including the inner barrier against primary process material. In such cases, the ego ideal has served its purposes, and recurrent disappointment leads to loss of self-esteem, guilt, and the more classical depression in which the internal object is aggressively dealt with.

If this is, in large measure, the course of events in adults, it is almost never the case in children. If secondary narcissism has not yet developed and if self-objectification has therefore remained primitive, both inner and outer ego boundaries remain insubstantial and the ego is less protected against homeostatically unbalancing stimuli from within as well as from without. In such cases the depression is much more perceptualized, and fresh charges of primitive material easily reach consciousness and proceed to overwhelm it or to be pushed into headlong action. (See Esman 1962.) From a phenomenological viewpoint, there is little self-esteem to be damaged if there has been little to begin with; the terrors of abandonment, starvation, and death that the patient experiences are not transposed into aggression, which consistently seeks either inner or outer objects, and the entire process appears much more primitive, disorganized, and bizarre.

If the symptoms signaling depression in adolescents are, in some ways, different from those in adults, they are, as many observers have noted, rather akin to the symptoms of schizophrenic illness in adults. Thus, one observes in both the dyshedonia, disturbances of ego boundary (depersonalization, estrangement, hallucinations); varying degrees of thinking disturbance; the terror of closeness, fusion, engulfment, abandonment, starvation, and death; pervasive ambivalence; sweeping suspiciousness; and the incongruity of mood and ideation — all of which are indicative of profound disorder of object relations. The adult schizophrenic is, of course, depressed, and his depression is so protean because it emerges from the same kinds of primitive fixations as does the depression of the child.

The phenomenology of the second, or *definitive,* phase of hospital treatment of adolescents (the phase of *introject work*) reflects, as I have come to believe, the natural history of the emergence and flowering of the protean depression described here. As the latter appears, the patient seems concomitantly more distant from the treatment figures and more disorganized and bizarre. Embedded in the adolescent's efforts toward distance and the bizarreness of the symptomatology is his eleventh-hour need to cause the staff to desist from blocking his resistances toward internalizing them; and it is crucially important that the staff redouble their efforts, lest the treatment founder.

CONCLUSION

This view of the natural history of intensive hospital treatment of adolescents is founded upon Simmel's observation that hospital patients are primarily narcissistically fixated, and it accords well with the course of active infantile mourning as described by Bowlby. Present observations allow the conclusion that the various phases through which the patients regularly pass during the course of their hospitalization correspond in more than a rough way to Bowlby's three stages. The phase of *resistance* (to treatment) corresponds to Bowlby's stage of *protest*; the phase of emergent *depression* (introject work) is akin to Bowlby's stage of infantile *despair*; and finally, Bowlby's stage of *detachment* finds approximate counterpart in the phase of *chronicity,* with ongoing regression and long-standing breakdown of any significant ability or effort to internalize.

During the phase of resistance to treatment, the patient protests the object loss attendant upon separation at the time of admission. The various resistances he uses to convey the aggression and hostility he feels concerning this loss serve at least two functions: First, they tend to further bind the lost object to him; second, partly as a result of the first, they retard or preclude the acquisition of new objects. Both resistances must be brought to a halt if the phase of resistance is to pass; this can be accomplished if, and only if, the meanings of the resistances are understood and appropriate interpretations are made to render their further use needless, in order to evoke the depression lying behind them (chapter 1). Many adolescent patients resist this difficult process through the development of unquestionably psychotic symptomatology, inherent within which is the message, "If you do not stop what you are doing to me, you will make me crazy." If this resistance is effectively dealt with in turn, the underlying depression will next emerge.

With the emergence of the depression, the patient begins to enter the second or *definitive* treatment phase of hospitalization — the phase of the *introject work* proper. The depression is, among adolescents, typically "impure" or "mixed" and is conveyed by a vast array of depressive equivalents, which together yield a protean clinical picture so different from the classical retarded depressions of later life. At least two features of preadult mental function conspire to produce this protean depression: the fluctuant insubstantiality of the mental and bodily ego boundaries of these patients and the absence of the firm binding of introjects, which renders the threat of their interchange more disturbing. Both factors lead to the use of conversion and somatization, and to access of primitive drives to motility.

As the patient proceeds to enter ever more deeply into the introject work, he begins to share profound feelings of personal guilt with the staff. He begins to convey, both verbally and otherwise, how "bad" he feels himself to be. He speaks of being dirty, seductive, evil, destructive, and murderous. He vents mounting hostility toward the treatment figures and, most important, begins to direct it toward his parents, present or past, living or dead. He repeats, both in direct and metaphoric ways, his feelings that the parental objects starved, abandoned, and killed him and demanded of him that he act out their own "bad" selves for them. By these routes, he begins to externalize the very core of what so much of his multi-layered illness was arrayed to conceal: his ambivalent "good" and "bad" selves, the introjects that composed the awful identity he had so long harbored until their pressures forced his symptoms upon him.

He can now say that he *hates,* without fear of vital reprisal from the treatment figures; he can also begin to say that he *loves.* The fear that externalizing these things will destroy him begins, then, to fall away. If the parents have begun to make analogous moves in their casework process, the time approaches when the intensive use of the closed ward is no longer necessary, and the patient may now begin to have greater physical freedom, including, of course, consideration for discharge from inpatient care. The time required for intensive use of the latter to bring the adolescent to this point of improvement may exceed one to three years, and extended out-patient psychotherapy for him and casework treatment for the parents may require several more years. It is only with these funda-mental ingredients that it is possible, at last, to very cautiously begin speaking of cure.

Notes

1. Some cogent formulations of parentification have been made by Rado (1956) and Berne (1961, 1964b).

2. This is not to gainsay the fact that outpatient psychotherapy has value for *some* adolescents, including a minority of those patients to whose problems this chapter is devoted. But if used solely or in the early stage of treatment, outpatient structure places almost insuperable difficulties in the path of any but sympto-matic treatment of the kinds of adolescent patient herein described.

3. It will be apparent that the occurrence of psychotic or borderline illness among adolescents is viewed here, in many if not all cases, as examples of the delayed appearance of an unresolved symbiotic condition, which is often diag-nosable on careful psychiatric study during latency. In these cases, the child's

symptoms may not have been particularly impressive, or the parents were unable or unwilling to seek professional help in those instances where the child was in prolonged, serious, and evident trouble. See also Fliess (1961) and Mahler (1952).

4. Among the factors that impair the staff's usefulness as substitute introjects, two emerge with special prominence in any work with preadult patients: (1) premature or total reliance upon the open or semiopen ward, which abets the patient's ongoing efforts to split and diffuse his transference to the treatment figures, the more readily to transform his intrapsychic difficulties in motility and hence to carry them elsewhere than on the ward, where they may be recognized and dealt with; and (2) the "vegetable soup milieu" (chapter 3), which, in effect, amounts to an effort to apply a caricature of guidance clinic structure in an inpatient setting. In such a structure, scant attention is paid to the differences in professional training between the psychiatrist, clinical psychologist, psychiatric social worker, psychiatric nurse, adjunctive therapist, and psychiatric aide or child-care worker. Rather, various staff members are viewed as more or less inter-changeable, and professional roles become obfuscated. In my experience, such role-blurring usually reflects unresolved interprofessional rivalries, which, in turn, convey deeper personal identity conflicts. The latter, communicated overtly or subtly to patients, wreak disastrous effects on the therapeutic effort by muddy-ing the staff figures' clarity as transference objects for the patients. For these rea-sons, membership in the ward treatment team is restricted to the psychiatrist, who, one concludes, is best equipped by his training to lead the team, and to the nurse and the aides or workers assigned to the ward. The remainder of the diag-nostic and therapeutic personnel have no responsibilities for the administration or management of the ward and hence have few reasons for entering it.

5. Mendelson (1960) provides a review of the psychoanalytic literature on depression.

6

Intensive Residential Treatment

Psychiatric treatment of preadult patients can be considered as having two major tasks, neither of which can in practice be separated from the other: (1) to assist the sick child to begin to resolve those fixations that have precluded ongoing psychosexual development and (2) to provide appropriate social and educational experiences through which a certain degree of such development may proceed while resolution of the illness is occurring. The goal of treatment is, of course, to help the adolescent to reinstitute developmental progress, which his psychopathology has either inhibited or abjectly thwarted.

More than a decade of experience in the intensive residential psychiatric treatment of early and middle adolescents has reaffirmed for me Simmel's view (1929) that psychoneurotic individuals, whether adolescent or older, do not usually seek or receive hospital treatment. Rather, the overwhelming majority of adolescent psychiatric inpatients suffer from one of the variety of schizophrenic disorders or are borderline or infantile-narcissistic individuals whose natural history would with high probability lead them into subtly or frankly psychotic adjustment in later life. It goes without saying that concomitant psychiatric casework treatment of parents is, whenever possible, an essential ingredient in the child's treatment; in some cases, combined family treatment accelerates the therapeutic process, as it brings child and parents together for mutual exploration of the intrafamilial problems from which the child's illness has developed and to which it in part gives expression.

Extended observations on the natural history of the hospital course of adolescents ill enough to require hospitalization have led to the discovery that the adolescent's intramural sojourn separates itself into several stages or phases (chapters 1–3, 5). Of these, I wish to describe briefly the two that have been most intensively studied over the past several years and about which we have accumulated the most thorough dynamic and phenomenologic information.

The *resistance phase,* as previously discussed, dates from admission through the end of the first six months to one year of residence. During this period, the child's and the parents' verbal and nonverbal behavior on the ward and in casework centers on their anger and anguish over separation and is found to resemble the responses of separated infants during Bowlby's stage of protest (1960a, 1960b, 1961, 1962). The rich complexity of patient and parental maneuvers during the resistance phase subserves their need to thwart or preclude change within themselves, to preserve the dyadic parent-child relationship which, in hospital patients, amounts to regressive fusions based in turn upon the most primitive preoedipal fixations. Indeed, a large number of these dyads represent long-concealed hypersymbioses, dormant during latency and wont to erupt belatedly as parental object-ties and their intrapsychic representations loosen during preadolescence.[1] Some of the parent-child dyads are autistic-presymbiotic, with a more ominous prognosis.

For both kinds of dyad, resistances to treatment are often kaleidoscopic and herculean, oriented toward preventing the treatment staff's perceived efforts to dissolve the fusions and hence to destroy the partners to them or for the autistic-presymbiotic adolescent, to take away the dereistic, magic-hallucinatory constructions that serve the child as substitutes for objects. Thus, the therapeutic resistances are life-and-death matters, and the staff members are perceived as plunderers and murderers.

Irrespective of the many forms the adolescent's resistance behavior may assume, ranging from adroit, pseudoadult dissimulation to frenetic attempts at alloplasticity on the ward, a common denominator becomes increasingly evident: Their aim is to split and divide the staff. Time-honored terms for this are transference splitting or simply manipulation. The usual interpretation of such actions holds that they aim to keep the staff figures "off base" or to hobble the staff's efforts to provide necessary external controls. Deeper scrutiny shows, however, that the adolescent's resistances aim to rend the staff into a congeries of fragmented part-objects. The resistances comprise direct-transference behavior to the hospital and to the ward and its therapeutic figures, and in them can be perceived the deeper and self-defeating need to experience the mother as a congeries of split-off part-objects. As the persistence of part-object relations is closely connected with the child's fear that he can destroy the maternal object or else be destroyed by it (Klein 1940, 1946), one realizes that the object-splitting resistances of the hospitalized adolescent are based upon very primitive oral-aggressive aims.

The outstanding problem of the child with symbiotic psychosis is profound, disorganizing anxiety when psychomotor development moves him toward beginning emancipation from primary dependence on the maternal figure; the child disorganizes because emancipation threatens his very existence, and he views himself, in his childlike way, as a mere part-object of the mother. Thus, failure of whole-object-representation characterizes the symbiotically fixated child. The same failure characterizes the resistance behavior of the hospitalized adolescent. It can thus be concluded that the roots of the psychopathology that lead most adolescents into the need for residential treatment are symbiotic, and in some, the roots are presymbiotic.

Experience shows that members of the therapeutic team—whether ward personnel, individual or group psychotherapist, adjunctive therapist, or teacher—must be prepared to work with a wide spectrum of regressive behavior among hospitalized adolescents based, in turn, on very early traumas and developmental fixations. In the case of the hypersymbiotic adolescent, the otherwise expected loosening of parental object-ties combines with mounting terror of abandonment to recapitulate, at this later age, the apprehensions of the classical, symbiotic three- to five-year-old so ably described by Mahler (1952). Both find expression in the welter of subtle frenetic techniques by which the hospitalized adolescent seeks to preserve or recapture the symbiotic union with the maternal object, techniques I have elsewhere described in terms of the resistance behaviors with which the staff must work (chapters 1–2).

Several ingredients are necessary for the intensive reconstructive treatment of the adolescent who needs residential care. First, as in the case of the classical symbiotic child, one must provide educational, occupational, and recreational experiences for properly selected groups of peers to encourage peer-age identifications and to promote the neutralization of raw instinctual impulses; thus, the establishment of opportunities for the patient to sublimate ushers in the elements of the latency-age experiences, which the hypersymbiotic adolescent has failed to achieve by virtue of the persistent regressive tie with the maternal object. Second, consistent recognition and appropriate interpretation of resistance behaviors must also occur. Individual psychotherapy, in the residential setting, may be delayed or not offered at all. Thus, the basic aim of these modalities is to wean the patient from the regressive hypersymbiosis with the maternal figure.

Although space does not permit detailed discussion of specific techniques of interpreting resistance behavior, several general principles may briefly be mentioned. First, in accordance with Aichhorn's and Goldstein's views, the staff strives to evoke the patient's positive transference to ward treatment figures, particularly but not exclusively to the psychiatrist, as quickly as possible (Aichhorn 1935, 1964, Goldstein 1959b). Liberal use of long- and short-term restrictions, including isolation (seclusion), early inhibits access of raw instinctual drives to motility, limits the patient's use of ward peers as a refuge from the staff members, and promotes the unlayering of overdetermined defenses by engendering regression through limitation of sensory stimuli (Charney 1963). Strict limitation of contacts with family members, whether in person or via letters, similarly inhibits the child's defensive use of such figures. Carefully individualized dosages of ataraxic medication will, in many instances, sufficiently reduce anxiety to the point at which the child feels less fearful of staff figures, thus lessening the need for distance from them and assisting him to communicate more coherently with them (Rinsley 1963).

Although all these measures are nonverbal interpretations, the ward staff, especially the psychiatrist, should gently and repetitively interpret to the child the latter's hierarchy of observable defensive maneuvers, particularly his repeated use of distance-promoting behavior and even his use of clearly psychotic symptoms both to attract and ward off staff attention to him. The early-established positive transference sustains the child amidst these powerful, early assaults on his modus operandi on the ward.

Assuming that the patient's and the parents' resistance maneuvers can be brought to light and rendered ineffectual, there follows a period of one to several years that is of the highest importance for the resolution of the core of the patient's psychopathology and for the exposure of at least partial resolution of the family's repertoire of pathological intercommunications. This period, which is termed the *definitive phase* or the *phase of introject work,* witnesses the emergence from the child and, one hopes, from the parents as well, of a variety of "bad" part-objects and is often accompanied by an apparently regressive turn of events. Thus, the patient evinces a wide range of regressive symptoms and may appear to be disorganizing. The whole process witnesses the emergence of the atypical depression described in chapter 5, which heralds the switch of introjects — the externalization of old "bad" part-objects and internalization of new "good" introjects, in part represented in the figures of those members of the therapeutic staff in whom the patient has come to make a libidinal investment. The phenomenology of this phase, with its atypical depression expressed in multiple regressive symptoms, bears a certain analogy to the stage of despair which Bowlby has described for separated infants and signifies the inception of mourning for the lost internal objects. Finally, the emergence of "bad" part-objects finds expression in the patient's many metaphorical communications that amount to, "I am bad," which bespeaks externalization of the elements of Erikson's "negative identity."

The residential treatment of the autistic-presymbiotic adolescent is a different matter. It will be recalled that the hypersymbiotic child, however ill, has indeed experienced the otherwise normal symbiotic object-relationship with a mothering figure that flowers in the first half of the first year, whereas the autistic child has not. The persistence, among autistic-presymbiotic adolescents, of the objectless (in Freud's term, the "auto-erotic") position necessitates that the treatment aim, with exceptional care and attention, at the formation of the anlagen of early object-ties. For these children, a highly simplified, compulsively arranged, and optimally predictable environment is an absolute necessity—not unlike that prescribed for the care of a patient with organic cerebral impairment. Psychotherapy begins early, the one-to-one relationship is stressed, and the positive transference serves as the fulcrum about which the entire therapeutic effort is balanced; group-educative and peer-relational tasks are either excluded or held to a bare minimum to minimize the potentially dangerous drain they exert upon the ego's tiny store of energy.

Although we have had some notable successes with this sort of adolescent, it is well to remember that the resistance phase is prolonged and, in some cases, apparently interminable; furthermore, introject exchange in what would otherwise be the later phase of treatment is so dangerous as to threaten psychological disaster, as one encourages the child to give up, as it were, the tenaciously held, fragmented, and magic-hallucinatory, part-objects that guarantee the very barest of ego function. It is these patients who faced with even the slightest push toward introject work pass over into a state comparable with Bowlby's stage of detachment, and they then proceed into chronicity. For them, careful nurturance of the positive transference and multiple feeding devices to replenish the ego's depleted energies are, as Federn (1952) emphasized, the foundation for prolonged efforts to build object relations.

Turning now to some orthogenetic implications, one sees the patient arriving at the hospital as a chronological adolescent but harboring fixations that date from infancy; hence, he brings with him a preoedipal view of the world. The hypersymbiotic adolescent has traversed the "I-am" (oral) stage and come to developmental grief somewhere in the "I-am-separate-and-distinct" (anal) stage; thus, although he has achieved a nonreflectively narcissistic self-awareness, his efforts at reflective self-investment have failed him (Rinsley 1962b). Furthermore, since differentiation of sexual role depends upon his negotiation of the anal (ambivalent) stage toward the oedipal stage, sexual identity is blurred, and the patient experiences himself as impotent and passive, lacking ability to control and to master, and hence vulnerable to both internal and external stimuli.

Another characteristic of the adolescent patient, which is often overlooked, is his exceptional family-centeredness. Psychologically bound to his mental representations of the primary parental figures, he proves unable to pass beyond the view that everyone does things as do his parents, a task ordinarily accomplished only toward the latter half of the latency period. He thus comes to project onto all adults, including the treatment figures whose ministrations will prove of signal importance to him, his fears and expectations of his parents. This is a powerful factor behind the direct and labile transferences he develops.

For such adolescents, an early and essential therapeutic task is to reach that point of awareness at which separation from the parent is no longer experienced as potentially lethal to either or both. This effort is largely begun during the resistance phase of treatment, throughout which the patient's protean protests neither lead him nor his parents (that is, the world) into dissolution. As internal objects next proceed to emerge during the phase of introject work, appropriate staff figures become internalized. Assuming that the staff can withstand the ordinarily tremendously regressive countertransference into which this phase of the patient's experience will lead them, the patient begins to develop the view that other adults do indeed differ from his parents. By this time, then, the patient has moved toward the accomplishment of several

developmental tasks: He has perceived that separation is not iden-
tical with disaster; he has begun to perceive that the compensatory
megalomania he has used as a defense against his feelings of vulnerable impotency is unnecessary; he has begun to define his sexual identity; and in beginning to recognize the differences between
his own parents and other adult surrogates, he has taken a long
step into latency with definite possibilities for the neutralization of
raw instinctual impulses so basic to the operation of sublimations.

For the autistic-presymbiotic adolescent, the main early therapeutic task is to build a relationship with some consistent therapeutic figure and to win the patient's love through an incredibly
complex variety of anaclitic and auxiliary perceptual and control
functions, the basic aim of which is to begin to help the patient
cautiously to externalize the welter of primitive, magic-
hallucinatory introjects with which he ekes out his psychotic existence. As these emerge, the pervasive fragmentation of the ego's
functions and experience slowly abates; ego nuclei now begin to
cohere in relation to the therapist, and the growth of primary
narcissism begins to provide to the child an increasing degree of
continuous self-experience. Of great importance is the growing
libidinalization of the ego, such that the child may derive pleasure
in self-experience and the ego may serve as object of both the
instincts and of what will, in time, become the superego. Thus, the
child achieves a meaningful "I-am," the foundation of early object
relations has been laid, and coherent self-experience in relation to
time, space, and causality becomes possible. In that minority of
these cases for whom success crowned our efforts, the subsequent
course of events proved to be the therapeutic growth of a symbiosis, with later resolution in the general manner described here.
But the tasks are so formidable and the skills required are so great
as, in very many cases, to preclude such a happy issue where
the statutory maximum time for residential treatment is limited to
four years.

For the parents of these adolescents, the therapeutic tasks are no
less formidable even if they seem rather less intensive and their
results less pervasive. The concomitant casework or family therapy
process must assist them to deal with their own resistances to

separation from the patient and thus to grant permission to their child to use the staff figures as parental substitutes. This implies resolution of the loyalty problem and renders unnecessary the patient's view of the staff figures and of the parents as adversaries, thereby curtailing this most significant manifestation of object splitting by all concerned. Failure in casework, whether because of a paucity of process-trained psychiatric social workers, the social worker's technical incompetence, or the parents' refusal or inability to participate, constitutes one of the most profound deterrents to the progress of the child's treatment.

Notes

1. As used here, Fliess's admittedly ungainly term, *hypersymbiosis* (1961), refers to the pathological persistence of the otherwise normal infantile mother-child *symbiosis* beyond its usual duration; *symbiotic psychosis* refers, of course, to the classical syndrome of Mahler (1952) in children between the ages three and five years.

7

Residential Treatment
in Theory and Practice

The historical basis from which I shall take my departure in this chapter includes the pioneering efforts of Ernst Simmel (1929) to apply the insights of psychoanalysis to the treatment of hospital patients, extended in turn by the Menninger brothers in Topeka (W. C. Menninger 1936b, 1937, 1939) and leavened by the development of the child guidance movement in the United States. Among the questions I propose to consider are the following:

1. What are the characteristics that determine an individual's need for residential, hospital, or inpatient treatment?
2. What, in turn, are the characteristics of the residential milieu that are conducive to lasting reorganization of the personality and not merely to those more superficial processes generally termed "sealing over," "transference cure," or, more banally, symptomatic dissimulation?
3. What is the natural history of the hospital course of those patients who undergo the experience of significant intrapsychic reorganization compared with that of those who do not?

4. Finally, what particular modifications of the hospital setting are essential for optimal psychiatric treatment of the adolescent with the more severe forms of psychopathology?

THE WEAK EGO

As Simmel (1929) noted almost fifty years ago, individuals who by whatever route eventuate in the psychiatric hospital are regularly found to suffer from a variety of difficulties that together comprise the protean syndrome of ego weakness (Rinsley 1968a). We generally diagnose such persons as borderline or "as-if" (Deutsch 1942), or else append to them such labels as schizophrenic, psychotic, character neurotic (psychopathic), immature, impulse-neurotic, polymorphous-perverse, or infantile-narcissistic (Gralnick 1966). Careful genetic-dynamic study of these individuals reveals the following characteristics of the *weak ego*:

1. Failure of normal repression.
2. Persistence of primitive mechanisms of defense, with reliance upon projection, introjection, regression, and denial.
3. Impairment of the ego's synthetic function, leading to disruption of self-environment relations and dissemblement of perceptual, cognitive-ideational, affective, and motoric functions.
4. Predominance of anxiety of the instinctual type.
5. Lack of "basic trust."
6. Pervasive impairment of object relations.
7. Failure of sublimation of "raw" instinctual impulses.
8. Persistence of primary process thinking with reliance upon transitivism and gestural and word magic.
9. Persistence of primary narcissism, associated with which are varying degrees of infantile-megalomania.
10. Serious difficulties with preoedipal and sexual identity.

The clinical manifestations of these underlying coping or defense mechanisms include pervasive inability to trust, depression, impaired tolerance for frustration, failure to interpose thought between instinctual need and direct action aimed at relieving it, and hence undue access of instinctual drives to motility; or the individual's behavior, if not excessively action-oriented per se, seems otherwise peculiar, dissembled, or bizarre. As a result, there ensue various degrees of disruption of interpersonal communication and social disarticulation. As a consequence, in the majority of cases, "others" – the family, friends and associates, or representatives of the wider social community – bring the patient to the hospital. It is precisely in these cases in which one discovers the apparent lack of motivation for that nice cooperation between patient and therapeutic figure that classical psychoanalytic therapists put forth as a prime requisite for successful therapy, supposedly indicative of "lack of insight" and thus illustrative of unsuitability for optimal reconstruction of the personality or cure.

If reliance upon these coping mechanisms bespeaks the seriously ill adult, it more or less normally characterizes the intrapsychic organization of children, where it is called immature or puerile. Inasmuch as the clinical manifestations are in both instances similar, the seriously ill adult is considered immature or regressed from a presumably higher level of psychosexual function. Like the psychotic adult, the child, by virtue of the immaturity of his ego, will tend to *act out*. Deficient in self-objectification and in well-developed secondary process or categorical ideation, which Piaget tells us develops only by early adolescence (Inhelder and Piaget 1958), the child proves incapable of conceptualizing his need for treatment and the motivation of his prospective therapist to help him. Hence, if judged by the standards of the dynamically oriented therapist of the "neurotic adult," the child will give the appearance of lack of motivation. Like the psychotic adult, the normal child and especially the sick child must depend on the auxiliary adult egos, who would treat him in the same fashion as he would otherwise depend upon his parents for love, including protection, support, instruction, and the proper application of external controls for his actions. This explains the intensity of the sick child's labile, direct parentifying transference to the prospective helping adult.[1]

The nature of this direct transference to treatment figures requires further elucidation. First, the life of the preadolescent or adolescent child is organized around the child's dependency upon parental figures, whether the latter are natural parents or surrogates; hence, their teachers, coaches, scoutleaders, and older siblings and peers come to be invested with needs, wishes, urges, and fantasies displaced from the primary parental objects or, more properly, from the latter's mental representations. This major aspect of children's transference assumes even more cogent significance for adolescents, one of whose major struggles involves powerful strivings toward emancipation from parental surrogates, leading in turn into pervasively ambivalent needs both to devalue and, paradoxically, to remain dependent upon them. Thus, the normally labile transference of children becomes the more so among adolescents, replete as it is with further decathexis of parents, multiple anxieties over psychobiological experiences and functions, and substitute object-seeking, leading to the shifting bipolarity of instinctual drives and their affective derivatives so characteristic for the adolescent (Blos 1941, A. Freud 1958).

Second, the seriously ill adolescent suffers from preoedipal fixations based, in turn, on traumata of a major degree earlier suffered at the hands of parents or equivalent surrogates. Hence, to the normal preadult coping and defense mechanisms and identity struggles of adolescence are added, in these cases, a welter of cognitive, affective, and behavioral difficulties that are derived from very early insults to the archaic ego of the child. These, in turn, contribute to the patient's transference an added measure of ambivalence and lability, such that his treatment figures come to be invested with an extra measure of unneutralized instinct, of expectations and fears that represent the externalized vicissitudes of the patient's own internal object relations.

Third, adolescence is a period of life characterized in part by the individual's search for intimacy, by his efforts to bring his reservoir of infantile partial aims and his seeking of partial objects under the hegemony of genital primacy. His need for peer and adult models for identification in part witnesses various degrees of dynamic-genetic regression, with circular de-fusions and re-fusions of instincts and notable tendencies to reinstinctualize (Spiegel 1951). Thus, reaggressivization and resexualization of previously autonomous ego functions contribute to the kaleidoscopic quality of the adolescent's self-seeking and object-seeking. Once again, these regressive tendencies are enormously accentuated among adolescents ill enough to require residential treatment, and they pose special problems for the adult treatment figures, whose countertransference is pulled hither and yon as a result of their needs both to enter and resist projective and introjective identifications with their young patients. These identifications are wont to lead the adult figures into extremes of bipolar attitudes toward the management of the patient, which, in turn, reflect the bipolarity of the patient's own instinctual organization – that is, undue authoritarianism or undue permissiveness. In the former, one glimpses the elements of the "new order therapies," exemplified in the writings of Szasz (1965), Glasser (1965), and Mowrer (1963a, 1963b), who emphasize behavioral conformity to accepted modes of conduct and the assumption of "responsibility" by the patient or who attempt to "build in" or strengthen the superego. In the latter, one glimpses a variety of antiauthoritarian reaction-formations, which find expression in a congeries of laissez-faire, permissive approaches to the care of patients. These involve the misapplication to adolescents of such varied modalities as classical psychoanalytic technique, "therapeutic community," and child-centered methods based presumably on "progressive" educational views and organismic concepts – which claim that, if left to themselves, children (including sick ones) intuitively and spontaneously "actualize themselves" or will otherwise make the right decisions for themselves, much as laboratory rats self-select appropriate diets.

The effect of overauthoritarianism is, of course, to preclude or forestall the patient's attempts to gain mastery by maintaining what amounts to an essentially megalomanic attitude toward the child and this, in turn, often reflects the adult's misguided efforts to defend against the infantile-grandiose, narcissistic wishes that the child projects onto him. The effect of overpermissiveness is basically the same, for if the adult spuriously invests the child with adultomorphic powers, the child will inevitably misapply them and hence will fail.

A fourth aspect of direct adolescent transference is of special importance in those cases in which the patient's fixations date from early infancy, prior to the inception of the normal mother-child symbiosis that ordinarily flowers in the latter half of the first year of life. These adolescents, developmentally deviant from the very earliest postnatal period, comprise a group of patients whom Fliess (1961) often would classify as autistic-presymbiotic, including the classical autistic children first described by Kanner (1943, 1949) and whom Bender (1947, 1953, 1956) would classify as pseudodefective. They are characterized by sweeping psychobiological deficiencies and dyssynchronies and are often mistakenly supposed to have "no object relationships." Careful clinical study reveals, to the contrary, a pervasive, bizarre, fragmented autistic pseudocommunity, populated by a welter of magic-hallucinatory internal objects, the majority of which are monstrous, terrifying, or "bad." The patient combines a congeries of self-perceptions and object-perceptions characterized by a most intense fear and suspicion of others and a profound degree of infantile-megalomania specific for the stage of primary narcissism; or else, one readily observes the persistence of the prenarcissistic condition that Freud (1914) termed autoerotic, during which the various erogenous zones pursue pleasure gain independently without benefit of any degree of psychic organization.

Although individual psychotherapy is the cornerstone of the treatment of such adolescents, the ward staff must wrestle with the patient's exceedingly primitive introjective and projective defenses, as the latter urgently seeks and yet is terrified by and must massively resist fusion with them. In these more primitive cases, the overall treatment pivots on the need to build those "good" objects derived from the patient's identification with the psychotherapist, and it is hoped that these will serve as nuclei about which the earliest, most archaic ego functions and representations will crystallize. Thus, the milieu supports the individual treatment process, beset as the latter often is with innumerable "misunderstandings" between the therapist and the other staff members, reflecting the extent to which staff members have become enmeshed in the patient's use of splitting defenses.

A fifth aspect of adolescent transference concerns the child's defensive maneuvers with respect to early object losses, which are regular features of the history of the residential patient of this age. By the term object loss, I refer to those situations in which key surrogate figures either died or were "lost" through parental separation or divorce or were, in effect, psychologically unavailable to the young child as a result of their own psychopathology. Early object loss leads the child into the persistent use of splitting, wherein the object loss is simultaneously and ambivalently both affirmed and denied (or disavowed) by the ego (Freud 1927, 1940). The splitting is, in these cases, associated with long-standing depression; the latter manifests itself in a wide variety of regressive symptoms peculiar to children (chapter 5), in contrast to the classical depressions of adults. As a result, the residential patient perceives adult treatment figures in terms of this background of loss, ambivalence, and splitting and shows enhanced degrees of alternating anaclitic clinging and negativistic pseudoindependence in respect to them. Thus, coupled with the patient's desperate need for objects is the fear that the objects he invests, hence upon whom he comes to depend, will in the end desert him.

In such cases, the patient brings into play a congeries of restitutive efforts that center on a further regression to defenses of an introjective and projective nature based on the mechanism of splitting. The "lost" object is reintrojected so that its actual disappearance may be denied. But along with the reintrojected mental representation of the object are also reincorporated aggressive attributes that the child has previously projected onto it, thereby comprising a hostile superego introject.[2] The clinical result is profound guilt. Thus, the patient feels that he has brought about the death of a natural parent, parental separation, or divorce or has visited upon his siblings a wide variety of insults and injuries; he feels himself to be "bad," which may mean destructive, homicidal, "crazy," stupid, and the like.

Much of the labile, kaleidoscopic, "manipulative" behavior of adolescent inpatients stems from such regressive and restitutive efforts. Their provocative alloplasticity, often called transference splitting or transference diffusion, in part represents ambivalent efforts to work through the traumata associated with early object loss. The patient's guilt leaves him poignantly susceptible to the recurrent fear that intimacy with a love object will repel the latter, that his love destroys, that there is no real prospect for object constancy, and that he is foredoomed to rejection and psychological starvation (Fairbairn 1954). As a result, one witnesses the adolescent patient's abiding suspicion of adults, coupled with his peculiarly transilient efforts to extract from them proof of their love for him while he counterphobically acts in a manner to ward them off (chapter 1).

SOME AXIOMS OF RESIDENTIAL TREATMENT

The aforementioned characteristics of the transference of the adolescent residential patient are essential for an understanding of the child's immediate postadmission behavior. In part because of his intense struggle over dependency needs, the adolescent, who is often sensitively aware of his need for help, nonetheless can admit it only in the most obscure and oblique ways. As a result, he often seems unmotivated or resistant. The form and variety of the adolescent's resistances are described in greater detail in chapters 1 and 5. But the basic issue concerns the salient fact that because early resistance behavior is heavily loaded with transference, the forms it assumes provide notable insight into the manner in which the patient has dealt with and attempted to regulate his relationships with key figures from the past, generally parents or equivalent surrogates, as these come to be expressed within the residential setting. Some learning theorists would perhaps say that the patient will perseverate in the use of outmoded, maladaptive, insufficiently drive-reducing adjustive techniques and that his illness in part expresses the narrowness of his coping hierarchy.

A first axiom of residential treatment would therefore hold that, to the degree to which the treatment setting otherwise tolerates or abets the patient's ongoing use of early transference resistances, their underlying significance will remain obscure and hence uninterpretable; further, that the patient will remain unengaged with the staff members. The obvious corollary to this axiom holds, therefore, that the residential milieu must provide controls for the patient's behavior, stringent ones in some cases, to preclude direct drive discharge through motility and to rechannel it via intercalated processes such as thought and verbal communication. To this end, the closed ward is essential because it alone provides the security of carefully titrated behavioral restrictions which must operate to force the patient back upon and within himself, so to speak.

A second axiom concerns the matter of the patient's contacts, both in person and via correspondence, with members of his family. Since the child's psychopathology develops within and in part gives expression to a skewed, pathological familial constellation, interruption of the hierarchy of pathogenic interactions among the patient and other family members must be put into effect as quickly as possible. To accomplish this with a minimum of serious trauma to all concerned, a concomitant psychiatric casework process is begun, within which the staff caseworker initiates the diagnostic study of the family while simultaneously assisting the family to deal with the often profound anxieties that rapidly develop when removal of a family member previously necessary for their repression or scotomatization has taken place. Often these anxieties propel the remaining parents and siblings into herculean, even bizarre efforts to undo their separation from the child, to so contaminate their contacts with him with double-binding communications as to decimate the patient's treatment by intimidating him into redoubling his resistance behavior. In some cases, the parents will attempt to bring attorneys, clergymen, interested friends, employers, public or political figures, other relatives, and a variety of other avuncular persons into the early diagnostic process or may threaten litigation or even violence in eleventh-hour efforts to intimidate the staff into releasing the patient. Careful study of the family members' own early resistance maneuvers reveals that they both cover and convey a welter of terrifying fantasies, which become projected onto the treatment milieu in general and the figure of the caseworker in particular, and they will attempt to communicate these fantasies to the patient unless steps are taken to preclude the latter (chapter 2). Thus, the staff must have the necessary legal armamentarium with which to enforce, if need be, the parent-child separation and, in this early period of inception of treatment, must carefully regulate the patient's family visits and correspondence.

A third axiom of residential treatment concerns the use of specific restrictions of the patient's behavior, a matter of importance throughout the entire course of the patient's residence but of even greater significance in the early period of treatment. In connection with the matter of restrictions, I shall have recourse to the following relevant if oversimplified graphic representation.

Figure 1

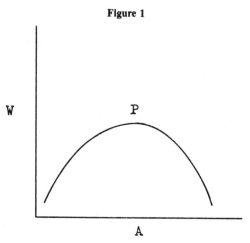

W represents what one could call *useful psychological work,* a term notoriously difficult to define and roughly analogous to the thermodynamic concept of free energy and to the psychological concept of goal- or task-oriented secondary process thought and action. A key component of W, from my point of view, is related to the patient's ability to respond to verbal restraint or control from the staff members and to comprehend the significance of interpretations that they offer to him. The A line denotes anxiety, in our cases, predominantly of the instinctual type, whereas P denotes a critical point of inflection. That portion of the curve to the left of P is called the ascending limb, whereas that portion of the curve to the right of P is called the descending limb.

For individuals situated somewhere on the ascending limb of the "work:anxiety" curve, each increment of anxiety leads to a corresponding increment of psychological work; put more succinctly, under such circumstances, anxiety motivates. Similarly, in the case of an individual situated on the descending limb of the curve, further increments of anxiety yield corresponding decrements of work; therefore under these circumstances, anxiety disorganizes.

The overwhelming majority of residential patients undergo referral for admission because the level of their instinctual anxiety has propelled them onto the descending limb of the work:anxiety curve, past the point of inflection, P. This level of anxiety has, in turn, induced the well-known traumatic state of the ego, with more or less paralysis of autonomous ego functions and regression to the use of those primitive defenses or coping mechanisms to which I have already referred. As the traumatic state is known to result from breakdown of the defense mechanisms of the ego in the wake of relatively excessive endopsychic and/or external stimulation, the immediate therapeutic task resolves itself into efforts to limit incident stimuli. For this general purpose, judicious dosages of ataraxic medication can be used, or the patient's over-stimulating peer interactions can be limited through restricting him to the ward or to his room; in cases in which the patient finds himself beset by panic of a degree that has lead to dissolution of his defenses against anxiety, a period of seclusion may be indicated (Charney 1963).

The psychoanalyst would view such a program as justifiably analogous to the function of the infant's maternal surrogate figure as a stimulus barrier against both excessive exogenous stimulation and endogenous "affectomotor storms" (Mahler 1952, Bergman and Escalona 1949). Concomitantly, it promotes the patient's investment in the staff figures, whose early function amounts to protecting him while allowing a comfortable degree of regression to proceed. Most important, however, is relocation of the patient to a point somewhere on the ascending limb of the work:anxiety curve. So situated, he begins to reassume an increasing degree of self-control, to communicate more coherently with the staff, and to experience relief from the terrifying feelings of loss of control that have characterized his pretreatment state.

THE RESISTANCE PHASE

As many authors have noted, the family member identified as the patient emerges from a long-standing pathogenic manifold of familial intercommunications, which Zentner and Aponte (1970) have termed the "amorphous family nexus."[3] Many of these families are dyssocial, alienated groups with varying degrees of effective social facade, whose membership is characterized by diffuse, shifting, interchangeable individual identities, multiple-binding communications, *pars pro toto* and *totum pro parte* roles, and superficially unpredictable lines of authority; they have therefore been termed skewed. Such families or pseudofamilies offer to their members a variety of protective gratifications, and the characteristic of the patient is his inability, for whatever reasons, to continue to use them; thus, the family appeals, with profound ambivalence, to the dreaded extrafamilial authorities or agencies for "help," or else the patient is wrested from them over their overt or covert protests. The purposes for which the help is sought are, of course, legion: The intricate if bizarre family nexus may be disintegrating, and the patient is "selected out" to communicate this, or one or more family members may perceive that the patient's continued presence in their midst threatens their composite existence; hence, he must at least temporarily be expelled. However, the patient may often, in fact, be the least ill family member, and the burgeoning conflict between his own ineluctable urge for growth and the family's pathogenic pressures on him force him apart from them by whatever means or route. Whatever the case, the family directly or otherwise carries its deviant member to the helping agency for its own purposes, which, in the case of families of severely ill adolescents, amount to a need either to get rid of him outright or else to induce the agency to refurbish him, so that he may once again assume his usual place, basically unaltered, within the family nexus.

The profound dislocation of the family's and the agency's respective expectations of the latter's functions of treatment contributes heavily to the wide spectrum of patient and family members' behavior that subserve the function of resistance to treatment. In the case of adolescent residential patients, the various resistance maneuvers subserve the need to preserve on-going fusion or symbiotic ties, based in turn upon the preoedipal fixations to which I have already referred. A particularly subtle manner in which the patient and the family will unconsciously conspire to accomplish re-fusion, described in detail by Zentner and Aponte (1970), is to behave in such ways as to attempt to incorporate the treatment structure into the family's nexus, to render the former into an arm of the latter. Thus, the generalization common to the aforementioned axioms becomes: The major purpose of identifying, interpreting, and preclude the patient's and the parents' early resistance behavior is to precede re-fusion among them, to thus detach the patient from the pathogenic family nexus and to promote his engagement with the treatment staff. As already noted, the treatment facility must have at its disposal and be prepared to use fully and definitively whatever legal means are available for those cases in which the family's and the patient's efforts to re-fuse assume herculean proportions.

The spectrum of the adolescent residential patient's resistance maneuvers, which ordinarily occupy a period of six months to a year following admission, and the metaphorical communications that they convey were described in chapter 1. I shall now briefly recapitulate them:

Identification with the aggressor. The patient in various ways attempts to imitate the adults' behavior, in an "as-if" effort to ward off the latter.

Leveling. The patient attempts to make siblings or peers of the treatment figures (the "buddy-buddy," "pal," or "we girls" phenomena).

Flirtatiousness and seductiveness. The patient attempts to sexualize the relationship with treatment figures.

Oversubmissiveness. Oversubmissiveness, obsequiousness, or sycophantic behavior (including "shuffling" or the "Uncle Tom" phenomenon common among Negro adolescents) comprise yet another counterphobic maneuver.

Persistent avoidance. More frequent among the most seriously ill adolescents, persistent avoidance includes frank negativism, muteness, marked aboulia and apathy, seclusiveness, sleepiness, disruptive efforts to provoke isolation, various forms of seizure and dissociative phenomena (including self-induced seizures in patients with epilepsy), absorption in daydreaming fantasy, and the like.

Scapegoatism. Includes such phenomena as denigration or vilification of ward peers ("He's stupid," "She's crazy") and efforts to manipulate wardmates into proxy roles by which the peer acts out for the subject ("behind-the-scenes manipulator" phenomenon); the purpose is to draw staff attention to others, and away from one's self.

Outright rebelliousness. The major function of wildly disruptive ward behavior in part subserves the need to ward off closeness to staff figures by attempting to force them into unremitting efforts to provide behavioral control; the underlying need for closeness is, however, glimpsed in direct, physical staff-patient contact that the disruptive actions provoke.

Transference splitting. Subsumed here are various forms of "playing favorites," a wide spectrum of staff splitting and manipulations of peers, gossiping, and tale carrying—aimed at keeping knowledge of one's self spread thinly enough to preclude any one of the treatment figures from obtaining a comprehensive view of one's self.

Somatization. Multiple body complaints serve to ward off staff attention to thoughts, feelings, fantasies, delusional preoccupations, and the like. Careful analysis of the complaints will, however, often uncover the hidden inner experiences.

Peer-age caricaturing. Also called "out-typifying one's self," peer-age caricaturing consists of a variety of actions that seem to convey the patient's need to be viewed as a "typical" adolescent; the behavior ever so slightly exaggerates such things as dietary fads, emotional lability, popular idealizations, and the general excesses adults are wont to associate with "typical" adolescent behavior.

Clique formation. Seriously ill adolescents are incapable of generating normal teenage peer groups. The "normal-appearing" small groups they are prone to form on the ward are usually found to serve the need to share data about themselves with each other, and these data never reach the treatment staff.

"Craziness and "pseudostupidity." The defensive function of disorganized ("crazy") behavior is to arrest, enthrall, or paralyze and hence to ward off the treatment figures. Similarly, the "pseudostupid" patient conveys the message, "I'm so stupid that you can't expect much from me (hence I can remain unengaged)."

"Intellectual" pursuits. These comprise basically autistic indulgence or absorption in literary, musical, graphic artistic, or scientific pursuits or projects, whether alone or with wardmates, the aim of which is to ward off and maintain distance from staff members.

Elopement. Running away is a complex, overdetermined phenomenon, connected with all sorts of aggressive, erotic, rescue, and reunion fantasies. When it occurs, it obviously terminates geographical contact between the patient and the treatment staff.

Parental Resistance Metaphors

As already noted, the patient's resistance behavior has enormous transference meaning. In addition, it expresses anguish over separation from his parents or from his fantasy constructs, which serve as dereistic substitutes for them. At root, the patient's resistance behavior conveys the expression of re-fusion or reunion fantasies. Concomitant with the flowering of the patient's resistances are those of the parents, whose fantasies are no less elaborate or regressive than are the patient's. Careful study of the parents' fantasies during the resistance phase of their child's treatment discloses that they are, as expected, compounded of primitive aggressive and erotic wishes, that they are at root preoedipal, and that they are exceptionally prone toward displacement or projection onto the treatment staff and the physical characteristics of the hospital (transference to the hospital per se) in general and onto the caseworker in particular. The latter will in general develop only if the treatment structure precludes transmission of the parents' resistance messages to the patient. My own study of early parental resistance metaphors has led me to classify them according as they in turn express (1) the parents' narcissistic or self-preoccupations; (2) the parents' view of the family's endogenous efforts to maintain its precarious equilibrium; and (3) the parents' particular ways of appersonating or depersonifying the child and consequently of attempting to put him to psychological use in ways that violate his own juvenile identity (chapter 2).

Insofar as the family is in various degrees dyssocial or in metastable equilibrium with extrafamilial objects and situations, revelation through whomever or by whatever means of the family members' idiosyncratic ways of maintaining the family group's pseudoequilibrium poses a severe threat to its perceived ongoing integrity. Their concern is that the child will "tell the family secrets," which is revealed in both their conscious and less than conscious efforts to admonish the patient against the development of trusting ties with the treatment staff. Thus, the patient is presented with a dilemma: If he acts on his nascent perception that the staff members can somehow be trusted, he courts disaster to his family, including loss of the parental figures; if he successfully resists treatment, he remains ill. The apparent paradox transpires that getting well, from the child's point of view, is worse than being sick, and a notable measure of the secondary gain of his illness lies in the preservation of his relationship with the parents and other members of his disordered family.

Rapid control of the patient's immediate postadmission behavior, regulation of contacts between parents and child, judicious

use of ataraxic medications when indicated, and carefully graduated increments of privileges lead the adolescent to a point at
which the aforementioned resistance maneuvers come into full
expression. As these develop, they are dealt with, in turn, by
appropriate further control of the patient's behavior coupled with
interpretations directed at their underlying transference significance. The major purpose of the latter, which we may consider to
represent the inception of the resistance work proper, is threefold:
(1) It has the effect of reassuring the patient that separation from
his family, in particular from his primary parental objects, will not
prove disastrous to him or to them; (2) it serves to stimulate the
patient's curiosity about himself, to "get him thinking" about his
past history and current behavior; and (3) it aims to promote the
patient's early identification with staff members, thereby further
detaching him from his symbiotic ties with his parent figures.

The patient's early identifications with staff figures, which find
their inception during the resistance phase of treatment, are different from those he will later make with them. During the resistance
phase, they assume the qualities of primitive superego introjects
and hence signify to the patient the operations of external surrogate egos which, like the "good" maternal objects of infancy, protect the archaic ego by limiting incident stimuli, curb self-injurious
actions and, in part through the discipline they inculcate, provide
reassuring nurturance. The resultant reduction of the patient's
instinctual anxiety moves him gradually toward the ascending limb
of the work:anxiety curve, and thus enables increasing increments
of responsive, interpretive work by the patient. This work can now
be increasingly done in collaboration with the adult treatment
figures and particularly with the psychiatrist.

Provided that the analogous resistance work is accomplished in
the parents' casework process, in most cases within six to eighteen
months, it transpires that the patient has developed sufficient trust
in the staff and the parents have developed sufficient trust in their
casework process, which represents the treatment structure to
them, that the parents begin in earnest to relinquish the patient to
the staff's care. Thus, the definitive resolution of the loyalty problem begins to appear. Parents and child have come to perceive that

they may indeed exist without each other, and the parents communicate to the patient in various ways that he may work with the staff without fear of injury to himself or to the parents or of reprisal from the latter.

Resistance Behavior as Protest

Ongoing clinical study of the adolescent patient's and the parents' resistance metaphors led me to the conclusion that these metaphors, expressed both verbally and nonverbally, could be viewed as more than crudely analogous to the behavior of prematurely separated infants, which Bowlby (1960a, 1960b, 1961, 1962) has termed, protest (chapter 5). Several factors seem indeed to support the analogy. First, the adolescent's otherwise natural tendency to recapitulate and hence to work through earlier oedipal and preoedipal conflicts appeared highly relevant; furthermore, such recapitulative working through is regressive, and fluctuating proneness to regression is a hallmark of the adolescent's struggle toward an eventually stable identity.

Second, as already noted, the patient's resistance metaphors seem to convey a powerful need to undo the parent-child separation and hence to bring back the child's "lost" objects and to reinvolve them. Thus, the resistance metaphors regularly tend to assume the quality of mourning.

Third, the persistent reliance upon the defense mechanism of splitting regularly characterizes the mourning reaction of the child as he ambivalently reaffirms and disavows the object loss he feels called upon to mourn. Persistent use of splitting similarly affirms the child's ongoing fixation at, or regression to, the early pre-depressive (paranoid-schizoid) position of infancy (Klein 1946), which signals the use of part-object relations. Thus, the adolescent's redoubtable tendency to split or manipulate represents the clinical emergence of his use of introjective and projective techniques for regulating his "good" and "bad" part-object relations. It comes as no surprise, therefore, that the fundamental psychological traumata upon which the adolescent residential patient's illness is based occurred during the infantile years, in a majority of cases during the predepressive period prior to the inception of the second year of life—a fact that careful historical and psychodynamic study of our patients has almost invariably revealed.

Viewed from a genetic-dynamic standpoint, successful management of the resistance phase of residential treatment precludes the patient's use of splitting and guides him ineluctably toward entrance into what must be considered as later manifestations of the original depressive position. As these changes occur, the resistance phase of treatment draws to a close, and the patient enters the next arena of his treatment—the phase of definitive treatment I have chosen to call the phase of introject work.

THE DEFINITIVE PHASE

As Aichhorn originally taught us, successful treatment depends on the respective capacities of patient and therapist for mutual identification. Resolution of the resistance phase of residential treatment thus proceeds from the patient's ability to identify with the treatment figures who are charged with his care; in particular, it proceeds from the child's trusting ability to have internalized in significant measure the external controls for his behavior that the residential milieu has supplied to him. Thus, a complex congeries of processes of growth is set in motion, common in the experience of the healthily developing child but deficient in that of the child who reaches the adolescent years hobbled by psychopathology serious enough to prevent successful negotiation of the oral stage of psychosexual development ("I am") and beginning entry into the anal stage ("I am separate and distinct; I can control and master"). It is my view, therefore, that an adequate intensive residential treatment process comes to develop, within an admittedly compressed span of time, the basic attributes of a healthy child-rearing experience.

A major characteristic of all children is their early infantile omnipotence, a residue of middle to late orality. The healthily developing child comes normally to project his omnipotence into the figures of his parents, leading to a sweeping overestimation of his loved parental objects.[4] The seriously ill child, essentially devoid of parental object constancy early in life, has found the normal projection of omnipotence impossible and has, in effect, clung to it. As the young child's omnipotence is comprised of primitive ("raw") aggressive and erotic instincts, their projection onto the residential treatment figures evokes the patient's fear that they will retaliate, injure, destroy, or absorb him—a fear that also in part accounts for his resistance to them. The resolution of the resistance phase of treatment thus implies the treatment figures' acceptance of the patient's megalomanic projections onto them, without acting on the primitive wishes associated with the projections; this situation cements strongly the bonds of mutual trust between the patient and themselves.

As the patient begins to part with the nucleus of "bad" internal objects that have long comprised the roots of his psychopathology, he also parts with what have been basic components of his early pathological identity. The loss of these parts of the self induces him to mourn for them; and the two major components of his mourning are the emergence of depression and the appearance of regression, both of which are, of course, inextricably interrelated.

Among adolescents, whether hospitalized or not, the emergence of depression heralds far more than the otherwise "classical" picture, combining as does the latter the subjectively felt loss of self-esteem, sadness, and various degrees of psychomotor retardation. Rather is the depression in these cases rife with splitting, and with denial or disavowal. Thus, the patient's mourning for the loss of his departing introjects conveys far more than the process of object removal (Katan 1951), as the objects that proceed to be removed are pejorative and their loss is accompanied, in the case of residential patients, by the most profound ambivalence; thus, the mourning becomes pathological. As pointed out in chapter 5, pathological mourning among adolescents is a protean process. It is accompanied by sweeping regression in all areas of psychological function—cognitive-ideational, affective, sensory-perceptual, and even motoric. The patient proceeds to assume a more primitive clinical appearance, which includes fluctuant clinging-dependency, marked negativism, notable swings of mood, and unpredictability. Of great importance are the experiences of depersonalization and estrangement (derealization); overt thought disorder may reappear, with classical associatve loosening, tangentiality, syncretism and concretism, and the occurrence of grandiose, self-referential, and nihilistic delusions. There occurs regressive reinstinctualization of bodily parts and functions, with all manner of somatic difficulties and, in some cases, frank somatic delusions. The patient now begins to speak of his "badness" and "evilness"; he talks of destructive wishes, and he berates himself for his past misdeeds and for the harm he feels he has visited on others. His terrifying experiences may indeed be likened to the drainage of pus from a long-concealed abscess as a necessary step in the healing of tissue that the purulent matter had previously infiltrated and split apart.

My extended observations of the behavior of the adolescent who has entered this phase of residential treatment have led to the conclusion that it is, at root, analogous to Bowlby's second stage of infantile mourning, which he termed the stage of despair. Common to both are the protean complexities of the "impure" depression of children. Indeed, the phenomena classically grouped about the concept of depression per se may be largely if not wholly overshadowed by the multiple regressive signs that portend the onset of a period of undoubted disorganization of the weak ego so characteristic of the residential patient of this age (chapter 5).

The emergence of "bad" internal part-objects and the concomitant introjection of "good" ones are of basic importance for the successful treatment to which the residential milieu is oriented. First, it strongly reinforces the patient's beginning awareness, during the resistance phase, that he and his parents are indeed capable of separate existence. Second, it moves the patient progressively from a condition of primary narcissism toward increasing self-objectification, which means enhanced ability to sense and test reality and to exert mastery over endopsychic and external events. Third, it signals the patient's entrance into the later, depressive position of infancy, during which he begins to perceive that his aggression, whether innate or derived from the aggressive cathexes associated with his "bad" introjects, is incapable of destroying what he comes increasingly to experience as whole-objects; thus he moves from part-object to whole-object relations. Underlying the above are the processes characteristic of this second, or later, form of the adolescent residential patient's identifications with his treatment figures — that is, the gradual metabolization and depersonification of his introjects as these become assimilated to his self-representations and hence become a part of his ego (Jacobson 1964, Kernberg 1966). Fourth, the identifications on which these critical processes and experiences are based have sweeping effects on the economic dispositions within the child's ego. They lead to de-fusion of instincts, with ensuing liberation of both aggressive and erotic energies for subsumption under the ego's synthetic function; thus, neutralized aggression comes increasingly to drive the defensive functions of the unconscious part of the ego, while neutralized libido comes increasingly to drive the ego's synthetic and perceptual functions, leading the ego toward increasing use of sublimations and growth of secondary autonomy (chapter 6, Rinsley 1968, Hartmann 1955).

It will be evident in what I have said that, from the standpoint of the residential patient, there are two exceptionally critical junctures in the residential treatment process, successful management of which has an important influence on the prognosis of the child's residential experience: (1) successful conclusion of the resistance phase, with subsequent entry into the definitive phase; and (2) the staff's capacity to withstand the protean, regressive turn of events in the definitive phase. A most important resistance with which all must deal is staff countertransference resistances to the often exasperatingly difficult regressive behavior of the patient as the exchange of introjects sets in in earnest. Staff members' efforts to bring the latter to a halt, whether by efforts to suppress it or through their own regressive identifications with the patient, must be precluded to a large extent if the patient is to work through his painful experience of mourning.

The mourning processes of the hospitalized adolescent ordinarily require the larger part of another year of residential treatment if not longer. As his mourning processes proceed and as his associated regression begins to recede, the patient becomes ready for increasing reassociation with his family, the members of which he has begun to view as distinct from himself and as increasingly "real" objects, whose limitations he may allow himself to understand without remaining enmeshed in them. His enhanced internal controls, based on identification with the staff members who have signified his auxiliary egos, lead him to a gradual expansion of privileges; thus, with careful guidance, he assumes increasing responsibility for what he does. The time now approaches at which continued full-time residential treatment becomes unnecessary, and, depending upon the circumstances of the individual case, the patient may be discharged to the day hospital, his own home, or foster placement; in many instances, he will continue his psychiatric treatment on an outpatient basis for a future period of time.

Although my remarks have comprised but a bare outline of the natural history of the complex residential experience of the adolescent in full-time hospital treatment, they nonetheless permit several conclusions concerning adolescent psychopathology and reconstructive as distinguished from symptomatic treatment in the residential setting (chapters 3 and 4). I am in thorough agreement with the important contributions of Masterson (1967a, 1968) regarding the etiological significance of *adolescent turmoil.* Masterson concludes that this omnibus term makes reference to a wide spectrum of personality difficulties of more ominous significance than is usually recognized. The more ominous psychopathological phenomena to which adolescent turmoil refers are commonly viewed as little more than manifestations of "transient situational" or "adjustment" problems — which are frequent enough among adolescents, of relatively superficial importance, and hence in need of superficial handling or management. I believe that this "situational" view of "adolescent turmoil" stems from several readily identifiable factors. First, from a diagnostic standpoint, the criteria for recognition of classical (schizophrenic) thought disturbance, set forth by Bleuler (1950) and developed by numerous careful students of categorical ideation, are as applicable to adolescents as to adults; failure to apply these criteria in the careful study of the formal processes of the adolescent's thinking regularly leads to an underestimation of the degree of the patient's psychopathology. A second factor involves failure to recognize those stereotypical characteristics of the pseudoamorphous, skewed, and psychotogenic family, within which the adolescent residential patient is regularly discovered to have grown up and to which his illness in part gives graphic and tragic expression. Yet a third factor concerns the adult's not inconsiderable difficulty in recognizing any sort of major psychopathology in children. Such a difficulty is in direct proportion to the extent to which any given adult must repress or even deny the variety of his own subjective difficulties during that age which is, now, personified in the patient he may be called upon to study. The adult countertransference to the presumably noisome adolescent finds expression in a variety of approaches to the problems, which appear with regularity in the psychiatric literature and infrequently with tragic consequences in the attitudes of professional workers who may be called upon to treat him (chapter 4).

Thus, one finds problems of underdiagnosis, to which I have already referred; one finds statements to the effect that "adolescents cannot be analyzed"; one finds well-meaning programs in which seriously ill adolescents are treated on adult hospital wards, motivated in part by the need to pare institutional budgets, which leads to the placement of sick children with sick adults and results in endless prolongation of the adolescents' resistance maneuvers; and one hears of short-term programs for adolescent treatment, in which little or no effort is made to help the patient and his parents to recognize and resolve the herculean problems of their mutual resistances toward separation. Finally, one hears the view, appropriate to the needs of the less seriously ill child, and thoroughly incorrect for the more seriously ill one, that it is better not to sunder a family by attempting to treat one of its members outside it. This view, in fact, represents a failure to appreciate the dereistic, dyssocial pseudoorganization of those families from which are derived severely ill children; for a child, whether adolescent or younger, who remains trapped within a profoundly disordered family unit, sanguine efforts at outpatient treatment are in many cases foredoomed to failure: the residual family members will exert powerful pressures on the child to resist the therapist's "dangerous" ministrations, and the pressures will succeed because the looser therapeutic structure is unable to cope with them. In such instances, the so-called community mental health approach, which advocates "bringing the treatment to the family in its own setting," proceeds to transport the treatment to the very worst place for its inception and fruition.

CONCLUSION

The following generalizations concerning the intensive residential treatment of adolescents who demonstrate the more severe forms of psychopathology can be distilled:

1. In the majority of such cases, physical or geographical separation of the patient from the remainder of his family members, notably his parents, is mandatory.

2. The patient should be admitted into a closed ward or cottage, within which careful scrutiny of his behavior and application of appropriate controls for his behavior become immediately operative.

3. A concomitant, dynamically oriented casework process with the patient's parents or with his responsible guardian surrogates should begin with admission into residence.

4. Intensive psychiatric and parallel casework study of the patient and his family should begin coincident with his admission, using the services of the full diagnostic team — including the admitting and ward psychiatrists, the clinical psychologist, the psychiatric social worker, the teacher of special education, and the ward or cottage nurse and aides or child care workers. Although in a few instances the patient needs to resist the immediate post-admission study, the deepening intrapersonal and interpersonal processes into which he feels himself to be plunged in most cases will be found to reassure him that those who are in charge of him are extremely interested in and concerned about him. Thus, the diagnostic process becomes at once an integral part of his treatment.

5. The initial therapeutic task facing the treatment personnel of the ward or cottage comprises the identification, recognition, control, and interpretation to the patient of those segments of his behavior that serve as resistance or warding-off devices aimed at preserving the pathological symbiotic ties with his mental representations of parental surrogates. This early resistance work also serves to uncover the nexus of pathological communications and object-ties characteristic for the patient's family and in which the patient has heretofore been immersed.

6. Particular attention needs to be given to the adolescent's early communications, which convey a premature need to identify himself with staff members. Although one may discover much that augurs positively in such messages from the patient as, "I like you," "I need your help," "You are nice (handsome, beautiful, powerful)," and the like, naive acceptance of them as indicators of more profound ego identifications early in hospitalization is a grievous error. It reflects in part the adult's own difficulties in recognizing the patient's counterphobic use of the resistance aspect of early positive transference. It is significant that one recently reported inpatient program, in which much is allegedly made of such early "positive" communications, actually "treats" adolescents for a maximum of six weeks (Abend, Kachalsky, and Greenberg 1968).

7. It follows that the closed ward, with its endogenous security devices, provides the optimal setting for the inception and at least part of the work of the resistance phase of treatment. The closed ward is also appropriate as the locale for the more regressive experiences associated with the definitive phase of treatment, during which the work of introject exchange begins.

8. The residential staff must be prepared to recognize and deal with the ineluctable regressive changes that accompany the patient's entry into the definitive phase of treatment. During this period, ward or cottage staff require considerable help with their countertransference, lest they proceed into a variety of maneuvers aimed unconsciously at warding off or terminating the patient's regression. If this occurs, the treatment quickly founders.

9. It is necessary to restate the fact that adolescents who require residential treatment are products of families, the pathology of which involves ill-defined, diffuse lines of authority and variable blurring and shifting of the roles and identities of their members. Hence, sick adolescents do not belong on adult mental hospital wards with sick adults whose psychopathology mirrors the disabilities of the adolescents' own parental surrogates—a locale that abets the adolescents' ongoing immersion in the same sort of pathogenic experiences that contributed so heavily to their illnesses in the first place. The sick adolescent needs healthy adults, not sick ones, until such time as his treatment leads him to extricate himself from them.

10. It must be remembered that psychiatric treatment in the general sense should constitute a growth experience for both the patient and for those who treat him. The residential treatment of the adolescent should point him toward the achievements of the latency period, during which the child makes notable strides toward the attainment of self-objectification, mastery, sublimation, growth of secondary autonomy, the beginnings of categorical ideation, and peer identification—which symbolize the further development of his identity as a person. Once this has occurred in earnest, the patient once again begins to move toward synchrony of his overall level of psychological development and his chronological age. And with this process completed, he reenters the arena of adolescence proper and can begin to struggle healthily, now, with the numerous problems characteristic for this critical stage of his maturation.

Notes

1. A cogent formulation of the significance of magical and parentifying expectations of the therapist is set forth by Rado (1956, 1962).

2. I use the term *superego introject* to refer to notably punitive, undepersonified or "unmetabolized" introjects of an archaic nature that have not become assimilated into the unconscious defenses of the ego. See Jacobson (1964) and Kernberg (1966).

3. For a concise review of major contributions to this exceedingly important area of psychiatric research, see Mishler and Waxler (1966).

4. There is considerable evidence in support of the view that the origin of belief in an omnipotent deity is derived from the parents' further displacement of the child's megalomanic projections into them. This displacement is, in turn, seen to result from the parents' need to ward off (or deny) the child's projections, which threaten to reawaken in the parents their own repressed infantile-megalomania.

8

Residential School

The term *education* (*Lat., a leading out*) is generally accepted to signify that process by which one acquires (learns), assimilates, and eventually transmits to the next generation those cognitive skills requisite for understanding one's self, one's particular culture, the world of which one's culture is a part, and the relations among the three. The basic cognitive skills — reading (lexics), writing (graphics), and arithmetic (ciphering) — underlie all that follows as the child progresses toward deepening mastery of the increasingly complex educational tasks that the school sets for him; irrespective of the particular educational theory, philosophy, or approach by which the school considers itself to operate, inability to have mastered these basic skills signifies educational failure.

For any particular child, educational failure may vary from mild or slight retardation in one of a few subjects to almost total inability to have learned the basic cognitive skills and hence to have mastered to any degree the higher-order semantic, synthetic, and quantitative processes and content to which they are fundamental. Educational failure may have its point of origin in the child and may result in turn from handicap, such as sensory deficit (blindness, deafness), deficiency of higher cognitive-perceptual integration (asymbolia), physical defect that limits educational exposure (Little's disease, muscular dystrophy), or mental disorder that obtrudes on and disorganizes the child's capacity to learn.

Educational failure may also result from pedagogical inadequacy, such as is found in substandard schools with deficient or inadequate curricula, poorly trained or psychologically disturbed teachers, administrative bureaucracies that stifle and stigmatize creative teaching, or educational philosophies and practices that slight the child's need for disciplined substantive learning in favor of undue emphasis on his "social adjustment." In fact, educational failure, of whatever degree, indicates that the educationally retarded child and the educational milieu to which he is exposed have been in various ways disarticulated, such that whatever the child's native potential for learning, the educational process has failed to help exploit it or, in other words, has failed to generate a genuine "learning atmosphere" for him.

Attendance at school occupies from one-sixth to one-third of the primary or secondary student's total day, during which the school serves as an admittedly specialized yet very real home away from home. Especially during the early primary school years, the young child quickly comes to view his teachers as more or less direct parental substitutes, and he displaces to and expects from them attitudes, thoughts, feelings, and responses analogous with those that have typified his own family relationships (A. Freud 1935, Devereux 1956). Thus, as the school milieu and the child's potentials and needs must mutually articulate if the educational process is to be successful, so must the milieu of the school and that of the home. No matter how brilliant and resourceful the school, its efforts will usually come to naught should the child return each day to a home environment that is indifferent or even antithetical to academic learning—a fact too evident to teachers in ghetto schools to warrant further elaboration here.

Another consideration is related to the extensive proliferation of welfare services and the implementation of mass education in American society, concomitant with the increasing degree to which parents have come to abdicate to extrafamilial individuals and agencies child-care and child-rearing functions traditionally accepted as the sole or basic responsibilities of the family surrogates (Roy 1967).[1] The school is, of course, one of the most important of these extrafamilial agencies, and to the extent that it assumes such functions — to the relative neglect of disciplined academic teaching — the stage is once again set for educational failure, exemplified in the paradox of the socially conformist child who, by virtue of the social promotion, manages to graduate from school unable adequately to read a newspaper.

We may now make note of the three "atmospheres," each of which is a necessary, if insufficient, condition for the success of the educational process: (1) the atmosphere of the child, which comprises the totality of the child's internal processes conducive to optimizing his educability, basic to which is his flexible receptivity to new learning; (2) the atmosphere of the school, where the child comes to experience the acquisition and mastery of cognitive skills as self-actualizing and self-gratifying, under the guidance of teachers who are psychologically sound, sensitive to his needs, and expert in what they teach; and (3) the atmosphere of the home, which is congenial and stimulating to the child's educational tasks, and hence reinforces the other two. The three components of this triad generally reinforce each other in the case of the child who experiences educational success. In some cases, however, the child appears to achieve despite malfunction of one of the three, usually the school or home atmospheres, and occasionally is found to have overcompensated for the perceived malfunction by organizing the educational experience along personal, private, or even autistic lines. Such an internal organization may, in turn, become part of and hence reflect progressive withdrawal, detachment, or alienation.

DEVELOPMENTAL CONSIDERATIONS

Entrance into school holds momentous significance for the child and for his family. It represents the latest in a series of fundamental individuative milestones, beginning with the child's actual delivery from the mother's body at birth and including weaning, the acquisition of speech, the development of motility, and the capacity to say "No" (Spitz 1957, 1959). It brings the child into contact with substitute parental figures whose uniqueness, idiosyncrasies, and differences from his own parents stimulate him to widen his experience with adults and to make comparisons among them. It expands his relations with nonsibling peers, thereby affording him a fresh stimulus for acculturation.

Entrance into school also initiates what will be a lengthy process for the child of accelerating and consolidating his shift from egocentricity toward more developed object relations. This process, in turn, comprises strengthening of his ability to sense and test reality, further growth of his self-identities and sexual identities, progressive self-differentiation and self-objectification, and a forward surge of his ability to control and master his own instinctual urges, hence to meet the demands that the external world makes of him. Entrance into school initiates, par excellence, the complex process of sublimation (Hartmann 1955, Fenichel 1945), which includes the canalization of primitive instinct into socially useful and desirable outlets, the growth of what Allport (1968) has termed functional autonomy, and the appearance of the capacity for the *Ding an Sich* (the attitude of the "thing for itself"), or the ability to value people and other objects in the light of their own particular structure, functions, and purposes.

The primary school years, roughly equivalent with the latency period conceptualized by psychoanalysis, similarly witness the child's progressive shift from reliance upon egocentric, preoperational modes of thought through progressively complex, differentiated ideation until, in early adolescence, genuinely abstract, categorical thinking makes its appearance (Goldstein 1939, 1959a, b, Kasanin 1946). This shift betokens the child's developed aptitude for genuine objectivity, reflected in his capacity for hypothetical and nosological reasoning, and signals the beginning of a mature ability to interpose thought between need and act and hence to tolerate and cope with frustration. In view of the subtlety and complexity of these developmental processes, it is hardly surprising that problems in the classroom, of whatever degree and whether academic or behavioral, serve as sensitive indicators that the child's psychosocial development has somehow gone awry. The classroom serves such a child as the locus within which his psychological difficulties may find ready expression.

THE CLASSROOM SETTING

The classroom setting may be viewed as a stereotypical social-environmental field. By definition, a class comprises one or more students whose main task is presumably to learn, and a teacher whose main task is presumably to teach. The physical structure of the classroom is generally predictable: Present are such devices as chalkboards, bulletin boards, erasers and chalk, student desks, and various visual aids and resource materials. Although he may mix freely with his students, the teacher, like them, has his place, usually at the head of his class. The classroom process operates according to a system of mutual rewards. The teacher is expected to establish and maintain disciplined control of the students, to assign them various tasks, and to reward them in various ways for suitable task performance; the students likewise reward the teacher through conformity to his disciplinary controls and proper performance of the tasks to which he assigns them.

It is well to remember that the young school-age child continues to function from a basically egocentric position; his adoption of smoothly operative internal controls is still a long way off, and his ability to view what he is expected to learn with reasonable objectivity (*Ding an Sich*) is vanishingly slight. He will conform and learn almost exclusively to please and be rewarded by his teacher. This salient feature of the child's classroom behavior reflects what is generally true for him at home in relation to his parents. It epitomizes the global, syncretic nature of the child's perception and cognition, and impels him to *parentify* his teachers as more or less direct extensions of the figures and personalities of his parents (A. Freud 1935, Devereux 1956, Werner 1948). As a result, the sensitive, intuitive teacher is often able to infer a good deal concerning parent-child relationships from careful observation of his students' behavior toward him; conversely, the teacher's responses to his young students ineluctably reflect his own surrogate-parental attitudes and expectations (Rinsley 1962a).

By definition, the parent-child (or teacher-student) relationship is an asymmetric dyad based on the former's authority and the latter's submission to it. It finds its origin in the healthy child's redoubtable need to project his infantile or childish wishes, fantasies, and expectations onto his parents. Beginning in earnest early in his second year of life, he projects onto them in particular the powerful infantile omnipotence he is known to harbor and thereby endows them with that very grandiosity he is beginning to learn he must eventually give up in order progressively to socialize. Through essentially the same process of infantile projection, the parents become repositories for the child's archaic ideals that, together with his projected omnipotence, establish them as near-deified beings. The child's *parentification* of his teachers thus represents a direct displacement of primitive wishes, fears, fantasies, and idealizations originally directed toward his parents; that he may offer them to both without fear of rejection or punitive retaliation constitutes a fundamental characteristic of the healthily developing child that Erikson (1963) has termed basic trust. Thus, the child's inherent developmental needs and experiences profoundly determine the teacher's authoritarian role in the classroom, just as they determine the parent's authoritarian role in the family. The fact of relational asymmetry, displaced to the classroom from its primary locus within the family, remains in effect with gradually decreasing impact throughout the remainder of the student's formal educational experience, no matter how far he proceeds in pursuit of academic learning.

In the case of the child who suffers from mental (emotional) disorder, these complex interrelated developmental processes and experiences have gone awry, but they have even more so in the case of the preadolescent or adolescent child who is disturbed enough to require separation from the parental home and admission into residential treatment. To summarize, (1) the child has failed appropriately to traverse those individuative milestones that antedate the significant further separation that occurs upon his entrance into school; (2) he has found it impossible safely to project his infantile fantasies and ideals onto his parents; thus, he is deficient in basic trust and is unable to parentify his teachers; and (3) as a result, the child remains inflexibly egocentric (narcissistic) and clings to his infantile omnipotence, which effectively precludes his entrance into the asymmetric relationship of the classroom and hence thwarts learning (Coolidge et al. 1962, Paulsen 1957, Sperling 1967). For such a child, the stage is now set for the appearance of that wide spectrum of symptomatic behavior that the clinician classifies as *school phobia.*

SCHOOL PHOBIA

The omnibus term school phobia refers to a wide range of symptomatic behavior signifying the child's inability or refusal to attend or remain at school. Its manifestations are legion, including persistent tardiness in awakening from sleep or arising from bed, washing, dressing, eating breakfast, gathering school paraphernalia, and actually departing for school; various psychosomatic symptoms prior to departure for or developing within the school or the classroom, such as headaches, nausea and vomiting, cardiovascular symptoms, and so on; feigned or simulated physical illness bordering upon true conversion or hysteriform manifestations; marked morning anxiety; and negativism and recalcitrance, conveyed in whining, querulousness, transparent delaying tactics, temper tantrums, and abject refusal to leave the home. Some of the more extended, less evidently school-phobic manifestations include sleep disturbances, including *pavor nocturnus* and nightmares, leading to morning fatigue; various actions within the school or classroom, the unconscious or conscious aim of which is to provoke separation or expulsion from school, including gross inattentiveness and withdrawal, failure or refusal to perform assigned classwork and homework leading to academic failure, gross or subtle hostility toward peers and teachers leading to peer-group exclusion and rejection, buffoonery, silliness, and pseudo-stupidity; and antisocial acts such as pilfering, destruction of the property of the school, teachers, or peers. Finally, school phobia is often communicated through frank truancy. Even this admittedly partial list of the sundry manifestations of school phobia serves to convey the wide spectrum of attitudes, feelings, and actions characteristic of the child bent upon avoiding classes.

The key to understanding the etiology of school phobia is discovered in the child's experiences at home; anxieties, apprehensions, fears, and expectations directed toward family members emerge as displacements onto the teacher (parental surrogate), classmates (siblings), or even onto the physical characteristics of the classroom or school building itself (home). Irrespective of the more precise clinical diagnosis in any given case, some, all, or a combination of the following underlying problems are regularly found to be operative.

Innate cognitive failure in school. The child with native cognitive retardation of whatever cause who finds himself in a class beyond his capabilities also finds himself in a traumatic, potentially overwhelming situation with which his limited ego resources cannot cope. He responds with mounting anxiety and, as expected, resorts to evasive or defensive maneuvers unconsciously aimed at relieving it. To understand the struggles of such a child, one must understand that certain of his actions represent direct expressions of his innate relative incapacity (primary deficit symptoms), whereas others represent expressions of his efforts to relieve anxiety associated with the disproportion he perceives between what he can do and what is expected of him (secondary symptoms) (Goldstein 1939, 1959a, b). Careful psychiatric and psychological studies are required to differentiate primary from secondary manifestations of the child's cognitive deficiency in order to plan a special educational program adapted to his needs. For some such children, the school-phobic secondary symptoms assume the structure of a systematized neurotic or psychotic illness, and where this attains sufficient severity and chronicity, psychiatric treatment is needed along with careful educational planning to maximize the child's use of his limited intellectual resources.

Pathological transference to the teacher. If the child's experiences with parents have generally been healthful, hence conducive to his proper psychosocial development, he will tend to view other parental surrogate figures as benevolent. If his experiences with parents have been otherwise, other surrogates are prone to assume the qualities of hated, feared, even persecutory personages, and the child will attack or avoid them or will ward them off. All three responses may paradoxically be conveyed through the child's counterphobic efforts to draw the feared teacher-surrogate into close contact by means of dependent, demanding, or obsequious behavior. The applicable remedial measures will depend upon the nature and severity of the family psychopathology, of which the child's symptoms are a partial expression, and will range from superficial family counseling to full residential placement for the child and concomitant treatment for the parents.

Pathological transference to classmates. Some school-phobic children have developed the view that the classroom is an arena for disruptive sibling rivalries. In accordance with such a view, classmates symbolize siblings with whom the child is locked in intense rivalry for the teacher's (parent's) attention and indulgence. In some cases the child suffers from masked depression expressive of despair over "winning out" over the classmates (siblings), and he proceeds either to withdraw from the competition or to disrupt the entire class in vain efforts to preclude his anticipated defeat for sole possession of the teacher's good offices. Numerous instances of classroom braggadocio, whining and cowering, bullying, buffoonery, chicanery, and exhibitionism thus represent expressions of classroom sibling rivalries. Remedial efforts may be successful at a superficial level with the child and the parents; where more serious psychopathology exists, intensive techniques of treatment are indicated.

Pathologically persistent infantile grandiosity. As noted previously, the healthily developing youngster proceeds trustingly to invest in his parents the infantile grandiosity (megalomania) characteristic of his early infantile life. Failure to have achieved this leaves him basically egocentric and fixated at a stage of fantasied omnipotence that, however subtly expressed, represents in effect a childhood delusion of grandeur. Such a child is profoundly mistrustful; suspicious of everyone, he views the world as a dangerous, predatory place, and he must have his own way. In his crudest form he becomes the obstinate, negativistic, and provocative youngster who proves to be intolerable in, and is often expelled from, school; in his subtlest form he emerges as the dissimulated and manipulative child who outwardly conforms to classroom discipline in order to outwit and fend off the mistrusted teacher-surrogate, to "defeat him at his own game." Such a youngster's prospects for developing serious mental disorder in later childhood, adolescence, or adulthood are great. For the more obviously paranoid child, intensive psychiatric treatment, usually residential in form, is mandatory; unfortunately, the well-dissimulated youngster often passes essentially undetected until more florid disturbances appear at a later date.

Persistent autism. The child with persistent autism lives predominantly if not exclusively within a self-encapsulated inner world divorced from meaningful relationships with persons and events outside himself.[2] His world is rich with frightening fantasy, and he relies upon primitive (regressive), affect-dominated, and idiosyncratic thinking well beyond that expected of youngsters at his chronological age. Less overtly alienated autistic children rely on a private, internally organized logic central to the structure of their perceptions and experiences while going through the motions of apparent attachment to the world outside; they are truly schizoid children, among whom are found a majority of the grandiose, paranoid youngsters referred to above.

For such children the classroom is a brutish arena, for it threatens to expose in the crucible of classroom experience the progressively alien and bizarre coping mechanisms on which they have come to depend. Such potential exposure threatens these children to a degree at which persistent, subtle and gross efforts at avoidance, evasion, detachment, and pseudocompliance develop. The denouement arrives when the cognitive-intellectual demands of the classwork overwhelm the child's intensely private, idiosyncratic ideational organization, thereby exposing his persistent failure to have learned the public, shared, problem-solving techniques of which his classmates are capable. In general, the brighter or more natively gifted the child, the later in his academic course the denouement will occur; for some brilliant autistic youngsters it may not appear until the college years, during which sudden or gradual scholastic failure signals the onset of overt psychiatric disorder. As the child's school-phobic difficulties are, in these cases, expressions of pervasive and long-standing illness, the classroom is offered to him only within an intensive residential center.

Fear of leaving the home. A frequent basis for the onset of school phobia is the child's underlying fear of what will occur at home during his absence. Careful study reveals a rich variety of fantasies centering upon parental loss, injury, or death, acts of violent aggression between the parents, and parental sexual acts that the child perceives as hostile, sadistic, or destructive. Many children with such fears have been appersonated or depersonified by one or both parents, leading in many cases to parent-child reversal of roles (chapter 2, Toussieng 1969, Weiner 1971). Some of these children have never separated from their primary maternal dependency and have continued in an essentially symbiotic tie with their mothers. Treatment varies according to the severity of the child's and the family's nexus of pathological relationships.

For the school-phobic child, each step toward separation-individuation, autonomy, and eventual maturity evokes fresh charges of anxiety and guilt as his powerful regressive ties to his parents come under the threat of disruption. It is appropriate in these cases to speak of the child's fear of success, or of his unconscious need to fail. It comes as no surprise, therefore, that such a child regularly expresses his profound fear of growth within the area so profoundly dedicated to it—the school (Rinsley 1971, Masterson 1971b).

CHARACTERISTICS OF RESIDENTIAL PATIENTS

The adolescent who requires hospitalization is invariably found to be seriously disturbed. The vast majority of such patients suffer from a form and degree of psychopathology most accurately indicated by the terms *borderline* or *schizophrenic*. Our findings further imply the following:

1. Regardless of his specific presenting symptoms, the adolescent is suffering from a degree of anxiety conducive to pervasive disorganization of the personality.
2. He has found it impossible to sustain significant relationships with others and hence has been unable effectively to communicate the extent of his subjective suffering.
3. He has usually signaled this suffering through various kinds of disordered action or overt behavior.
4. He requires thorough and careful protection, including external controls, to ease his anxiety and promote meaningful communication with those who seek to help him.
5. He comes in most cases from a family in which one or both parents suffer from serious mental disorder; as a result, both parents are psychologically or physically unavailable to him.

Borderline and schizophrenic refer to an adolescent residential population, most of whom, following Mahler (1952), may be divided into two major diagnostic subgroups.

Group I: Presymbiotic (Autistic-Presymbiotic), Nuclear or Process Schizophrenia of Adolescence

Group I includes adolescents whose pervasive illness has been present since infancy. They are severely psychologically disorganized; they show cognitive, perceptual-sensory, affective, and motoric developmental dyssynchronies; and may display the "soft" neurological signs often found in children Bender (1947, 1953, 1956) terms pseudodefective. *Presymbiotic* applies to these adolescents from recognition of their long-standing failure to have developed a satisfying relationship with a consistent mothering figure; *autistic* applies to them because they live in an inner world replete with horrendous and frightening "bad" objects and hence are incapable of meaningful relations with other persons. The prospect of closeness or intimacy with other persons terrifies them and provokes them to withdrawal or attack. These adolescents are admitted to the hospital with a chronic history of developmental lags and of psychosocial and educational failure and many have been stigmatized as brain damaged or retarded. The great majority achieve postadmission Wechsler Intelligence Scale for Children (WISC) Full Scale IQs in the borderline retarded range or below (chapter 10, Rinsley 1971).

Group II: Borderline and Symbiotic
Schizophrenia of Adolescence

Residential adolescent patients classifiable under the rubric of borderline and symbiotic schizophrenia[3] have experienced the elements of a need-satisfying, mother-infant relationship; their psychopathology reflects their essential failure to have separated from it or to have undergone any significant degree of individuation (Masterson 1971). Some of these adolescents are overtly psychotic, whereas others present their psychopathology in the form of hyperactive, impulsive, megalomanic, destructive, asocial, or antisocial (pseudopsychopathic) behavior or through a wide range of anxiety-laden, phobic, hysteriform, and obsessive-compulsive (pseudoneurotic) symptomatology (Mahler 1952, Mahler and Gosliner 1955, Bender 1956, Ekstein, Bryant, and Freedman 1958). Whatever the symptomatic facade may show, careful study reveals that these symbiotic youngsters rely heavily on an autistically organized inner world, the content of which centers on mother-child fusion and reunion fantasies which must at all costs be protected from the scrutiny of others. Within this category are found some adolescents labeled as "brilliant but crazy," including the odd or strange "model student" and occasional examples of the "childhood genius," whose purported genius reflects massive pseudointellectual overcompensation rather than genuine originality and creativity.

Just as the Group I adolescent is often misdiagnosed as feebleminded, mentally retarded, or brain damaged, the Group II adolescent is frequently misdiagnosed as psychoneurotic or suffering from some sort of phase-specific "adjustment reaction" or "turmoil state" supposedly confined to adolescents (Masterson 1967a, Weiner 1971). The postadmission WISC Full Scale IQs of

Group II adolescents range from borderline through superior scores. Some are intellectually gifted but have achieved below their educational potential because of the inroads of their illness, whereas others have achieved brilliantly in academic work at the expense of otherwise healthy peer group and wider social and interpersonal relationships. Sudden or insidious decompensation occurs in these adolescents, as it often does in younger primary school children, when the requirements of both the school and the wider social environments threaten to overwhelm the youngster's precarious, guarded autistic personality organization (chapter 10, Rinsley 1971).[4]

The educator would be justified in regarding these rather detailed classifications as little more than an exercise in psychiatric nosology were it not for the fact that they play a fundamental role in the selection of an adequate special educational program for the adolescent residential patient. The thesis I will now proceed to develop asserts that the group structure, frequency of meeting, and curricula of residential school classes depend significantly on the natural history of the youngster's psychopathology, as well as on the nature and extent of his response to the residential therapeutic environment.

RESIDENTIAL SCHOOL: GENERAL CONSIDERATIONS

Dunn (1963) has said that attending school is the child's occupation. Conversely, children anticipate that classroom education will be a substantial part of their life experience, an expectation no less valid for our population of residential patients than for otherwise healthy youngsters. The problems associated with providing an adequate educational experience for the former are, to say the least, formidable.

First, adolescent inpatients arrive at the residential setting with prior educational achievements that range from academic superiority at the senior high school level to near illiteracy; thus, the special educational program offered to them must flexibly provide curricula appropriate for an exceedingly wide range of educational needs.

Second, as already noted, the seriously ill adolescent brings to the classroom degrees of anxiety, mistrust, suspicion, alienation, and egocentrism well beyond those expected of an average adolescent classroom population, as well as cognitive, sensory-perceptual, and emotional encumbrances from which the latter will not suffer at all. The residential teacher must therefore possess extreme psychological-mindedness, intense motivation, endless patience, expert knowledge of his subject, intimate self-knowledge and self-comfort, freedom from significant psychopathology, and genuine affection and empathy for children, whether they be well or ill, if he is to deal effectively with the countertransference demands of his work and provide appropriate external controls for his students.[5]

Third, the majority of inpatient adolescents have had at least some experience in regular school classes, however academically unsuccessful it has been, while some have been genuinely good students. Accordingly, residential classes will physically resemble ordinary ones; the classroom will not be an occupational therapy shop, a recreational area, or a group therapy room. A basic corollary to these physical environmental considerations has to do with the teacher's own identity, for the fundamental need of all children, especially sick ones, is that their adult surrogates possess well-defined self-identities as well as sexual and personal identities. In accordance with this need, the residential teacher will view himself primarily as an educator who imparts and catalyzes formal learning, no matter the degree to which he must concomitantly function as individual or group psychotherapist or serve in a mixed, even kaleidoscopic array of other roles as a consequence of the transference needs of his students. It follows, therefore, that polemics concerning whether residential school should be termed "educational therapy" or "therapeutic education" or whether the teacher should be termed a therapist, educator, or teacher are irrelevant (Morrow et al. 1972). Nowhere more obviously than in an intensive residential psychiatric setting are the close similarities among child-rearing, pedagogy, and therapy to be discerned.[6]

Fourth, although the basic function of school concerns the teaching and learning of cognitive skills, this function must intimately interdigitate with the therapeutic tasks and goals of the residential milieu as a whole. Education, like occupational and recreational therapy, becomes an arm of treatment. Thus, residential school classes are prescribed for the child as part of his overall therapeutic program. Since the child's residential psychiatrist bears the responsibility for coordinating and directing the latter, he is responsible for the formal school prescription as well. Some relevant questions to which the residential psychiatrist will desire answers before school classes are prescribed include the following:

1. Is the child psychologically able to utilize school with profit in the residential setting—that is, without impeding the course of his treatment at that particular point in his residential experience?
2. If so, should the child be scheduled for a one-to-one (teacher:student ratio) class, or may he be expected to handle a group (higher-ratio) class with one or more classroom peers?
3. Should the child be placed in a class with peers of the same or the other sex or in a class with both?
4. Should the classroom process emphasize more formal academic curricular studies or therapeutic relationship?
5. How often should the class meet?
6. What subjects should the child study? For example, should the prescription include English (to promote communication, decrease withdrawal, and provide actual and fictional identificatory personages, heroes, and ideals), mathematics (to expose and work with formal thought disorder and to provide the graded continuity of learning inherent in a mathematics sequence), history (to stimulate exploration of the collective and personal past and to serve as an adjunct to the genetic-dynamic explorations of the child's psychotherapy), and typing (to strengthen eye-hand coordination and the perceptual-kinesthetic aspects of the bodily schema)?

7. Should homework be assigned, and, if so, how much? To what extent may the child be expected to study and perform his assignments essentially on his own in the ward or cottage?

My comprehensive studies of the course of treatment of severely ill adolescents in an intensive residential setting (chapters 3–7, Rinsley 1962a, 1971) have indicated that too-early referral of the adolescent to off-ward or off-cottage adjunctive activities, including school and occupational and recreational therapies, may seriously complicate these activities to the point at which their specific and more general therapeutic values are significantly impaired. These studies indicate that adolescent inpatients, during the first year or so following admission, proceed in various ways to resist the impact upon them of the ward or cottage structure and the adult therapeutic figures who articulate it. The adolescent's resistances are communicated through a wide range of overt and covert, and both verbal and nonverbal, actions and metaphors unconsciously directed toward splitting and dividing (manipulating) staff members, thereby fending them off. The adolescent's resistances proceed to interdigitate with the anxieties, doubts, and guilt that the parents or other responsible parental surrogates come to express in their concomitant family therapy process, and the two combine to inhibit both the adolescent's and the parents' acceptance of the residential center and its staff as genuinely trustworthy and potentially helpful. Analysis and elimination of this resistance phenomenon generally require a period of not less than a year, during which the adolescent will be prone to incorporate any offered school experience into his particular pattern of resistance. Thus, although one may prescribe school for the adolescent inpatient during this initial or resistance phase of residential treatment, the teacher must maintain constant vigilance to discern classroom transference behaviors by which the adolescent communicates his need to press the school experience into service as a resistance to his treatment.

The answer to the initial question, "Is the child psychologically able to utilize school with profit in the residential setting?" thus resolves itself into two subsidiary questions: (1) Has the treatment thus far succeeded in remitting enough of the adolescent's post-admission anxiety to permit him greater freedom to use his native intellectual abilities in pursuit of learning? (2) Are the adolescent's particular patterns of resistance to treatment understood to the extent that the staff, particularly the teacher, can preclude the classroom process from becoming enmeshed in them? As already noted, residential classes for the population of adolescent inpatients presently under discussion must provide a wide range of subject matter suitable for grade levels from one through senior high school. Some classes offer elementary or core curricula, oriented toward the needs of youngsters with minimal educational achievement, whereas others offer recognized academic subjects capable of presenting a challenge to the intellectually gifted adolescent inpatient. Some classes may consist of a teacher with but one student (the one-to-one class), whereas others will contain more than one student.[7]

The approach to residential school, now to be described, is derived from more than fifteen years of accumulated experience in the special education of seriously ill adolescent inpatients. Every effort is made to provide each patient, in suitable form and optimal degree, with both school (residential classroom) and home (ward or cottage) atmospheres conducive to optimal learning. To accomplish this complex task, both the residential school and the ward or cottage environments must be closely interdigitated. Ideally, they should be in close geographic proximity, so that ward or cottage staff members and residential teachers have frequent opportunities for direct and ongoing communication about each adolescent who attends classes in order to recognize, clarify, and evaluate how the patient's behavior in one atmosphere is related to his behavior in the other. Intimate communication between the teachers and the ward or cottage staff members conveys but one portion of the shared knowledge of the adolescent which all adults in daily contact with him must possess. Such knowledge develops from frequent, regularly scheduled conferences and meetings, as well as from unscheduled, informal ("curbstone") contacts among adult staff members during which important data about the adolescent are transmitted.

Although the higher-ratio classes function according to a recognized curriculum, both its content and sequence must be flexibly determined by the teacher himself in accordance with knowledge of the individual student's psychological characteristics, prior educational achievements, and current level of intellectual function. In the one-to-one classes, classroom practice is even more flexible, as the teacher often subordinates curriculum as such to the therapeutic and transference needs of the student. Rigid specification of such variables as total number of teaching hours and hours and days of student attendance, as commonly established for regular classes by local or state boards of education, are largely irrelevant to pedagogical practice in an intensive residential setting.

As a member of the treatment staff, the teacher is responsible for administration of the full gamut of behavioral, activity, and privilege restrictions whenever the adolescent patient's behavior, whether in the classroom or elsewhere in the teacher's presence, necessitates them. It is surprising to discover the number of residential centers in which this essential part of therapeutic structure is either overlooked or, worse, expressly interdicted. The result hobbles the teacher's responsibility to provide quick, flexible, and appropriate external controls for a youngster in need of them, thereby setting up the classroom as a locale for acting out.

Class attendance is mandatory, save in those rare circumstances in which the adolescent patient is disturbed to the point of requiring seclusion with around-the-clock supervision in the ward or cottage. Patients who are briefly or for more extended periods of time restricted to their rooms or to the ward or cottage areas for therapeutic reasons are released from such restrictions for the period of daily class attendance. The basis for this practice stems from the need to preclude the patient's propensity to avoid classes through the expedient of provoking behavioral restrictions.

The patient is expected to remain in class throughout the full class period, generally forty-five to fifty minutes. In a properly taught class, the teacher develops sufficient rapport with the students and maintains a degree of control of student behavior that would make grossly disruptive episodes unusual. When they do occur, however, the teacher removes the patient from class, secures his safe escort to the ward or cottage, and may restrict him to the latter or to his room to assist him in regaining behavioral control. The youngster continues to be responsible, during the period of his restriction, for completion of the day's assigned classwork, with which he may receive temporary additional assistance from the teacher at her discretion, and with the approval of the residential psychiatrist. The latter now begins to explore with the patient the basis for his loss of control in class. The psychiatrist and the teacher will often meet together with the youngster and mutually explore with him the anxieties, preoccupations, and subjective experiences that have contributed to his classroom difficulty (the so-called three-way meeting). Is is interesting to observe how quickly classroom difficulties prove amenable to intensive short-term study.

An hour after a thirteen-year-old male adolescent required restriction to his room for cursing at his teacher, the latter, the youngster, and the psychiatrist met for a "three-way." After a few minutes of diligent, sensitive questioning, the boy fearfully admitted that he had hallucinated his hated father in the person of the teacher, had next experienced sudden panic, and had "blown up" in an effort to "get out of there." The adults present complimented him on his ability to share this experience with them, assured him that his hallucinatory experiences need not impair his schoolwork, and encouraged him to complete the day's assigned classwork during the period of his restriction. With careful follow-up analytical work with his psychiatrist, the boy did not repeat his loss of control in class, although he continued with his momentary hallucinosis until his need to utilize it was understood and could be eliminated.

A fifteen-year-old female patient, after several weeks of "model" classroom behavior, began to present a surly, negativistic attitude toward the male teacher, which quickly served to undermine the latter's authority and to evoke similar behavior from several classmates. After several days' work it was discovered that the girl had been experiencing intense sexual feelings directed toward the teacher, to such a degree that they literally paralyzed her attention to the classwork. In this case the girl had displaced strong erotic transference feelings from her psychiatrist to the teacher; when this was understood, accepted, and worked with by the psychiatrist, the classroom difficulty quickly abated.

Timely completion of assigned homework is mandatory. If left unattended, problems with this important aspect of schoolwork, like disruptive classroom behavior, will rapidly impair educational performance. Once again the psychiatrist, with or without the simultaneous presence of the teacher, explores with the patient the basis for his refusal to perform or complete home assignments; often such exploration uncovers the immediate precipitating factors and allows correction of the overt difficulty. As in the case of disruptive classroom behavior, resistance to homework most often reflects the presence of classroom transference problems. If the problem persists beyond one class period, the patient is placed on supervised study on the ward or cottage. Supervised study commences immediately following the evening meal, and involves limited segregation from the mainstream of ongoing ward or cottage activities while the patient works at his lessons under the watchful eyes of ward or cottage staff members, generally aides or child-care workers. In the majority of instances, one or two evenings of scheduled supervised study, along with continued exploration by the psychiatrist, will resolve the homework problem. Our experience indicates that if it persists beyond this point, the problem signifies the operation of major patient-staff and home-school splits indicative of inappropriate placement in class or sometimes premature prescription for residential school. In the face of intransigent refusal to perform homework assignments, termination of the patient's class placement is indicated.

As in the case of all off-ward or off-cottage scheduled activities, the ward or cottage staff are responsible for having each youngster prepared to attend residential classes on time and in an appropriate physical condition. The teacher will expect the patient to present himself at class awake, properly dressed and fed, and with school paraphernalia in a state of readiness for the day's classwork.

THE REFERRAL FOR RESIDENTIAL SCHOOL

Concomitant with the psychiatrist's intensive individual examination and the psychiatric social worker's family evaluation, the newly admitted adolescent inpatient receives a thorough battery of intelligence, achievement, projective, and thematic tests. These include the WISC, the Wide Range Achievement Test (WRAT), the BRL Sorting Test (for evaluating categorical ideation), the Bender Visual-Motor Gestalt Test, the Rorschach Test, the Thematic Apperception Test (TAT), and the House-Tree-Person Test. From four to six weeks following admission, at a scheduled diagnostic case conference, the psychological test and casework findings are presented, and the examining psychiatrist summarizes these and presents in detail his own genetic-dynamic formulation of the case accompanied by his formal diagnosis, prognosis, and therapeutic recommendations. The patient's comprehensive residential plan is subsequently developed following careful consideration of the etiology, dynamics, natural history, and familial-social foundations of the adolescent's psychopathology. Included in this plan is the question of whether the patient should be referred for residential school. Finally, careful scrutiny is accorded the patient's educational history, as gleaned from earlier school reports, previous grade placement, estimated intellectual potential as inferred from current test results, known and inferred psychological factors contributory to whatever degree of educational retardation the patient has previously demonstrated, and present achievement test results (Boomer 1969, Hirschberg 1953). If residential school is prescribed as part of the adolescent's therapeutic program, the referring residential psychiatrist will consider the more concrete matters of timing of the referral, class structure, course content, and frequency of class meetings.

The teacher's gender identity is of little or no significance for the success of most adolescent inpatients' residential school experience. The basis for this conclusion stems from the relatively primitive nature of the adolescent inpatient's transference to the teacher; put more simply, the adolescent will inevitably proceed to parentify his teachers according to his own needs and as they represent to him at different times either paternal or maternal surrogates or more archaic personages, irrespective of their own native gender. As in all therapeutic and quasi-therapeutic experiences, the skill and sensitivity with which the helping person deals with the patient's transference largely determine its course and outcome.

For Group I (presymbiotic, nuclear, or process schizophrenic) adolescents, a single one-to-one class with a highly trained teacher is usually prescribed. Experience shows that the Group I adolescent is unable to sustain himself and hence experiences an ever-present threat of psychological disorganization amidst the welter of peer-competitive experiences to which he is subjected in a class with other children. The major emphasis in the one-to-one class is on therapeutic relationship; the speed and depth with which it develops depend critically on the teacher's ability to handle the youngster's primitive, regressive transference and to provide appropriate external controls to remit the marked anxiety he experiences. In other words, the teacher must provide a stable atmosphere for learning. As already noted, most Group I adolescents perform in the borderline retarded range of intelligence or below; hence, most one-to-one classes for them will generally present a circumscribed range of basic core-type material, such as spelling, elementary arithmetic, reading, and writing during those class periods in which the teacher-student relationship is adequate to sustain the student's limited capacity for intellectual work.

The one-to-one class should convene no less than three times a week, at exactly the same hour, in order to sustain transference development and optimize the regularity, hence predictability, of the classroom experience for such pervasively disorganized adolescents. The Group I adolescent referred for a one-to-one class should not be referred for other one-to-one therapeutic activities, including individual psychotherapy, so long as it is necessary for him to remain in such a setting, which exerts a critical drain upon his limited psychological resources. Finally, although the one-to-one class may be organized according to the usual semester system, its therapeutic nature renders it a relatively long-term process for which no arbitrary time limits can or should be set. Efforts to propel the presymbiotic adolescent prematurely toward regular or higher-ratio classes, thereby terminating the one-to-one process, may prove deleterious to the patient's educational and general therapeutic progress.

It is evident that the effectiveness with which the Group I adolescent learns in school is but one expression of the depth and genuineness of his relationship with his teacher to a degree far in excess of what is obtained in higher-ratio school classes and in regular or public school classes for noninstitutionalized youngsters. The psychotherapeutic skills required of the residential teacher deserve careful supervision for the classroom process, best provided by a staff psychiatrist or clinical psychologist skilled and experienced in the treatment of adolescents; such supervision may be obtained through an intensive individual process or in group process control.[8] The fundamental goal of the one-to-one class is to catalyze those basic identifications with the teacher around which the nuclei of effective ego functions may proceed to crystallize; if the latter occurs, the child will learn.

For Group II (borderline and symbiotic schizophrenic) adolescents, the residential psychiatrist will usually prescribe a higher-ratio class, with at least two and not more than six students (Burnett 1965). In contrast with Group I adolescents, symbiotic adolescents often flourish in the higher-ratio class, which serves as a group structure conducive to desymbiotization, with attendant separation from regressive parental ties. It is well to remember that the major therapeutic goal for Group II adolescents is resolution of such regressive ties, which have persisted throughout the preschool and latency years, leading to concomitant socialization and strengthening of object relationships. Thus, the more normal features of childhood development are reflected in the greater resemblance of the higher-ratio residential class to regular school classes, including a stronger adherence to and emphasis on curricular content. Within such a context, the teacher's psychological skills and sensitivity must, of course, match those required of him in the one-to-one class as he labors with the mixture of both pathological and age-appropriate transference responses to which his students will be prone.

TESTS AND GRADES

Nowhere is the adult's insensitivity to the needs of children more evident than in that pejorative manifestation of latter-day mass-educational theory known as social promotion. It is impossible even to guess how many intellectually retarded and mentally disordered children are literally pushed from grade to grade, without regard for their native cognitive competence or for what and how much they may have managed to learn. The result, so well and sadly portrayed by our population of adolescent inpatients, is the muddled, disturbed youngster who finds himself in an academic grade well in excess of his developed knowledge and skills, a phenomenon that has in the profoundest sense an effect in direct contrast with that which sanguine practitioners of the social promotion claim for it. At root, the social promotion reinforces the child's narcissism and mistrust; it informs him that he may indeed get something for nothing and that his teachers care little for whether or what he has learned.

It hardly needs emphasis, therefore, that the social promotion and related practices, such as ungraded classes and tests graded without regard for the student's actual performance, find no rational place in a therapeutic setting for seriously disturbed adolescents. On the contrary, our experience confirms the need in such a setting for appropriately spaced examinations, consistent performance standards, and final semester or course grades, even for those adolescents whose education proceeds in the one-to-one class. One may justify these operational recommendations in two ways.

The majority of successfully treated adolescent inpatients eventually return to junior or senior high school following completion of their residential experience, indicating the importance of validly earned course credits for their future educational endeavors.

Clear-cut, age-appropriate, and predictable criteria for academic performance strengthen the child's inchoate self-objectification, serve to orient him in respect to his peers, promote his capacity to compare himself with others, and protect him from a degree of ambiguity with which his cognitive capacities are not yet prepared to cope. These criteria supply the differentially graded hurdles by which he comes gradually to be introduced to the countless judgmental standards against which he must measure himself in later life. For the sick adolescent, such criteria comprise a fundamental part of his treatment, hence the impropriety, especially in a purportedly therapeutic environment, of unstructured, ungraded, child-centered classes devoid of disciplined teaching and learning. Accordingly, scheduled examinations and test and final course grades find a basic place even in the one-to-one classes as indicators that the students have accomplished a measurable degree of honest academic work.

A striking example of the perceptiveness of a thirteen-year-old schizophrenic girl came to light through her abject refusal to continue with her class. Diligent inquiry brought forth her statement, "I got a B on . . . the . . . test but I got only five questions right, and Barbara got a C but she got nine questions right. . . . To hell with that . . . teacher . . . she's a fake!" The teacher later admitted that she had assigned the test grades on the basis of "what the child is *expected to do*" [italics added]. She saw the point of the ensuing question: "Well, if you have no objective grade standards, why do you give grades at all . . . who is kidding whom here?" Thereafter, her grades reflected honest performance, and the patient settled down to her classwork.[9]

CONCLUSION

The view of special education in an intensive residential psychiatric setting set forth in chapter 8 proceeds from several generalizations concerning both educational and psycho-therapeutic processes and the close relationship between them.

1. It is assumed that the predominant function of the classroom process, whether in a residential treatment setting or elsewhere, is to impart literate cognitive skills by means of an asymmetric relationship between teacher and student.

2. The mentally ill adolescent is admitted into residential treatment for the prime purpose of alleviation of his psychopathology and not primarily to pursue academic or vocational education. Thus, although the majority of adolescent inpatients will attend school, some, for varying periods of time during their course of hospital treatment, will not.

3. It is recognized that all forms of psychiatric treatment may be viewed as learning experiences; conversely, all forms of classroom learning, particularly within a residential milieu, have therapeutic implications. Hence, residential school becomes and functions as an arm of treatment in the wider sense, and the teacher serves his students as a full member of the residential therapeutic team.

4. The residential teacher accepts a child into class only on the residential psychiatrist's formal referral, based in turn on the latter's thorough knowledge of the child's psychopathology, educational history, course in residential treatment, and levels of actual and potential intellectual performance. Possessed of this shared knowledge, the teacher is equipped to schedule an appropriate class load and to plan a suitable curriculum for the child, as well as to adequately anticipate and cope with the symptomatology that the child is likely to show in the classroom.

5. The residential teacher should possess a working knowledge of developmental and abnormal psychology, particularly of that age group of children he is called upon to teach, and should be sensitive to children's verbal and nonverbal (behavioral) metaphors. The residential teacher must participate as a full therapeutic team member in all scheduled and informal diagnostic and therapeutic meetings and conferences devoted to each of the patients he teaches.

6. A considerable and, in some cases, overwhelming part of the adolescent inpatient's classroom behavior reflects displacements

and projections indicative of regressive transference to the teacher. Conversely, the latter's countertransference responses can pose serious problems for his effective performance with his students. Thus, careful, intensive individual and group process supervision, provided by expert clinicians, is essential for the recognition and resolution of these well-recognized problems, and for assisting the teacher in acquiring a degree of intimate self-knowledge and self-comfort conducive to his optimal performance in his primary role as an educator.

7. Residential classes convene in a classroom setting closely integrated both geographically and architecturally with the wards or cottages that serve as the main treatment areas.

8. Nowhere more evidently than in an intensive residential psychiatric milieu is the teacher called upon to serve as a true "healing pedagogue," for within it the remainder of the therapeutic atmosphere supports and catalyzes his educational labors, and the latter are an important contribution to the alleviation of psychopathology. Thus, treatment and education ineluctably combine to guide the residential patient toward resolution of his illness and resumption of that notable portion of his psychosocial development which it had so long precluded.

Notes

1. The recent and often heated controversy over sex education in the schools provides a case in point.

2. It will be evident from the text that the term *autism* is used here in the general sense of dereism (Bleuler 1950) and not in the manner in which it has been employed by Kanner (1943, 1949) and others (early infantile autism).

3. Included in this category are adolescents whom Masterson (1971b) characterizes as suffering from "borderline syndrome."

4. In a recent work, Easson (1969) proposes the following categories of adolescents who require residential (inpatient, hospital) treatment:

1. The severely handicapped, neurotic adolescent.
2. The disturbed adolescent with ego defects and developmental arrest.
3. The disturbed adolescent with severe conscience defects.
4. The psychotic adolescent, further grouped into

      a. The process psychotic (nuclear schizophrenic) adolescent.

      b. The reactive psychotic adolescent.

This classification appears tedious. Careful reading of Easson's clinical descriptions of patients in the first three groups strongly suggests that most, if not all, of them are in fact borderline or frankly psychotic, and the recovery statistics he cites, particularly for adolescents in categories 2 and 3, support this inference. Indeed, Easson's category 1, 2, 3, and 4b inpatient adolescents appear to correspond, as a group, with Group II (borderline and symbiotic schizophrenic) adolescents, whereas his category 4a inpatient adolescents correspond with Group I (autistic-presymbiotic, nuclear, or process schizophrenic) adolescent inpatients.

      5. Sarason, Davidson, and Blatt (1962) observe that extant collegiate and university training programs for teachers fail to equip them with the complex psychosocial skills that even ordinary classroom teaching requires, a point further underscored by Toussieng (1969). Most authorities agree that adequate training programs for teachers in residential treatment centers are essentially nonexistent. Therefore, such centers must assume full responsibility for the training and supervision of residential teachers in the skills required for successful work with inpatient children (Morrow et al. 1972).

      6. It cannot be overemphasized that the stability of the residential teacher's role as teacher facilitates his availability to the adolescent patient as a transference figure, hence reinforcing his important subsidiary role as a therapeutic figure. (See Morrow et al. 1972).

      7. My experience indicates that, for a population of borderline and psychotic adolescent inpatients, the optimal number of students is four, with an allowable maximum of six (Burnett 1965).

      8. It must be emphasized that, no matter how impressive their prior educational credentials, teachers who expect to work in an intensive residential setting require intensive, ongoing (in-service) training and supervision by qualified psychiatric and clinical psychological staff members. For some classroom processes, such as the one-to-one class, a one-to-one or small group supervisory process will prove effective; for others, larger group process control will suffice. Supervision will usually focus on transference-countertransference communications and behavior and on the symbolic aspects of teacher-student interaction. Such supervision, which promotes the teacher's acquisition of a high level of intimate self-knowledge and self-comfort, is conducive to the success of his pedagogical efforts.

9. The practice referred to in this case obviously applies only in those classes in which all the students are expected to cover, hence be examined in, essentially the same material. In some high-ratio classes in which students may work at different rates, examinations must be individualized, although they must still be based upon honest, predictable performance standards.

9

A Comprehensive View of Residential Treatment

DEVELOPMENTAL AND DIAGNOSTIC CONSIDERATIONS

Irrespective of presenting symptomatology, the adolescent who is a candidate for residential treatment is invariably found to have failed at the interrelated developmental tasks of separation-individuation and emancipation (Masterson 1971b, 1972b). The more precise extent of that failure depends on whether his difficulties arose prior to or after the inception of the mother-infant symbiosis during the first postnatal year of life. Following the formulations of Kanner (1943, 1949) and Mahler (1952, 1958, Mahler and Gosliner 1955) in the case of infants and younger children it is possible to divide the great majority of adolescent inpatients into two major etiologic-diagnostic groups.

Group 1. Presymbiotic Adolescents

Adolescents diagnosed as presymbiotic (autistic-presymbiotic, Fliess 1961) are traditionally viewed as suffering from nuclear or process schizophrenia. Their pervasive psychopathology has been present since early infancy; they are severely disorganized, show perceptual-sensory, cognitive, affective, and expressive-motoric dyssynchronies and often display the "soft" neurological signs found in schizophrenic children whom Bender (1947, 1953, 1956) has termed pseudodefective. The term *presymbiotic* applies to them from recognition of their failure to have achieved a satisfying relationship with a mothering figure, hence to have received the protection of the maternal stimulus barrier during the period of maximal vulnerability of the infantile ego. As a consequence, there remain profound chronic defects of the ego boundaries, with persistence of introjective-projective defenses and reliance upon magic-hallucination, scotomatization, and denial. The term *autistic* applies because these adolescents live within an inner world replete with a welter of mixed ideal and horrific bad internal objects, which are fused with endopsychic sensations and images, and hence with their primitive perceptual notions of their bodily processes, organs, and products. As a result, meaningful relations with others are impossible, and the prospect of closeness or intimacy is likely to provoke inordinate clinging, withdrawal, or attack. These adolescents are admitted to the hospital with long histories of developmental lags and psychosocial and educational failure; many are stigmatized as brain-injured or retarded. The overwhelming majority receive postadmission WISC full-scale IQs in the borderline retarded range or below (chapters 5 and 7, Rinsley 1971). A variety of diagnostic labels are regularly accorded the presymbiotic adolescent (Rinsley 1971). (See Table 1)

Group 2. Symbiotic (Borderline) Adolescents

Adolescent inpatients classifiable under the rubric of symbiotic (borderline) have indeed experienced the elements of a need-satisfying mother-infant object tie; their psychopathology reflects their failure to have separated from it and hence to have undergone any significant degree of individuation. Some of these adolescents are overtly, even floridly, psychotic, whereas others present their psychopathology in the form of hyperactive, impulsive, megalomanic, asocial, or antisocial (pseudopsychopathic)

Table 1

AUTHOR'S TERMINOLOGY	EQUIVALENT DIAGNOSES	OFTEN MISDIAGNOSED
Presymbiotic psychosis of adolescence	Nuclear schizophrenia	Mental retardation, moderate to severe
	Process schizophrenia	
	Child schizophrenia pseudodefective type (Bender 1956)	Psychosis with Mental retardation
	Childhood schizophrenia, (organic group) (Goldfarb 1961)	Organic cerebral impairment
	Schizophrenia, childhood type	Chronic brain syndrome, owing to various causes
	Schizophrenia, catatonic type (occasional)	Various syndromes of ego and developmental arrest (Easson 1969)
	Schizophrenia, hebephrenic type (occasional)	
	Kanner's syndrome: infantile autism (rare) (1943, 1949)	
	"Atypicality" (Rank 1955)	

behavior or by means of a wide spectrum of anxiety-laden, obsessive-compulsive, phobic, and hysteriform symptomatology (pseudoneurosis) (Bender 1956, 1959, Masterson 1971b, 1972b). Irrespective of specific symptoms, careful study discloses heavy reliance upon an autistically organized inner world, the content of which centers upon mother-child fusion and reunion fantasies, which must at all costs be protected from the scrutiny of others.

Within this group are found some adolescents labeled as "brilliant but crazy," including the odd or strange "model student" and occasional examples of the "childhood genius," whose purported genius reflects massive pseudointellectual overcompensation rather than genuine originality or creativity. Just as the presymbiotic adolescent is often misdiagnosed as feebleminded, mentally retarded, or brain-damaged, the symbiotic adolescent is frequently misdiagnosed as psychoneurotic, characterologically disordered, or else suffering from some sort of phase-specific adjustment reaction or turmoil state supposedly specific for adolescents (Masterson 1967a, b, Weiner 1971). The postadmission WISC full-scale IQs of symbiotic adolescent inpatients range from borderline through superior scores.

Some are indeed intellectually gifted but have achieved below their educational potential as a consequence of the inroads of their illness, whereas others have achieved brilliantly in academic work at the expense of otherwise healthy peer-group and wider social and interpersonal relations. Sudden or insidious decompensation occurs in these adolescents, as it often does in younger symbiotic primary school children, when the requirements of the school and the wider social environment threaten to overwhelm the youngster's precarious, guarded, autistic personality organization (chapters 5 and 7, Rinsley 1971). Table 2 records some of the numerous diagnostic labels regularly assigned to the symbiotic adolescent (Rinsley 1971).

Historical and examinational findings regularly demonstrate the following characteristics of the adolescent who is a candidate for intensive residential treatment:

1. Major signs of ego weakness, including substantial reliance on such primitive defenses as projection, introjection, regression, and denial; impairment of the synthetic function of the ego, with ensuing disruption of self-environmental relations and decomposition of perceptual, cognitive, affective, and motor functions; predominance of anxiety of the instinctual type with associated failure of normal repression; impairment of object relations; serious impairment, or lack of, basic trust; persistence of primary-process (autistic; dereistic) thinking, with reliance on transitivism and gestural and word magic; and persistent infantile grandiosity and serious difficulties with self- and sexual identities (Rinsley 1968a).
2. Major problems with instinctual drives, including burgeoning or extreme failure of inner controls, that lead to profuse if fluctuant acting out, confusion, and turmoil; and schizoid patterns indicative of massive ego constriction, leading to withdrawal and alienation.
3. Failure of interpersonal relations, including inability to utilize intrafamilial and wider social and peer relationships in the service of self-control and self-direction (Easson 1969).

4. Inability to effectively utilize offered environmental supports for ego functioning, including those of the family and the wider cultural environment, particularly the school (Easson 1969).
5. Presence of latent or overt classical thought disorder, which conveys failure to have achieved a significant measure of abstract categorical (operational) thinking by early adolescence. (When viewed against a background of sudden, progressive, or chronic psychosocial distress, the presence of classical thought disorder may be considered pathognomonic for the adolescent who requires intensive residential treatment.)

Table 2

AUTHOR'S TERMINOLOGY	EQUIVALENT DIAGNOSES	OFTEN MISDIAGNOSED
Symbiotic psychosis of adolescence	Borderline syndrome of adolescence (Masterson 1971b, 1972)	Adjustment of reaction of adolescence
	Reactive schizophrenia	Adolescent turmoil
	Childhood schizophrenia, pseudoneurotic type (Bender 1956) pseudopsychopathic type (Bender 1959)	Psychoneurosis (anxiety, phobic, hysterical, depressive, obsessive-compulsive, "mixed," and so on)
	Schizophrenia, childhood type	
	Schizophrenia, chronic undifferentiated type	Various schizophreniform conditions
	Schizophrenia, catatonic type (occasional)	Personality disorder, especially delinquent, antisocial, schizoid, and the like
	Schizophrenia, hebephrenic type (occasional)	
		School phobia (rare)
		Various syndromes of ego and developmental arrest (Easson 1969)

DIAGNOSIS OF THE FAMILY

Irrespective of social class, the family of the adolescent inpatient will almost invariably be discovered to have raised and dealt with him as if he were something or someone other than who he in fact is — that is, to have appersonated or depersonified him (chapter 10). A consequence of parental psychopathology, such depersonification operates according to a general pattern, which Johnson and Szurek (Johnson 1949, Johnson and Szurek 1952) first described in the case of the delinquent or antisocial child and adult, and severely inhibits and distorts identity formation (chapter 10, Schmideberg 1948, Stragnell 1922).

Detailed study of the families of adolescent inpatients discloses their similarity to the pervasively disturbed families described by Bateson, Lidz, and Wynne (Mishler and Waxler 1968), the relationships within which have been subsumed under the term "amorphous family nexus" (Zentner and Aponte 1970). Such families are organized essentially along autistic lines, with such features as pervasive use of double-bind communications; blurring of age, generational, and sexual roles; shifting and fluid individual identities; patterns of irrational thinking with distorted perception of the extrafamilial world; inadequately controlled or pathologically overcontrolled instinctual urges; and diffusion and obfuscation of leadership and authority. In summary, the adolescent's psychopathology represents his prior internalization of these pathogenic patterns, his immense ambivalence toward them, his inability to communicate about them, the secondary gains of his efforts to comply with them, and his miscarried efforts to break free of them.

THE RESIDENTIAL MILIEU:
GENERAL CONSIDERATIONS

The genuinely therapeutic residential milieu is not a school, foster care home, detention facility, recreational center, or correctional institution, although at various times it functions in all these roles. Rather, it comprises a small psychiatric hospital, the staff of which represents a group of competent professionals, and each with a well-defined role and whose main tasks include the detection, control, clarification, and interpretation of the patient's symptomatic behavior. The setting should be reasonably self-contained, with an ongoing in-service training program for its staff, in order to limit or eliminate the classical clinical-administrative dichotomies that seriously complicate and often vitiate the performance and goals of intensive treatment (Gralnick 1969).

The fundamental, general functions of the residential milieu for the seriously ill adolescent include the following (Noshpitz 1962):

1. Removal of the patient from the pathogenic family nexus and from the extra-familial environment, the demands and expectations of which have overwhelmed him.
2. Shelter and protection, including interpersonal, pharmacological, and physical devices to graduate and limit incident stimulation — hence, to offer protection against ego trauma (chapter 1, Rinsley 1963, 1968b, Noshpitz 1962).
3. Appropriate, consistent (therefore predictable) external controls, the purpose of which is to transduce communications inherent in symptomatic verbal and nonverbal behavior into secondary-process language.
4. Opportunities for controlled therapeutic regression, with emergence of transference responses — which in turn reveal the spectrum of the adolescent's particular and over-determined coping mechanisms, including those that represent his resistances to treatment (chapters 1, 2, 5, 7, Rinsley 1971).
5. Recognition and diagnosis of the manifold of pathogenic, depersonifying communications and role and identity confusions characteristic of the patient's family nexus.
6. Appropriate, intensive use of the techniques of confrontation, clarification and interpretation vis-à-vis the patient and his parental surrogates, in order to expose and alter their appersonative patterns of communication.
7. Promotion of the adolescent's need to identify with the residential staff as good objects, with concomitant

emergence of his endopsychic nucleus of bad (internal) objects (chapters 5 and 7, Rinsley 1971).

8. Provision of such ego-supportive modalities as ongoing education (residential school), recreational and occupational therapies, and, for some older adolescent inpatients, vocational training as part of their overall treatment.

THE RESISTANCE PHASE

Irrespective of the route by which the adolescent and his parents have entered the combined residential treatment process and whether voluntary or otherwise, they quickly develop a variety of resistances to it. (See chapters 1-3, 5-7, Rinsley, 1971.) These resistances, whether gross or subtle, intense or fleeting, serve to disguise and protect the pathogenic family nexus — the congeries of wishes, needs, fantasies, and role distortions that all parties to the nexus share in common, including the secondary gains subserved by the symptoms of the family members and especially the patient. In the case of the presymbiotic adolescent, the resistances, often herculean, ward off staff members' access to the enormously primitive inner world of part-object representations, exposure or loss of which the adolescent perceives as a threat to his very existence. In the case of the symbiotic adolescent, the need is to draw attention from the welter of primitive re-fusion and reunion fantasies that comprise the matrix of his psychopathology. In the case of the parents, the resistances aim toward deflecting the family therapist's or the caseworker's attention from the various depersonifying themes characteristic of the parent-child relationship as well as to deny or assuage the guilt associated with them.

Resistance behavior conveys the adolescent's particular spectrum of archaic, overdetermined coping devices, particularly in relation to authority or surrogate figures from the past. Its recognition, clarification, and interpretation are best carried out in a closed ward or cottage, where comprehensive external controls and carefully titrated privileges bring the adolescent into engagement with, and prevent his avoidance or evasion of, staff members.

The most important forms of resistance behavior that adolescent inpatients regularly demonstrate are the following (chapters 1 and 7, Rinsley 1971):

1. Identification with the aggressor, including some forms of early positive transference, and imitation or mimicry of adult staff members in a counterphobic effort to ward them off.
2. Leveling, which represents the adolescent's effort to depersonify staff members into peer or sibling figures.
3. Flirtatiousness and seductiveness, which convey efforts to sexualize relationships with staff figures, thereby deflecting their attention from other actions, fantasies, preoccupations, and sensory-perceptual experiences.
4. Oversubmissiveness, which has obvious counterphobic intent.
5. Scapegoatism, either active—by which the adolescent sets up a wardmate or motivates him toward proxy acting out—or passive—exemplified by the adolescent who masochistically collects injustices or actually sets himself up to be assaulted or punished by peers or staff members.
6. Outright rebelliousness, ambivalently aimed at warding off staff members through provocative or wildly disruptive behavior, as well as provoking patient-staff contact through application of necessary physical restraints or controls.
7. Transference splitting, a notable form of which is often called manipulation, including gossiping and tale carrying and various efforts to split staff members or even whole shifts of aides or child-care workers, thus concealing thoughts, feelings, and other subjective experiences in the ensuing confusion.
8. Persistent avoidance, including classical negativism, apathy, somnolence, daydreaming, various seizure and dissociative phenomena, refusal to eat, and efforts to provoke restriction and isolation.

9. Somatization, by which physical complaints become the metaphorical vehicle for body language communications as well as a means of deflecting the staff tion from thoughts, feelings, fantasies, and delusional preoccupations.

10. Peer-age caricaturing, also termed "out-typifying" one's self, by which the adolescent attempts to deny or ward off attention to disturbing subjective experiences through actions that appear as slight exaggerations of behavior traditionally viewed as "typical" of teenagers.

11. Clique formation, in which peer-group or small-group interactions are used to preclude engagement with staff members.

12. "Craziness" and "pseudostupidity," the aim of which is to arrest or paralyze staff attention to disturbing inner experiences with the message "I am too crazy (stupid) to bother about, so why don't you leave me alone (or let me out of here)."

13. "Intellectual" pursuits, including literary, graphic artistic, and scientific pursuits and projects, which have basically autistic significance — notably if indulged in without careful staff supervision.

14. Elopement or running away, a complex, overdetermined act in response to a variety of aggressive, erotic, reunion, and rescue fantasies. Although running away may and often does have positive therapeutic meaning, its occurrence during the resistance phase of treatment almost always betokens an anxious need to preclude therapeutic engagement.

Analysis of the adolescent inpatient's resistance behavior and metaphors requires the staff's sustained and comprehensive attention to every nuance of his daily actions and interpersonal relationships. Concomitantly, the parents (or in some cases, other surrogate figures) bring to the caseworker or the family therapist resistance communications, which, in turn, reflect their own anxiety, guilt, and patterns of depersonifying their child. The latter comprise the following general categories (chapters 1 and 10):

1. The child as "thing," inanimate object or externalized part of one's self, a narcissistic part-object lacking an identity of its own apart from that of the parent. (This category of depersonification is found among seriously disorganized, or psychotic, parents.)
2. The child as parent figure, which reflects the classical parent-child reversal of roles (Schmideberg 1948).
3. The child as spouse, which reflects serious age and generational conflicts with notably incestuous overtones and actions.
4. The child as sibling, in which the parent lives out with the child earlier sibling rivalries and conflicts derived from the inability to have separated from symbiotic ties with his or her own parents—that is, the child's grandparents (Masterson 1971b, 1972b).
5. The child as lifelong infant, reflective or the parent's own unresolved infantile needs and anxiety over assumption of genuinely adult goals and values.

In symbiotic cases, the adolescent's and the parents' resistances serve to protect the parent-child tie, separation or emancipation from which evokes fresh charges of anxiety and guilt in both, which lead in turn to further regressive efforts at mutual clinging. Successful working through of the separation requires rigid control of parent-child contacts and correspondence; when accomplished, it signifies beginning resolution of the so-called loyalty problem, such that the parent in effect bids the child to trust and begin to identify with the staff members, and the child proceeds to so act. Even within an intensive, interpretive, and carefully supervised residential milieu, such resolution ordinarily requires six to eighteen months of concentrated work by all concerned.

In presymbiotic cases, the problem is more difficult, and the outcome of the resistance work more problematic. Often, there are no available parents whom the adolescent can begin to objectify and from whom he might separate; hence, the resistance work must center on the enormously difficult task of separating him from the welter of magic-hallucinatory, mixed, idealized, and terrifying internal objects with which he lives. Although no time limits can be assigned to this process, some adolescents in this situation have managed to accomplish the resistance work within a five-year period of intensive residential treatment.

In both symbiotic and presymbiotic cases, successful completion of the work of the resistance phase of residential treatment betokens the inception of the adolescent's significant and enduring identifications with the staff members and of the parents' identification with and acceptance of their child's treatment, personified in the family therapist or the caseworker. The stage is now set for the beginning of the next, or definitive, phase of residential treatment, the hallmarks of which are (1) accelerating emergence of the adolescent's heretofore suppressed autistic preoccupations and coping efforts and (2) the progressive clarification and amelioration of the family's pathogenic nexus of mutual depersonifications (Rinsley 1971).

THE DEFINITIVE PHASE

Entrance into the definitive phase of residential treatment initiates what often proves to be a period of regressive storm and stress for the severely ill adolescent. It means giving up the core of bad introjects central to his psychopathology, the efflorescence of anxiety and guilt—which his symptoms have in part held from conscious awareness—emergence of the last vestiges of the powerful infantile-megalomania common to unseparated personalities devoid of basic trust, and the onset of various degrees of regression in all areas of psychological function (chapters 5 and 7, Rinsley 1971). The whole process signals the ultimate failure of the adolescent's traditional splitting defenses and confronts him with the anxiety and guilt that attend the inception of whole-object relations. Thus, the adolescent proceeds to grieve or mourn the loss of his introjects, however pathogenic they may have been, with emergence of the exceedingly painful "mixed" or "impure" depression of childhood (chapter 5, Masterson 1971b, 1972b). During this period, he begins to speak of how "bad," "evil," and "destructive" he has been, and by his regressive experiences and actions mounts an eleventh-hour plea to the staff to remit the therapeutic pressure on him, to desist from further efforts to empty him of his objects. The staff members understandably find it difficult to continue, as their powerful countertransference to the adolescent's experience of impending annihilation motivates them to restore him to his former state. Of signal importance in sustaining this introject work are the identifications with the staff the adolescent has developed toward the end of the prior resistance phase of treatment.

Of particular impact on the adolescent during this phase of his treatment is the failure of the secondary gain of his illness, a result that ensues in part from the parents' ongoing work in the family therapy or concomitant casework process, such that they begin to signal to him that they no longer need to depersonify him. Thus, he becomes doubly bereft as he perceives the departure of his bad introjects as well as his parents' failure to continue reinforcing his symptomatology. If he traverses this period successfully, the adolescent will have begun to objectify himself and his parents and hence to have given up his infantile ties to them.

THE RESOLUTION PHASE

Completion of the definitive phase of residential treatment ordinarily requires another year of intensive therapeutic work. As it begins to draw to a close, the adolescent becomes prepared for increased and unsupervised visits and passes with his family and for the assumption of ever-wider responsibility for his own actions. His earlier identifications with the staff have supplied him with the nucleus of "good" introjects, which he had long lacked, and his increasing capacity to objectify himself and his parents now serves to preclude reimmersion in whatever remnants of the family's original depersonifying nexus of communications may persist. By now he has successfully worked through the paradigmatic "loss" of his original archaic pathogenic internal objects, which will have strengthened him for the mourning he must now perform as he begins to separate from the residential staff and milieu that have become so important to him. The latter will require several months of combined interpretive and supportive therapeutic work, accompanied by concomitant working through by the family as they prepare to reacquire their child.

Masterson (1971b, 1972b) independently described three analogous phases in the intensive psychiatric treatment of the adolescent with borderline syndrome: his phase 1, testing, corresponds with the resistance phase; his phase 2, working through, with the definitive phase; and his phase 3, separation, with the resolution phase above described. Lewis (1970), also working in a residential setting, confirmed the phasic nature of adolescent residential treatment, with particular emphasis on resistance and later introjection.

THE BASIC GOALS OF RESIDENTIAL TREATMENT

For the presymbiotic adolescent, the full residential setting provides a highly concrete, compulsively styled, and maximally predictable environment, as free as possible from peer-competitive experiences and organized to support the one-to-one, or individual, therapeutic process essential for the treatment of the nuclear schizophrenic adolescent. The individual therapist may be a psychotherapist, psychoanalyst, specially skilled residential teacher, or occupational or recreational therapist whose work with the patient interdigitates closely with that of the other residential staff members and who receives intensive individual or group-process supervision to promote recognition and resolution of the enormously difficult countertransference problems that such work entails. The goal of the individual therapeutic process comprises catalysis for the crystallization of basic ego nuclei and points toward establishment of the patient-therapist symbiosis symbolic for the earlier mother-infant symbiosis, which the adolescent had never achieved. Once established, the patient-therapist symbiosis requires extended efforts directed toward eventual desymbiotization, which signals the adolescent's first real efforts toward separation-individuation. The whole process may be diagrammed as in Figure 1 (Rinsley 1971). In the case of the presymbiotic adolescent,

Figure 1

Resistance Phase	Definitive Phase	Resolution Phase
Establishment of symbiosis ↓		
Beginning resolution of symbiosis	→ Continued resolution of symbiosis	→ Desymbiotization and separation

establishment and beginning resolution of the patient-therapist symbiosis occur during the resistance phase of treatment. During that period, the patient comes to develop and work through the transference psychosis, symbolic of the enormously primitive and archaic experiences resulting from early object loss. Among the various factors contributing to the exceptional difficulty of this work, three emerge with particular clarity: (1) The patient's early resistances assume herculean proportions; (2) staff counter-transference of similar proportions emerges exceedingly rapidly; and (3) many such adolescents are products of thoroughly disorganized, fragmented pseudofamilies, or else have long since lost contact with parents and other family members; as a result, there is often little, if anything, in the way of family therapy or concomitant casework treatment, and the resistance phase of treatment becomes prolonged.

For the symbiotic adolescent, who is essentially locked within a prolonged, unresolved mother-infant fusion tie, the therapeutic goal comprises desymbiotization with attendant separation and individuation. To this end, the major focus of the work of the resistance phase of treatment becomes the recognition and interpretation of the adolescent's fantasies, which center on megalomanic control of and reunion with family members, particularly the mother. As these recognitions and interpretations proceed, the residential program increasingly emphasizes progressive socialization, graduated expansion of privileges, peer-competitive participation (including residential school and occupational and recreational therapy classes), and increased personal responsibility. Although individual psychotherapy may be prescribed and is often helpful, it is not considered essential for the symbiotic adolescent, who often works best with a skilled residential psychiatrist directly in the ward or cottage area on a day-to-day basis. In particular, willy-nilly prescription of individual psychotherapy is contra-indicated, especially during the resistance phase of treatment— lest the adolescent proceed to incorporate it into his splitting defenses, thereby vitiating its impact upon him. The process may be diagrammed as in Figure 2 (Rinsley 1971).

Figure 2

Resistance Phase	Definitive Phase	Resolution Phase
Recognition and expo-sure of symbiosis ↓		
Beginning resolution of symbiosis →	Continued resolution of symbiosis →	Desymbiotization and separation

CLINICAL-ADMINISTRATIVE STRUCTURE OF THE RESIDENTIAL SERVICE

Effective intensive residential psychiatric treatment represents the opposite of the pathogenic familial-social nexus, within which the adolescent's psychopathology has developed and to which it gives expression. This treatment includes establishment and maintenance of stable staff roles, clear-cut and predictable lines of authority, firmly and equitably enforced rules of dress and con-duct to which patients are expected to adhere, and rapid and effec-tual staff communication and consensus regarding every aspect of the patient's daily experience and behavior. Within such a setting, the residential psychiatrist assumes leadership of the ward or cottage therapeutic team, which is composed of the nurse and psychiatric aides or child-care workers. The residential psychiatrist possesses final authority in determining and implementing the overall therapeutic plan for each patient, in collaboration with the other ward or cottage staff members, and prescribes indicated educational and adjunctive therapeutic activities and classes. The residential psychiatrist collaborates closely with the caseworker or family therapist and with his patients' group and individual psychotherapists, none of whom carry administrative responsibility for the ward or cottage treatment areas.

Ideally, an intensive residential psychiatric service should be reasonably self-contained; if the adolescent service is a part of a larger general, teaching, or public or private mental hospital, its staff should be able to evolve and implement its clinical-administrative program devoid of coercion or pressure to conform to general institutional rules inapplicable to an adolescent residential program. Its ongoing diagnostic and therapeutic work should be carried on, with but rare exception, only by full-time staff members. By and large, part-time visiting or attending staff, lacking comprehensive daily knowledge of the patients, complicate the therapeutic work by falling easy prey to the adolescent's redoubtable tendency to manipulate them and to split and divide them from the full-time staff members.

If the residential setting also serves as an affiliated teaching service, it becomes essential for the various trainees, particularly the general and child psychiatric residents and fellows who serve as residential psychiatrists, to receive intensive supervision by experienced senior staff members who are themselves actively immersed in the therapeutic work of the service. Such supervision, which may often assume therapeutic qualities, serves to expose and minimize the serious transference-countertransference binds that trainees are prone to experience in their work with seriously ill adolescents (Hendrickson 1971, Hendrickson, Holmes, and Waggoner 1959, Holmes 1964). The same is true as well for the various full-time staff members themselves, for whom individual and group-process in-service training and supervision are ongoing needs.

GROUP AND FAMILY THERAPY

The therapeutic ward or cottage program comprises a more extended form of group therapy. For the hospitalized adolescent, formal, dynamically oriented group psychotherapy has a definite place, subject to several qualifications:

1. Formal group psychotherapy is optimally conducted with a mixed- or same-gender group of adolescents numbering not more than six, with or without a recorder.

2. Group psychotherapy is contraindicated for presymbiotic adolescents until they are well along in the definitive phase of treatment.

3. Group psychotherapy is of little therapeutic value and may indeed exert negative therapeutic effects in the case of symbiotic adolescents during the resistance phase of treatment—that is, before they have engaged with the ward or cottage staff. The exception is the psychotherapeutic group conducted directly in the ward or cottage treatment area and integrated into the mainstream of daily ward or cottage activities.

4. With hospitalized adolescents, the conduct of the group sessions should follow a carefully prescribed and enforced structure regarding time and place, promptness of arrival, and behavior during the sessions. Although the patients may in various degrees participate in setting and maintaining the structure, a passive, or laissez-faire, approach to it by the therapist is contraindicated. The notion of participatory democracy in an adolescent residential service is often an illusion that disguises staff countertransference and scotomatizes the adolescent inpatient's very serious difficulties with ego functioning (Rinsley 1972). The therapist must therefore unequivocally convey to the group that he is in full and complete control of it at all times.

Again, regularly scheduled meetings between the hospitalized adolescent and his parents, under the supervision and with the scrutiny of the caseworker, constitute a form of family therapy of particular diagnostic and therapeutic value to all concerned, especially as such meetings serve to promote exposure and resolution of the parents' and the adolescent's resistances. The parents should have their own meetings with the caseworker for discussion of problems not directly related to their difficulties with their child, as well as for consideration and analysis of the events that transpire during the patient-child meetings, so that these may be correlated with the details of the child's ongoing work in the ward or cottage.

RESIDENTIAL SCHOOL
AND ADJUNCTIVE THERAPIES

The therapeutic and specific values of residential school and of occupational and recreational therapies lie in their firm integration as part of the overall therapeutic program of the residential treatment service, and not as ends in themselves (chapter 8, Hirschberg 1953, Rinsley 1971). Thus, the teachers and the occupational and recreational therapists have concomitant status as full therapeutic team members, and the specific skills they impart or catalyze subserve the adolescent's particular therapeutic needs.

In the case of the presymbiotic adolescent, the disorganizing effects of peer competition necessitate assignment to the one-to-one class. In school, the specific goal of imparting basic cognitive skills succeeds only if the student-teacher relationship flourishes. Often, the residential teacher becomes, in effect, the adolescent's psychotherapist as he labors to catalyze the youngster's blighted capacity to learn. The same general considerations apply to occupational and recreational therapies, in which the therapist utilizes specific professional skills and modalities to generate and reinforce the nuclear object relationship so essential for the process schizophrenic adolescent.

In the case of the symbiotic adolescent, residential school and adjunctive therapies represent opportunities for desymbiotization. In them, the symbiotic adolescent is urged toward competition and socialization, with ensuing exposure of his infantile grandiosity and opportunities for relinquishing it through the consensual process. In all cases, the therapist must set and maintain a firm structure in which the adolescent is expected to perform and must be skilled in therapeutic process in addition to the specifics of his particular professional expertise.

SOME PITFALLS
OF RESIDENTIAL TREATMENT

The variety of pitfalls common to residential therapeutic services for adolescents amount, on careful analysis, to symbolic repetitions of the antecedent depersonifications to which the adolescent inpatient has previously been exposed. To them, the patient responds either directly or metaphorically with the message, "You don't understand me!" Under such circumstances, the patient has three alternatives: (1) He may dissimulate and appear to comply; (2) he may proceed to act out and "raise the roof"; or (3) he may run away (chapters 1, 4 and 5). Some of the common pitfalls are:

1. Substantive and euphemistic misdiagnosis or under-diagnosis of the borderline or frankly psychotic adolescent with such labels as character disorder, psychoneurosis, adjustment reaction, or some form of deviant development (Masterson 1967a, 1967b, 1968, 1971b).
2. Countertransferential adultomorphization of the adolescent, reflected in laissez-faire, overpermissive, pseudo-analytic, and pseudodemocratic approaches, which profoundly overestimate the youngster's coping and adaptive capacities and scotomatize his difficulties with self- and sexual identities.
3. Open-ward treatment of the adolescent during the resistance phase of his work, prior to engagement with the ward or cottage staff.
4. Capitulation to the warding-off demands inherent in the adolescent's regressive actions and experiences during the early part of the definitive phase of treatment, thereby terminating his underlying need and efforts to desymbiotize.
5. Failure to regulate and control parent-child correspondence and visits, and consequent failure to effect parent-child separation, with resultant persistence of their mutually depersonifying communications.
6. Failure or unwillingness to utilize necessary legal controls to ensure the adolescent's continued residential treatment

during those times when his and his parents' fear of exposure of their pathogenic nexus motivates efforts to remove the patient against medical advice.

7. Premature or willy-nilly use of individual psychotherapy for the symbiotic adolescent during the resistance phase of treatment.

8. Use of part-time, visiting, or attending staff members and of school classes and adjunctive therapies not intimately integrated with and subservient to the basic therapeutic purposes of the residential service.

Part III

Diagnosis
and Etiology

10

Patterns of Depersonification

My father is a bastard
My ma's an S.O.B.
My grandpa's always plastered
My grandma pushes tea
My sister wears a moustache
My brother wears a dress
Goodness, gracious
That's why I'm a mess![1]

The general thesis I will attempt to develop and illustrate in chapter 10 is that the preadolescent or adolescent child who develops significant psychopathology does so as a consequence of having experienced a notable degree of depersonification or appersonation throughout childhood (Fliess 1961, Giovacchini 1970, Kessler 1966, pp. 421–438; Mahler and Rabinovitch 1956, Mahler 1968, Masterson 1971b, Sperling 1950, 1955, 1970). Put another way, it may be said that such a child has been perceived and accordingly dealt with as something or somebody other than what he in fact is, which means that he has suffered various degrees of distortion of his developing identity. The data to be presented and the inferences drawn from them are clinical, developed from experience with 100 adolescent cases in intensive residential psychiatric treatment in a psychodynamically oriented residential treatment service, including intensive parallel or concomitant casework and family therapy of parents or other responsible surrogates.

The adolescent inpatients who have served as clinical subjects for this study were found to be suffering from borderline or schizophrenic disorders. No attempt will be made to assess the relative etiological weights of environmental, "reactive" or "exogenous" factors or of purported "innate," "process" or "nuclear" developmental lags or deviations.

Several assumptions, familiar to clinicians, will be seen to underlie what follows:

1. Children with significant psychopathology, including the adolescent inpatients who have served as clinical subjects for this study, have experienced a degree of depersonification sufficient to have seriously distorted their evolving identities.

2. In keeping with the formulations of Mahler (1952, 1968, Mahler and Gosliner 1955, Mahler, Furer, and Settlage 1959) and Fliess (1961), the adolescent who eventuates as suffering from nuclear, process or pseudodefective schizophrenia has never experienced a healthy, need-satisfying mother-infant symbiosis. Such an adolescent receives the diagnosis, *presymbiotic* (*autistic-presymbiotic*) psychosis of adolescence (chapters 8 and 9, Rinsley 1971b, Bender 1956, 1959).[2]

3. Again following the aforementioned authors, the adolescent generally termed borderline, pseudoneurotic, or pseudopsychopathic has indeed experienced a mother-infant symbiosis but has never managed to separate from it, or to individuate. Such an adolescent receives the diagnosis, *symbiotic* psychosis of adolescence (chapters 8 and 9, Rinsley 1971b, Bender 1956, 1959).

4. Common to both groups of severely ill adolescents is failure of separation-individuation. The presymbiotic adolescent's a priori inability to have developed a need-satisfying mother-infant symbiosis by definition precludes separation from it; in the case of the symbiotic adolescent, such failure has occurred a posteriori.

5. In the cases studied, it has been repeatedly affirmed that the adolescent's severe defects in the capacity for object relations correlate with analogous defects in one or both parents. In a more concrete sense, the parent who is unable to perceive himself or herself as a parent is unable to perceive the child as a child; hence, neither is able to perceive the other as real.[3] Thus, the nexus of pathological family relationships serves as the matrix from which our patients' psychopathology could be said to have developed (Zentner and Aponte 1970).

Extended experience with the families of adolescent inpatients has confirmed their close similarity to the families of schizophrenic persons as described in the work of the three classic writers on this complex subject: Bateson, Lidz, and Wynne. A brief consideration of their contributions is therefore in order.[4]

Bateson. Fundamental to Bateson's work is the concept of the *double bind,* which refers to a learning context in which the growing child is repeatedly subjected to incongruent, mutually exclusive messages from which no escape is possible and concerning which no further discussion ("metacommunication") can be developed. Within such a setting, the child is forced, in effect, to deny important aspects of his self and his experience. Bateson's formulations emphasize the maintenance of family equilibrium or homeostasis through the elaboration of rules governing what, when, and how family members intercommunicate, the existence of which rules is denied. Parallel casework or group therapeutic experience with these families invariably reveal the notable extent of their members' perplexity, as the latter find themselves motivated, influenced, and controlled by covert metaphorical communications often at variance with what is actually or directly stated.

Lidz. Lidz's observations and inferences reflect a major concern with generation, age, and sexual roles within the family, the blurring or confusion of which leads the developing child into serious difficulties with his evolving identity. Lidz describes two distinctive kinds of pathogenic families, the characteristics of which are not mutually exclusive: the *skewed* family, organized around a central, dominant pathogenic person, generally the mother, and the *schismatic* family, characterized by chronic parental hostility and mutual withdrawal. In both, the family's pervasive psychopathology reflects itself in patterns of irrational thinking and in distorted perception of the extrafamilial world, both of which are taught to the growing children. Of particular importance in such families are barely contained murderous and incestuous fantasies which threaten direct eruption as the child enters adolescence.

Wynne. Wynne assumes that a stable, coherent family environment is essential to permit and encourage the growing child to test and select a variety of roles as parts of his developing identity. In the pathogenic family, however, roles are found to be either excessively rigid or loose and ambiguous; failure of true role complementarity is concealed behind a facade of "pseudomutuality"; communication and interaction are fragmented and disjointed; and irrational shifts in attentive focus preclude genuine continuity of relationships. The child conforms to the family nexus as a result of pressures to maintain the facade and hence denies the basic meaninglessness of the relationships, and the imposition of family sanctions effectively isolates him from extrafamilial sources of socialization (the "rubber fence" phenomenon).

DEPERSONIFYING PATTERNS

The mutually complementary descriptions of pathogenic families just considered may be subsumed under Zentner and Aponte's phrase, *amorphous family nexus*. This term refers to "families with a primitive, poorly differentiated, and too broadly encompassing nexus. The individuals in these families have no meaningful self-image outside of the family nexus. Within this nexus, they do not clearly differentiate themselves from other members" (Zentner and Aponte 1970). Diffusion or obfuscation of roles thus comes to reflect the family members' primitive perceptions and hence their psychological uses of each other.

The adolescent inpatient's long history of depersonification in turn reflects his earlier, ongoing relations with parent figures or, more accurately, with his mental representations of them. Of particular importance are the mother's perception of and capacity for appropriate intellectual and emotional response to the infant, which comprise basic aspects of the mother-infant object tie from which is later derived the mother-infant symbiosis during the infant's first postnatal year of life. The mother's perception of and response to her child are, of course, intimately related to the integrity of her own identity as a loving, feminine, maternal adult who is appropriately emancipated from her own antecedent mother-child symbiosis and whose spouse values, hence catalyzes her maternalism. Where these values are deficient or absent, the mother proceeds in various ways to depersonify her baby, to press him into use for the satisfaction of her own thwarted psychological needs, and to fill in the gaps in her own identity. Thus the child becomes for her something or somebody other than what he really is.

Careful study of the adolescent inpatient's and his parents' verbal and nonverbal metaphors, particularly during the resistance phase (chapters 1, 2, 4–7, Rinsley 1971), amply confirms the pervasiveness of their nexus of mutually depersonifying relationships. As a result, it has been possible to formulate a nonexhaustive classification of *spurious identities* with which the adolescent has come to be invested throughout his childhood years. These spurious identities are by no means fixed or invariant; they often change with time and in accordance with the needs of other family members, particularly the parents, to maintain them and the child's degree of compliance with and resistance to them. They may be classified as follows:

1. The child as inanimate object (thing)
2. The child as parent figure
3. The child as spouse
4. The child as sibling
5. The child as lifelong infant

THE CHILD AS INANIMATE OBJECT (THING)

A parent's perception of the child as a *thing* may represent an actual view of him as an inanimate object, such as a toy or other prized possession; often it also bespeaks a view of him as a bodily part-object, such as a breast, a piece of excrement or a phallus, and, in some cases, an organ or system of special sense or motility, such as an eye, an ear, or even voluntary muscle. Parents who so perceive their child are at best borderline personalities whose child represents to them a vehicle through with their most primitive narcissistic needs seek gratification, or through which their own unsuccessful efforts toward desymbiotization may in fantasy come to fruition. Again, by means of projective identification (M. Klein 1955), the child may symbolize an object of fantasied attack, of terror or of revulsion—the carrier of the parent's own projected instinctual needs—whose very existence must be scotomized or denied (disavowed) (Fliess 1961), as in some cases of postpartum psychosis, or even physically abolished (the so-called battered child, child murder) (Terr 1970).

Thus, the seriously disorganized mother of an adolescent boy told the caseworker, "Without Malcolm I would feel lost . . . I would feel dead . . . I always wanted to be a boy myself and *he's just like my little thing . . .*" [italics added]. She also told the caseworker that she could not recall her son's face when apart from him, during which times she experienced depersonalization and estrangement, which she had attempted to banish via quixotic efforts to visit him.

The mother of a psychotic thirteen-year-old girl had insisted, at the time of the latter's admission, that her daughter was pregnant (she was not). This communication had proved puzzling until, several weeks later, its meaning became clear from the following remarks by the mother during a casework hour: "I just know Jan is pregnant because I can feel the baby inside me like it was my own . . . it's like Jan is still inside me . . . ." [You mean it's like you never gave birth to Jan?] "That's right . . . it's like she was never born . . . ." The mother later avowed that she had "never felt better" than when carrying her daughter. The mother had never psychologically separated from her daughter, and the mother's narcissistic wishes had come to be projected into the adolescent girl through the delusion of the latter's pregnancy.

Another case, strongly reminiscent of Fliess' examples of "abolishment" of the child (Fliess 1961), concerns a thirteen-year-old boy whose psychotic, bedridden mother had assigned him the duty of attending her menstrual function by attaching and removing new and soiled sanitary napkins! As a regular feature of this performance, the mother would slap his hands as he went about his task, saying to him, "Naughty . . . bad . . . mother should whip you . . . ." This activity had persisted throughout the latter half of the boy's latency years until his admission, at which time he was found to be preoccupied with gruesome, bloody, and mutilated genitals, as well as with more general themes of violence, murder, and mayhem.

The "as-if" nature of the parent-child relationship in cases of inanimate depersonification of the child reflects the close relationship between inanimate objects and the mental representation of internal and surface bodily parts (Deutsch 1942). In such cases, the child is viewed as a *fragment* from which the parent unwittingly seeks to borrow various aspects of his or her identity.

In the first clinical example cited above, the mother had projected her own phallic wishes onto her son. Her unremitting efforts to bind him to her could be seen to represent her wish to possess a phallus of her own, reflective of her disrupted feminine identity. Thus, she could hardly function in the role of the boy's mother. Her seductive, incestuous behavior toward him served to ward off underlying fears of castration, which the boy's separation from her, via ongoing maturation, had come to symbolize. The role of the phallus as a displaced feeding object (breast) for the mother came to light much later in the course of her parallel casework treatment. Thus, separation from the boy symbolized loss of the maternal figure for this symbiotically fixated woman.

The archaic, preoedipal identity problems common to parents who thus depersonify their children are legion. For some such parents, the child serves as proof of the parent's actual existence and serves to remit parental feelings of nihilism and emptiness; thus, the message of such a parent is, "Without children (or pregnancy) I feel dead, nonexistent." The first clinical example cited above illustrates this difficulty in the mother's basic preoedipal identity.

For some parents, delivery of the infant signifies one's own separateness and uniqueness, hence ability to control and master one's self and environment. In such cases, delivery of the baby has the significance of the parent's first anal gift to the grandparent, signifying the acceptability of the self and its corporeal products; in addition, it possesses the magic-omnipotence that both parent and child associate with feces. Thus, the child is pressed into service to bring about the long-feared yet hoped-for emancipation of the parent from primary dependency upon his or her own parents and hence becomes the bearer of the parent's own infantile-megalomania, becoming thereby both powerful and dangerous.

A condensate of these fantasies is illustrated in the case of a fourteen-year-old psychotic boy whose mother, beset with the fear that her infant's breast-feeding would "tear me apart," attempted to wean the three-month-old baby by anointing her nipples with dog feces.

Again, for some parents, pregnancy may symbolize highly erotized and displaced oral wishes and fantasies, with unborn fetus cast into the role of a parasite who will consume its mother. Further, as pregnancy terminates menstruation, it removes what is for some adults a prime indicator both of femininity and castration. The price to be paid for the latter is exacted, in the end, at the time of parturition, when the fantasied mutilation of the woman's genital is now perceived to occur.

Thus, the mother who takes pains to inform her school-age youngster, often in dramatic fashion, of the dangers and agonies of the child's delivery ("When I had you it almost killed me . . ."). One mother confessed to the caseworker that she had fully anticipated that giving birth to her daughter would kill her, and that the most terrifying aspect of it was the episiotomy ("When I saw him ready to cut me there, I just knew I'd die. . . .").

Of great importance, in many cases, is the parent's depersonification of the child into a vehicle for the expression of the parent's own repressed, disavowed or otherwise unacceptable wishes—a phenomenon ably described by Johnson (1949) and Johnson and Szurek (1952, 1954). Here the child becomes a particular extension of one of the parent's own ego functions—the neuromuscular or motor-effector apparatus. Under such circumstances, the child's (later, the adolescent's) psychopathology comes to be reflected in antisocial or "delinquent" behavior aimed at retaining or retrieving the parent's approval (love) as well as remitting the parent's displaced guilt through provocation of disapproval and punishment from the wider social environment.

Inanimate depersonification of the child, which traditionally has its inception in early infancy, at worst so decimates the child's early, groping efforts toward homeostatic object-seeking as to fixate him at a presymbiotic stage of development. At best, it binds the child in a symbiotic condition by precluding the expected transition from part-object relations to whole-object relations, with ensuing failure of depressive working through and attainment of object constancy (Fraiberg 1969, M. Klein 1935, 1940, 1946, Money-Kyrle 1966).

THE CHILD AS PARENT FIGURE

The parent's perception and psychological use of the child as a symbolic parental surrogate represent the classical parent-child reversal of roles (Schmideberg 1948).[5] Condensed within them one discovers any or all of the otherwise normal expectancies and needs that the child ordinarily directs toward his parents, including the following:

Oral needs. Oral needs include feeding and nurturance; protection from endopsychic and external stimulation ("stimulus barrier"); differentiation of the human facial gestalt (three-month smiling response [Spitz 1957, 1959, 1965]); early differentiation of the uniqueness of the maternal person and awareness of her absence (eight-month anxiety [Spitz 1957, 1959, 1965]); the beginnings of mother-infant separation through weaning, acquisition of speech and development of motility; flowering and beginning resolution of the mother-infant symbiosis (Mahler 1968); the beginning of object constancy with transition from the predepressive (paranoid-schizoid) position of part-objects to the depressive position of whole-objects (Fraiberg 1969, M. Klein, 1935, 1940, 1946, Money-Kyrle 1966); and completion of transition through the sensorimotor period (Piaget 1954, 1957).

Anal needs. Anal needs include further self-differentiation and individuation, with growth of self-mastery and environmental mastery as symbolized in the development of sphincter control, the fundamental process by which the child progressively cedes his infantile-megalomania (grandiosity) to the parents, thereby establishing them as omnipotent ideals with consequent growth of basic trust in their benevolence; development of reaction formations, the forerunners of later sublimations essential for progressive socialization; the beginning of secondary narcissism (self-objectification); inception of the exceedingly important defense of repression; and the beginnings of preoperational thought (Piaget 1954, 1957).

Phallic (oedipal-incestuous) needs. Phallic needs include the flowering of gender identity, development of the capacity for specifically genital satisfaction, the rise of typical infantile sexual theories, the taboo of incest and the appearance of the male and female castration complexes, and further development of preoperational thought (Piaget 1954, 1957).

Latency needs. Latency needs centering upon further and substantial growth of self-objectification and reality-testing, massive broadening of social horizons, development of the attitude of the *Ding an Sich* (the thing for itself) as evidence of further individuation (chapter 8), and growth of concrete operational thought (Piaget 1954, 1957).

Like the parent who depersonifies the child into a thing or a bodily part-object, the parent who parentifies the child thereby demonstrates profound failure to have emancipated from the primary parent-child tie. Through the mechanism of regressive identification with the child, such a parent hopes to receive from the child those narcissistic supplies that the child would normally be expected to receive. Among these are food and external controls.

> The mother who reports feeling "happily filled up" only when pregnant, or who reports feeling ecstatically becalmed or tranquilized while nursing her baby, therewith communicates the baby's role, not only as a food item for her per se but as a succoring, anxiety-relieving object as well.

> It is common, upon arrival of a first child, for young parents to say, "Well, the fun is over—now we've got to settle down!" Such statements betray the new or prospective parents' view of the baby as a sort of stern, demanding superego figure who will exert controls upon them and hence will force them to "grow up." Such a view of the child need not be pathological unless the child becomes a major vehicle for the magical enforcement of a spurious adulthood on the parents, including serving as a means whereby raw aggressive and erotic instincts are held in check—thus, the case of a husband who for years harbored preexplosive homicidal urges toward his wife, which he carried out shortly following the marriage of their only son.

As mentioned, parents with major problems with object constancy are unable to endure the extinguishment of their child's image when he is away from them and attempt repetitively to relive through their offspring the same problem these parents had with their own mothers. One observes in them a recapitulation of the primitive infantile fantasy—out of sight, out of mind, which means, in effect, that the separated child no longer exists, is dead, or has been killed. Thus, the parent's infantile rage and terror over separation or departure from the grandparental surrogate become projected into the child and then denied through endless clinging to him.[6]

Of great importance in parentification of the child are the parent's conflicts over, and unconsummated needs for, self-objectification, control, and mastery. In such cases, one observes the parent's unremitting efforts to idealize and adultomorphize the child, to project into the child the parent's own reservoir of magic-omnipotence and infantile-grandiosity. Such a child becomes, in the parent's mind, a powerful, omniscient being, with whom through identification the parent seeks to achieve a proxy sense of mastery and accomplishment. But through the very process of adultomorphization, the parent poses for the child impossibly high standards and expectations of intellectual and emotional achievement that lead to ineluctable failure, which only further infantilizes him. Or else, the dyssynchronous motivations supplied by the parent drive the child into a variety of cognitive, affective, and motoric dyssynchronies, which may render him a developmental freak.

Parental overexpectation, particularly of the intellectual sort, is common among intellectual, driving, and achievement-oriented upper-middle-class parents, and need not be pathogenic unless the child finds it impossible to meet their demands, either because of native incapacity or because the child is never rewarded when he does ("double bind").

A particularly pathetic form of depersonification of the child, not uncommon among lower-middle-class mothers in the 1930s, assumed the form of efforts to render their daughters into facsimiles of Shirley Temple, the brilliant child movie star, despite the absence of beauty or talent. Other examples include parents who force upon their children endless hours of daily scholarly study or of musical, athletic, and gymnastic practice to the utter disregard of the child's inclinations or abilities.

An especially malignant form of adultomorphic depersonification of the child finds expression in what amounts to a pervasive laissez-faire attitude toward the growing child's need for disciplined external controls. In such cases, the child is passively encouraged toward (that is, is not discouraged from) actions or behavior that are per se potentially injurious to him. Parental laissez-faire may thus reflect underlying competitive and destructive wishes toward the child.[7]

> The father of a schizophrenic, brain-injured fourteen-year-old male inpatient saw no objection to permitting the child during the latency years such "adult" pursuits as cigarette smoking, drinking, and attempting to drive the family car. At age ten, the youngster had sustained a severe head injury, necessitating partial temporal lobectomy, following an accident while piloting the father's motorcycle! Casework revealed that the father's laissez-faire attitude toward his son masked homicidal wishes toward the boy, whom the father had long perceived as a rival for the wife's attention and care.

Another manifestation of this sort of depersonification of the child, described by Schmideberg and confirmed in some of my own cases, concerns the parent who proves reluctant or totally unable to make needed decisions for the child as a defense against revealing the parent's own perceived "imperfections." The child thereby comes to be viewed as a totally innocent or blameless being, and the consequent lack of discipline with which he is dealt often leads to acting out with little or no responsibility therefor assumed either by the parent or the child (Schmideberg 1948).

Thus, one not rarely observes a parent who stands by as the toddler-age child proceeds to damage or destroy other people's possessions such as household or retail store items or even the parent's own home and its furnishings, because one ought not curb or interfere with the free expression of the youngster's natural and insatiable curiosity! An extreme example of this concerned the adoptive father of a fourteen-year-old male inpatient who, several weeks before the boy's admission, threw up his hands in utter helplessness as the boy proceeded to set fire to their home!

Some of the more familiar pathological uses of children as adultomorphic parental figures center upon the more classically incestuous themes inherent in the role reversal, with numerous possible dynamic permutations. One of these is the phenomenon of heterosexual parent-child incest, involving sexual intercourse or various sorts of partialistic (polymorphous-perverse) acts between parent and child. In general, the younger the child is, the more polymorphous-perverse are the acts and the more obsessive is the parent's need to indulge in them, the more severe is the parental psychopathology, of which the pedophilic acts are partial expressions. It is well recognized that the choice of a child as a direct sexual object reflects despair over inability to have established a meaningful genital relationship with a mature adult and thus indicates major problems with identity, in turn derived from the adult's own emancipatory failure.

Within the context of parentification, sexual misuse of the child is generally thought to express the displacement to the child of prior incestuous wishes toward the grandparent; if with an opposite-sexed child, it reflects the chronic persistence of "normal" oedipal wishes; if with a same-sexed child, it reflects the persistence of "inverted" oedipal wishes. Often it reflects the involved parent's frustrated aggressive and erotic needs, displaced from the spouse to the child ("My child loves me better than you do!"); or even in some cases to deny parenthood altogether, ("This is not my [your] child—indeed, he is not a child at all, hence I am free to use him sexually!"). Whatever the specific dynamic meanings of the incestuous acts themselves, they signify failure of the consanguineous incest barrier, whether with natural, adoptive, or foster children.

Of relevance in this connection is the parent's sexual misuse of the child in fantasy, leading by means of metaphorical verbal or nonverbal communication to anachronistic or pathological sexual behavior by the child (Litin, Griffin, and Johnson 1956, McCord, McCord, and Verden 1962).

Thus, the child with excessive sexual curiosity, or who indulges in antisocial degrees of sex play with peers, is often discovered to be acting out similar wishes in the parent, for whom the child serves as an expressive vehicle.

Again, sexual parentification of the child may find expression in the adolescent's sexual promiscuity or delinquency, by which the child acts out the parent's own incestuous wishes, or whose behavior symbolically reflects the parent's own preoccupation with and view of grandparental sexual behavior (Johnson 1949, Johnson and Szurek 1952, 1954). Maternal prostitution fantasies may thus come to find expression in the teenage girl's own sexual promiscuity. Often such behavior symbolizes an unremitting search, not for a phallus but rather for a feeding object (breast), which in turn reflects the daughter's need for or prior use of a male (paternal) object as a substitute maternal figure as a result of serious earlier disruption of the mother-daughter relationship.

An example of these mechanisms, operative in a male adolescent, could be perceived in the case of a fifteen-year-old borderline schizophrenic Negro inpatient with a history of extreme sexual promiscuity and premature ejaculation. The boy's much-married father fancied himself a sexual athlete, with an endless procession of "girlfriends" occupying his ramshackle home. Intensive treatment revealed that the boy had used sexual promiscuity as a counterphobic means of warding off fantasied assault (castration) by the father ("If I am like you, you won't attack or hurt me!"); failure of this defense came to be expressed through the premature ejaculation. Underlying it was a deeper, pathological identification with the latent-homosexual father, who had "driven off" the boy's mother. The at times near-frenetic use of peer girls and older women in part conveyed the boy's wishes to "punish" and frustrate the departed mother as well as to reunite with her.

Another example concerns a fifteen-year-old girl, with a diagnosis of borderline (symbiotic) psychosis and a long history of purported sexual promiscuity with peer boys and older men. The maternal grandmother had been the "town prostitute." Following a brief period of sexual promiscuity in adolescence, the patient's mother had married an austere, ascetic, and religiously fundamentalistic man whom she considered "Christlike." After many months of treatment, the patient admitted that she had never had sexual intercourse but had clearly perceived the mother's need to prostitute her and had playacted. It then became clear that the patient's preservation of her virginity expressed her partly conscious wish to possess the ascetic father and to eliminate the mother. The girl put it clearly: "My mother thought I was like her mother, and I guess she used me to feel less guilty herself. . . ."

THE CHILD AS SPOUSE

Along with parentification, depersonification of the child as a symbolic husband or wife represents a sub-category of adultomorphization; indeed, the two are often discovered to overlap (Sperling 1952, 1970). Generally speaking, success in acquiring a marital partner signifies a major step toward consummation of the young adult's ongoing urge toward emancipation individuation. The successful conception and bearing of children are, of course, prime indicators of biological maturation, and the traditional grandparents' pride signifies for them the success of their own childbearing practices.

There are at least two sets of circumstances in which the parent's depersonification of the child into a symbolic spouse is most likely to occur and to have a particularly pathological effect upon the child's psychosocial development. The first concerns narcissistic, unemancipated parents who obsessively and repetitively press the child into service as a means of wresting independence from their own parents, as if the only way to grow up is through pregnancy and childbirth.

Thus, numerous "forced" or unduly early (adolescent-age) marriages, spectacularly unsuccessful from a statistical standpoint, serve as misplaced emancipatory vehicles for immature, psychologically disturbed individuals who are ill-prepared for the rigors and responsibilities of child-rearing. For the young woman, the child signifies a spurious psychobiological maturity, a specious "proof" to her mother that she is indeed a woman. For the young man, the child often serves as "proof" of his mastery and potency—in such cases also a denial of castration.

In many such cases, one observes the curious and fascinating displacement to the child of emancipatory and rescue wishes and fantasies originally directed toward the husband or wife.

Two related variants of this phenomenon are the so-called "black widow" and "black widower" phenomena, occasionally expressed in spouse-murder following the arrival of one or more children but more usually illustrated in the case of the parent who proceeds to provoke rejection or abandonment by the spouse after delivery of the child. Thus, a mother who had produced six children (including a fourteen-year-old psychotic boy) by five different husbands frankly referred to her many marital partners as "studs," stating, "I wanted children so bad I could taste them and I guess I just used them [the husbands] for that!"[8]

Often the parent for whom child = spouse clings desperately to the child, with the apparently paradoxical result that the emancipatory child-object remains infantile and serves as a chronic reminder to the parent of his or her spurious adulthood and independence.

Some cases of parent-child incest are discovered to represent situations of this sort.

The second set of circumstances surrounding depersonification of the child as a spouse concerns the biological parent who is bereft of a real spouse as a consequence of abandonment, separation, divorce, or death. In such cases, the parent clings to the child as a substitute for the departed husband or wife. Often such a parent is discovered to be attempting, through such behavior, to grieve or mourn the lost spouse, with attendant magical wishes to retrieve and reunite with the latter as symbolic for the underlying wish to reunite with a "lost" parent (the child's grandparent). Thus, the clinical syllogism, *child = spouse, spouse = parent, hence child = parent,* represents a salient example of the blurring of age and generational boundaries, which Lidz has described.

> The young, attractive, divorced mother of a four-year-old boy brought him to the psychiatrist because of extreme negativism, *pavor nocturnus,* and assaultiveness toward her. Not only was the mother sleeping with the boy, but she went about the house nude in his presence as well and even regularly admitted him into the bathtub with her! Hers had been an adolescent marriage with early pregnancy and the child's arrival had been a major factor underlying the eventual divorce, sought by the immature husband who had perceived his new son as a threat to his precarious relationship with his wife. Part of the dynamics in this case was revealed by the mother's remark to the caseworker: "Billy [the boy] looks just like his grandfather [the mother's father, who had deserted the family when the mother was seven years old]." Intensive psychotherapy of the mother would later demonstrate her unconscious need to drive away her husband as symbolic of the earlier loss of her father, for whose desertion she had long felt responsible. Underlying identification with the lost father had engendered in the mother a latent masculinity, partly manifested in her exhibitionistic behavior toward her young son — the unconscious aim of which was to work through her fantasy of possessing a phallus of her own.

THE CHILD AS SIBLING

Parental depersonification of the child into a sibling (peer) is frequent in disturbed families, and it may be taken to represent a pathogenic extension of the healthy parent's need to disavow unconscious dependency needs through denying them in the child. In such cases, one witnesses what amounts to sibling rivalry between a parent and his or her natural or adopted child. The nature and significance of this rivalry in turn depend upon whether the parent perceives the child as an older or a younger sibling or indeed even as a co-twin.

When the parent perceives and deals with the child as an older sibling, the child receives the identity, for the parent, of a transitional identificatory object (older brother or sister) onto whom are displaced the parent's wishes, needs, and fantasies originally directed toward the grandparents. In some such cases, the parent often seeks to extract "older-sibling secrets" from the child, frustration of which leads to resentment of the child's own solitary and peer-group games and play; as a consequence, the parent may attempt to dissuade the child from such age-appropriate activities either by isolating or adultomorphizing him. In other cases, the depersonifying parent may "set up" the child as the spouse's "favorite," thereby revealing that the need to parentify the spouse lies at the heart of the effort to depersonify the child as a sibling ("You prefer our child to [love him or her more than] me!").

The youthful-appearing forty-year-old mother of a fourteen-year-old symbiotic girl fondly told the caseworker: "Ethel and I look so much alike we could be taken for sisters. . . ." Indeed, mother and daughter had often frequented local bowling alleys where they together sought out the company of teenage boys for on-the-spot double dates. Invariably at these times, the daughter actively "procured" the boys for both, whereupon the mother would coyly and seductively proceed to compete with the daughter for *both* boys! The mother could also admit that she felt jealous of her daughter's solitary dates, following which she would make strenuous efforts to pry loose from the girl the details of the latter's behavior while with the boy, especially putative sexual behavior.

When the child is depersonified as a younger sibling, one generally witnesses the emergence, via the child, of the parent's intensely competitive, retaliatory, and punitive wishes centering upon earlier sibling rivalry for the grandparents' love and supplies. In many cases, the parent eschews the unconscious, self-appointed role of "big brother" or "big sister," thereby withholding from the child counsel, guidance, and advice essential for the latter's self-development.

> The father of a psychotic fifteen-year-old boy told the caseworker, "Sure, I never taught him anything—why should I? He'll have to find out how to be a man by himself, like I did."

Of significance are examples of parents who attempt to supply their hospitalized child's clothing needs by bringing articles that are soiled, worn, or outsized. One mother stated, "Well, what does she expect—she ought to be thankful for hand-me-downs—that's all I got when I was a kid!"

We have seen several cases of child-battering by both mothers and fathers in which the dynamics could be traced to an older sibling's (the parent's) intense rivalry with a younger sibling.

When the parent depersonifies the child as a co-twin (especially if the parent is in fact such), one generally discovers a variety of early preoedipal wishes and conflicts indistinguishable from those that typify inanimate depersonification of the child. In such cases, the parent perceives and responds to the child-twin as an extended part of himself or as a thing.

The feelings of parents who were biological twins that they were "only half as good" as other children, with associated fantasies of having been deprived, damaged, or mutilated, are often displaced to the child, where they assume the form of the parent's conviction that separation from the child is indeed impossible. In the case of fraternal, opposite-sexed twin children, intense oedipal and oral wishes often come to be displaced from the opposite-sexed parent to the twin child. Thus, both opposite-sexed adolescent co-twins, aged fourteen years, were admitted into residential treatment with lengthy histories of florid psychotic decompensation and familial incest; indeed, the girl proved to be three months pregnant, and it was impossible to determine whether her father, her brother, or someone else had impregnated her.

Depersonification of the child as a sibling finds not infrequent expression in instances of parent-child incest as a repetition of the parent's earlier, juvenile sex play with siblings and preadolescent peers, particularly in cases in which the incestuous acts are predominantly or solely polymorphous-perverse.

Thus, the father of a fourteen-year-old inpatient girl had for some years indulged in a caricature of childhood sex play with her, limited to partialistic acts aimed at "teaching her all about herself." The girl blandly described it as "like we were playing 'Doctor.'"

The genetic-dynamic common denominator in cases of parental depersonification of the child as a sibling is discovered in the person of a grandmatriarch (more rarely, a grandpatriarch) from whom the parent has never been able to separate (Benedek 1956, Friedman 1966, Giovacchini 1970). In such families, obfuscation of age and generation roles finds expression in the grandmother's need to view her children and grandchildren as peers or siblings.

A fascinating example concerns the case of a thirteen-year-old Negro girl who had been admitted in a psychotic condition following an attempt to poison her father by placing Drano in his pizza and with whom she had been engaging in partialistic incest for several years. A significant part of her illness centered upon her extensive delusional preoccupation with her deceased, psychotic maternal grandmother. The latter had been viewed by her own children (including the patient's mother) as a clairvoyant personification of God. The grandmother had selected the patient as "My favorite child," to whom she had bequeathed her preternatural powers. Thus, there had evolved a symbiosis involving the grandmother, the mother, and the patient; the latter two had assumed the identity of peers who had attempted to deal with their intense sibling rivalry in part by exchanging places with each other for possession of the father.

THE CHILD AS LIFELONG INFANT

Analysis of the foregoing modes of depersonifying the child reveals their common origin in the parent's ultimate need to perceive and preserve the child as an infant in perpetuity, to use the child for the gratification of powerful narcissistic needs. For some such parents, fear of one's own maturation, aging and ultimate mortality provoke regressive identification with the infantile or immature child; keeping the child infantile thus serves as a guarantee of one's own agelessness.

Infantile depersonification of the child often serves the adult's need to ward off or deny feelings of inadequacy, ineffectuality, or impotency through megalomanic overcontrol of the child.

> The seriously disorganized mother of a fifteen-year-old male inpatient told the caseworker, "I never felt grown up until I had Billy—whenever I look at him he makes me feel like a real woman!" (Note the magical adultomorphic power which the mother attributes to the boy, whom she had otherwise successfully infantilized throughout his life.)

It is generally accepted that persistent overindulgence or frustration of the growing child's needs have significant infantilizing effects and that even more regressive of the child is their unremitting and unpredictable alternation. Persistent overindulgence and overprotectiveness rob the child of essential opportunities to experience the growth that results from appropriately graded frustrations, whereas persistent frustration of the child's expanding congeries of coping devices has essentially the same effect. One may conceptualize these extremes in terms of antipodal attitudes toward the child, as described in the following discussion.

The message of total acceptance: "Nothing you do displeases me." As noted, some parents early and repeatedly convey to the child that everything he does is pleasing, acceptable, desirable, or above reproach; they thus communicate to him that he is faultless and blameless and that he can do no wrong. In such obscene pandering to the child's narcissism, one perceives the parent's projection into him of ambivalent, hostile and ideal wishes and fantasies; it conveys the parent's submission to the child's will and, as a consequence, induces and maintains a pathological hypertrophy of the child's control of the parent. It furthermore constitutes a lie that the child ultimately detects but is continually stimulated to make the most of. With such an approach to the child, the parent conveys an inability to accept, hence control, the child's infantile-grandiosity, thereby fixating and reinforcing it. Unable thus to cede to the parent the infantile-omnipotence that the latter perceives to be alien and frightening, the child invariably comes to infer that his fantasies, wishes and impulses are so dangerous as not to be shared with or entrusted to others.

Thus are spawned the "Little King" and "Little Queen" syndromes, accompanied by burgeoning anxiety and guilt, as the child perceives that he is free to place in action whatever aggressive and erotic impulses may arise within him; he may thus fantasize that he is whatever he wishes to be and proceed to act as if the fantasies are realities. Largely devoid of appropriate external controls, the child never really learns to interpose thought between need and act and hence to develop secondary process and tolerance for frustration.

As already noted, that variety of adultomorphic depersonification of the child which finds expression in an attitude of laissez-faire generally conveys the parent's underlying competitive and destructive wishes toward the child. Of related importance is the parent's need to produce and utilize a "blameless" or "perfect" child in order to remit feelings of guilt with the associated need to be punished. The inevitable restrictive and punitive sanctions that the child's acting out provokes from an aggrieved extrafamilial environment thus provide the parent with proxy satisfaction of his or her own guilt-laden needs.

Graphic examples of this problem are found among parents who ceaselessly project blame for their children's difficulties onto various aspects of the extrafamilial environment, such as the school, the church, other people's children, and the like. Some such parents engage in litigation with or may physically assault teachers, principals, school counselors, clergymen, or other authority figures from a need to provoke their punishment. Their paranoid acts betray their use of their "ideal" children as triggers for the retributive explosion they are convinced a hostile environment holds in store for them.

The message of total rejection: "Nothing you do pleases me." Communicated in its most direct form, the message of absolute or total rejection of the child as a real, pleasing or interesting object is incompatible with the child's survival and is manifested in some tragic cases by the parent's physical abandonment of the child to exposure and starvation. In a rather less thanatic form, the parent may transmit the message either through actions that convey scotomatization (abolition) of the child or that signify the parent's need to keep the child at unreachable emotional distance. Whatever the case, the parent's message amounts to, "You are bad (harbor 'bad' things inside you that frighten me) and I must not relate myself to you!" Irrespective of the basis for such a view of the child, the latter responds with powerful efforts to introject the departed (dead) parent, along with desperate clinging to the "bad" internal objects which comprise condensed self-object-representations and parental part-object-representations. The result is a process of pathological infantile mourning interminable in its extent and rife with the persistent operation of splitting defenses.

After several years of intensive psychotherapy, a fifteen-year-old girl, a presymbiotic adolescent inpatient, had begun to menstruate. She had been deserted by her unmarried parents in infancy, with the usual succession of boarding and foster placements. The girl was finally able to tell her therapist that she had feared menstruating ". . . because I was afraid to lose my family. . . ." It then developed that she had fused the archaic mental representations of her family, especially her parents, with her cloacal products — that is, feces, urine, and menstrual effluvium — in a desperate, long-standing effort to cling to them.

The child who has, in effect, been scotomatized by the parent remains developmentally arrested at the stage of magic-hallucinatory wish fulfillment, with a welter of condensed and substitute delusional part-object constructs that have thwarted the development of object constancy and hence have precluded the development of object relations. However pathogenic these constructs have been, such a child (later, the presymbiotic adolescent) has long clung to them with a tenacity which often renders therapeutic efforts to externalize them into a life-and-death struggle.

IMPLICATIONS FOR SUCCESSFUL RESIDENTIAL TREATMENT

This review of the process of depersonification is derived from experience with combined intensive residential and concomitant casework treatment of 100 adolescent inpatients and their families. The several categories of depersonification here presented are congruent with the findings of other investigators experienced in the psychodynamics and sociodynamics of seriously disturbed families and are neither rigidly fixed nor mutually exclusive. Rather, they are observed to overlap and interdigitate in accordance with the natural historical evolution of the pathological family nexuses to which they give expression.

The processes of successful residential psychiatric treatment of presymbiotic and symbiotic adolescents, including necessary ameliorative modification of the distorted object relationships within their families, have been set forth in chapters 1-3, 4-9, and Rinsley (1971). The points listed below provide a brief review:

1. Separation of the adolescent from the pathogenic family nexus through admission into full-time residential treatment.

2. Working through of the significance for the patient and his family of the former's physical separation from them, including careful attention to the defensive and restitutive maneuvers which come into play as a result.

3. Scrutiny of the patient's and the parents' early resistances to the residential therapeutic structure, including its personnel, rules, and physical characteristics as manifestations of transferentially overdetermined coping devices that furnish notable insight into family members' perception and psychological use of each other.

4. Careful staff control and supervision of parent-child visits and correspondence to comprehend, control and interpret their mutually pathogenic communications — hence to develop a comprehensive knowledge of their patterns of mutual depersonification.

5. Gradual definitive psychological separation of the patient from his archaic mental representations of family members, particularly parents, leading ultimately to their mutual objectification, hence strengthening of their age- and role-appropriate identities vis-à-vis each other. For the presymbiotic adolescent, this means establishment of a symbiotic relationship within the context of the residential setting, emancipation from which also begins in earnest during residence. For the symbiotic adolescent, it means vigorous therapeutic pressure toward desymbiotization (separation-individuation) from the inception of the residential experience (chapter 9, Rinsley (1971).

6. With the establishment of separation-individuation, the goal of discharge from residential treatment comes within reach, with the strong prospect that the adolescent will prove capable of avoiding reimmersion in whatever remnants of the family's original pathological nexus may yet remain and hence will resume the psychosocial growth his depersonification had early interrupted.

Notes

1. From the Broadway musical, *West Side Story.* Quoted by permission of G. Schirmer and Company, publishers.

2. Some of our patients here classified appear to be adolescent examples of the "more benign" child psychosis described by Geleerd (1946, 1958), Mahler, Ross and DeFries (1949), and Weil (1953a, b).

3. It is well to remember that mutual parent-child depersonification need not spring either predominantly or solely from psychological causes. For example, the badly damaged, deformed, or "monstrous" infant born of otherwise psychologically healthy parents will seriously violate the parents' antenatal, anticipatory gestalt of a normal, healthy baby, and hence may appear to them as "unreal." Again, a physically bizarre or monstrous neonate suffers from deficient or perverted "sending power"; the image such a baby presents is strange and atypical and its repertoire of appropriate responses to early mothering peculiar, deficient, or largely absent. Thus, the parents' and in particular the mother's empathic responses to the otherwise gruesome or bizarre infant will vary from the pathologic to the well-nigh absent, as they must be to a stillborn infant who is by definition devoid of innate response. Some authorities view the baby with early infantile autism in like fashion by postulating an innate, almost total inability to "invest" in others *ab initio* and who develops essentially into an unperson pervasively devoid of the capacity for object relations.

4. For an excellent review of these authors and their collaborators, see Mishler and Waxler (1968).

5. For a penetrating and sensitive description of a schizophrenic adolescent trapped in a parent-child role reversal, see Friedman (1966).

6. Especially in symbiotic cases, the parent will proceed to act out and hence attempt to attenuate these fantasies through both legal and, at times, extralegal efforts to remove the child from the hospital against medical advice or will rather so interfere with his treatment as, in effect, to preclude the inception of the desymbiotizing process (chapters 2 and 7, Rinsley 1971, Zentner and Aponte 1970). The problem becomes particularly acute when parent and child perceive the beginning loosening of their symbiotic tie. When this occurs, the residential center or hospital must be prepared to go to full legal lengths to keep the child in residence.

7. The countertransferential manifestation of these unconscious wishes is nowhere better observed than in some residential settings that are essentially

devoid of external controls or are actually designed to operate with undue permissiveness toward seriously disturbed adolescents.

8. Note Kraepelin's statement (1921, p. 60) in reference to individuals suffering from the manic phase of manic-depressive psychosis: "Incomprehensible engagements, also pregnancies, are not rare in these states. I know cases in which the commencement of excitement was repeatedly announced by a sudden engagement. 'Each child has a different father,' declared a female patient. From these proceedings serious matrimonial quarrels naturally arise."

11

On Adolescent Schizophrenia

Numerous writers on adolescence, including Geleerd (1957, 1961), Harley (1961), Eissler (1958), Ackerman (1958, 1962), Erikson (1956), Josselyn (1952) and Anna Freud (1946, 1958), view adolescence either as a psychologically disturbed state or period, or as a time when the individual undergoes some sort of "normative crisis." From their writings have emerged such terms and phrases, presumably characteristic of the adolescent personality in our culture, as identity crisis, identity diffusion, turmoil, bipolarity of instincts, storm and stress, role diffusion, ego exhaustion, and so on. The implications of such a view, characteristic for what has been termed the "turmoil school" of adolescence, are several. First, the turmoil writers assume that all adolescents are in various degrees psychologically disturbed or ill. Some, including Anna Freud (1946), describe the pubertal ego in such fashion as, in effect, to amount to psychosis with attendant and significant ego weakness and consequent failure of the ego's synthetic function.

Second, it follows that insofar as all adolescents are more or less psychologically ill, the precise diagnosis of psychopathology in an adolescent, except in extreme cases with florid symptomatology, is a difficult undertaking bordering, at times if not always, the impossible. Further, if diagnosis is difficult, prognosis becomes problematic indeed, and even the experienced clinician will often find himself at a loss either to understand at any given time and in depth the nature and extent of the adolescent's psychopathology or to make adequate predictions concerning its outcome.

Third, the turmoil writers adduce the presumed disturbed condition of adolescents in support of the related notion, still put forth in the literature, that adolescents are not well motivated for psychotherapy or psychoanalysis. In this argument can be discerned the echoes of Freud's early claim that patients suffering from the "narcissistic neuroses" (meaning, in current terminology, those who are clinically borderline or schizophrenic) are unamenable to transference analysis and hence to analytic cure. According to the turmoil writers, analytic treatment in depth is precluded by the adolescent's low frustration tolerance with ensuing tendencies toward acting out in the transference and elsewhere, by his bipolar affective shifts, ever-proneness to regression, shifting and unpredictable resort to partialisms, and related difficulties with ego functions. The argument is, of course, circular: The adolescent's borderline or frankly disorganized condition is invoked to support the notion of his unanalyzability, whereas the latter is, in turn, adduced to support the notion of the precarious state of his ego. From this it follows that therapeutic technique with the adolescent must depend on the presumably limited nature of his ability to cooperate in his treatment; hence, one cannot expect to treat him consistently in depth, and more sustained analytic efforts must await his adult years.

Fourth, the relatively subdued, "quiet," undemonstrative adolescent, who is clinically devoid of the overt signs of turmoil presumed to characterize the adolescent state, should be viewed with some clinical suspicion, if not alarm. Indeed, Anna Freud (1958), Beres (1961), and Lindemann (1964) assert, in effect, that the relatively quiescent, undisturbed adolescent is undergoing deviant development, whereas Fountain (1961) claims that adolescents may be distinguished from adults through impaired frustration tolerance and ineffectual reality testing.

Fifth, granting the above inferences and conclusions, it becomes possible to derive at least theoretical support for the view that there exists a true adolescent subculture with its purportedly inevitable "conflict of generations." This view, supported by Keniston (1965) and Coleman (1961), among others, perceives the adolescent as a sort of "as-if" personage who, neither fish nor flesh, finds himself mired between the child he once was and the adult he is later to become—devoid of the presumably quiescent moorings of his latency years, biologically developed yet psychosocially unprepared for orderly adulthood. Beset with conflicts, developmental dyssynchronies and surges of instinct, the adolescent becomes, according to this view, an alienated quasi-person, a muddled, kaleidoscopic transitional phenomenon. From this it is but a short step to "explanations" for a host of phenomena supposedly characteristic for adolescents, including teenage argot, music, and subcultural values and those features of adolescence typical for the development of the well-known peer group.

The turmoil writers on adolescence have, of course, applied the hard-won insights of psychoanalysis to explicate the adolescents they have met in the clinic, consulting room, or residential center. From this work have emerged the following formulations:

1. The upsurge of instinct at adolescence, both relatively and absolutely, places enhanced stress upon the as yet immature ego, resulting in various degrees of genetic-dynamic regression with the emergence of instinctual and defensive bipolarities of sweeping extent and impact (A. Freud 1946, 1958).

2. In part as a result, the adolescent proceeds to recapitulate, or is compelled to repeat, conflicts and efforts toward their resolution typical for antecedent stages of psychosexual development, including the phallic-oedipal-incestuous, anal, and oral stages. It is particularly the proneness to regression to preoedipal stages, notably the early anal (anal-sadistic) and oral, that imparts to the adolescent personality its bedevilingly "as-if," borderline, even overtly psychotic features. These features in turn comprise the basis for the assumption that adolescents are exceedingly difficult to treat in depth.

3. Of notable influence upon the adolescent is that process Katan (1951) has termed "object removal," which may in part be understood in terms of decathexis of parental mental representations (Jacobson 1964, pp. 170–193). Those components of the latter that function as relatively loosely bound or "unmetabolized" ("undepersonified") superego introjects have in the past served the child as purveyors of what internal controls he has managed to develop (Rinsley 1968a, Kernberg 1966). Upon their "removal," the adolescent ego is faced with fluctuant and impending breakdown of controls upon instinctual pressures and, hence, on the actions demanded for their immediate reduction. The process of object removal, together with the associated anxiety over primitive urges to reincorporate and re-fuse with the departing object-representations, in part account for the adolescent's well-known need to devalue the parents and the social and cultural values associated with and derived from them.

4. A fourth psychoanalytic tenet, in part also derived from consideration of the regressive-recapitulative features of adolescent personality, concerns the adolescent's redoubtable tendency to the use of identification, leading to a predominant reliance upon narcissistic object choice. Put another way, it may be said that the adolescent selects his associates from a profound need for self-validation and self-justification. This, along with anxiety over the possibility of sustained intensity in his object relations — which reawakens fantasies of re-fusion or reunion with his departing object-representations — accounts in part for the adolescent's proneness toward association within loosely bound peer groups and conveys the fleeting, labile, and egocentric quality often characteristic of his friendships. It also accounts for the adolescent's peculiar "openness" to new experiences and for the perfervid if often obsequious grovelings before older "charismatic" and demagogic "leaders" and younger purveyors of supposedly adolescent styles of dress and music.

Until recently, the writings of those theorists and clinicians representative of the turmoil view of adolescence have comprised the accepted psychoanalytic contribution to an understanding of this important period in the development of individual personality. It may be said, however, that the turmoil view of adolescence is now giving way in the face of increasing evidence that it applies, with the full weight of its observations and conclusions, to but a particular and selected subgroup of adolescents who suffer from serious psychopathology.

Growing and serious doubt that the view of the turmoil writers applies to the general population of adolescents is associated with the research and writings of Berger (1963), Schwartz and Merten (1967), Hess and Goldblatt (1957), Meissner (1961, 1965), Offer (1967), Offer, Sabshin, and Marcus (1965), Douvan and Adelson (1966), Elkin and Westley (1955), Masterson (1967b, 1968, and Masterson and Washburne (1966). Although the work of these investigators covers a heterogeneous variety of subjects and methodologies, one may nonetheless draw from them several cogent conclusions that have important implications for the study, understanding, clinical diagnosis, and treatment of adolescents.

First, although psychoanalytic insights and formulations basic to the turmoil view of adolescence apply in some measure to all adolescents, they account most cogently for the more extreme experiences and behavior of the disturbed adolescent, whose clinical appearance represents a caricature, or an overstatement of the "normal" or healthy adolescent. It is thus possible to accept the psychoanalytic account of the adolescent experience without necessarily subscribing to the turmoil view of it.

Second, the majority of nondisruptive and nondisrupted adolescents, rather than undergoing "deviant" psychosocial development, on the contrary represent the rule of healthy adolescent growth. They do not experience significant parent-child dislocations, claim relatively few feelings of alienation and isolation, and tend to accept the sociocultural values of their parents.

Third, the turmoil-ridden adolescent and his unduly subdued confrere are representatives of two highly selected subpopulations that have come to the attention of extrafamilial helping agencies, including the psychoanalyst's consulting room. They comprise deviant or sick subgroups, atypical for the general population of adolescents. Because they are sick, they have in exaggerated measure struggled with and failed to resolve the numerous endopsychic and interpersonal problems with which the majority of adolescents successfully cope.

Fourth, since the turmoil-ridden adolescent is seriously psychiatrically ill, he requires intensive and often prolonged psychiatric treatment for difficulties that center, at best, on failure to have achieved age-appropriate degrees of separation-individuation and hence emancipation. His problems are not expressive of some sort of temporally circumscribed, phase-specific "adjustment reaction," and he will not grow out of them (Masterson 1967b).

Fifth, there is no convincing evidence of a developed adolescent subculture, based upon presumed intergenerational conflict and driven by presumed, deep-seated feelings of alienation, depersonalization, and detachment. Where these are discovered to be present they are expressions of serious psychopathology. By the same token, there is no good evidence that the more exaggerated forms of "adolescent protest," including acts of a grossly destructive or antisocial nature, should be viewed as in any way fundamentally different from similar behavior when displayed by chronological adults. Again, notable psychological perturbation in an adolescent is not merely an expression of adaptive efforts to cope with the conflicts inherent in psychosocial growth or to create rites of passage, however crude, by which to traverse the adolescent period. Instead, perturbation constitutes prime evidence that the adolescent's coping efforts have already gone profoundly awry.

PRELIMINARY THOUGHTS ON DIAGNOSIS

Several factors may be viewed as having contributed to the degree of obfuscation that surrounds the different diagnoses of borderline and relatively unflorid schizophrenic psychopathology among adolescents. One of these is the historical association of adolescent psychiatry with child psychiatry, in particular with the psychoanalytically based child guidance movement with its necessary emphasis upon process and dynamics as over against the nuances of diagnostic nosology, a position epitomized by such writers as K. A. Menninger, Mayman, and Pruyser (1963), who seriously question the applicability of traditional diagnostic categories.

A second factor has to do with the inapplicability of the Bleulerian primary diagnostic criteria (Bleuler 1950), particularly those that concern formal ideational organization, in the differential diagnosis of major psychopathology in preadolescent children. The child psychiatrist is wont to evaluate the adolescent by means of essentially the same criteria of process and content to which he is limited in the case of the younger child, thereby ignoring the fact, amply demonstrated in the monumental studies of Piaget (Inhelder and Piaget 1958, Piaget 1954, 1957), that abstract categorical ideation (Piaget's circular operational thought) normally develops by early adolescence. Thus, failure to apply Bleuler's criteria or, worse, viewing overt or latent classical thought disorder as more or less expected of the adolescent regularly leads the clinician into the profoundest diagnostic errors.

A third factor concerns the substantial degree to which the turmoil view of adolescence readily obscures the diagnosis of serious adolescent psychopathology. If all adolescents are in various degrees psychotic, or at least profoundly "disturbed," there is really no good reason for alarm should the adolescent be found to reason autistically, at least at times, or otherwise display the tangential, associatively loosened, overinclusive-overexclusive, syncretic, and concretistic thinking characteristic of schizophrenia among adults!

Helen

Helen was a bright, attractive fourteen-year-old who was seen in an hour-long consultation interview with the complaints of increasing uncooperativeness, seclusiveness, deteriorating schoolwork, "running around," preoccupation with the health of her pet dog and canary bird, and obsessive concern with her menstrual odor. Her mother reported the onset of these problems shortly after the father's sudden death in an automobile accident eight months before, following which Helen was not observed to have grieved.

During the interview, the girl described how she "hated" her "domineering" mother and clearly discussed how she had turned to her deceased father as a maternal substitute ("He was more of a mom to me than she was!"), becoming increasingly sexually involved with him in fantasy. The dynamics were not at all obscure: a chronically and seriously impaired mother-daughter relationship, failure of separation-individuation from the ambivalent maternal tie, displacement of maternal wishes to the father, and conscious fantasies that she had indeed killed him through her wishes for further intimacy with him. Helen's thought processes were overtly logical, but a brief animated tour de force with similarities questions revealed, in her answers, the following:

Bird-Airplane: "Well, you've got a bird . . . I mean birds fly like airplanes except they haven't got rigid wings, like, they have different power for flight. . . ."

Knife-Fork: (Answer) "Both cut things, don't they . . .?"

Circle-Square: (Answer) "Well, I studied those in geometry . . . geometrical figures, OK? Also you can fit one inside the other so you got a polygon or something. . . ."

This clinical vignette will illustrate what later postadmission psychiatric, clinical psychological, and casework studies brought out in detail—namely, that Helen had begun what was to become a long course of deviant psychosexual development (had started to become ill) in her preschool years. She had in effect remained symbiotically tied to, hence psychologically unseparated from, her mother; her immense envy of the mother had led her to turn to the father, thereby competing with the mother for him as well as seeking a substitute source of narcissistic supplies from him; the male sexual organ had thereby come to assume the symbolic role of a feeding object (breast), toward which Helen felt as ambivalent as she had toward the mother's breast; the unexpected death of the father had reactivated the aggressive aspect of her ambivalence, leading to overwhelming guilt, and inability to mourn the "lost" object toward whom she had felt genuinely murderous rage as paradigmatic of her failure to have desymbiotized from the beginning.

These herculean forces had lain in check throughout Helen's latency years, largely unexpressed as a result of the relatively expensive efforts Helen had made to hold them in repression partly through her otherwise superior intellectual endowment, which was now rapidly crumbling as a consequence of her burgeoning illness. The concomitant casework study and ensuing family therapy further developed the results of Helen's own clinical examinations: Helen's mother, herself unemancipated and tied in an infantile bond to her own mother (Masterson 1971b, 1972b), had attempted to emancipate by marriage to a distant, aloof man who symbolized a basically ungiving maternal figure. Thus, Helen's psychopathology in part represented a recapitulative living out of her mother's own failure of separation-individuation. Helen's cure rested upon exposure, interpretation, and resolution of her archaic pathogenic identification with her mother—a process that required close to three years of intensive residential treatment and family therapy.

Helen's genetics-dynamics were consistent with her clinical diagnosis of borderline schizophrenia and with her long-standing failure to have desymbiotized. The clinical syndrome she presented could be termed a *symbiotic psychosis of adolescence.*

In contrast with Helen's clinical syndrome is that of the boy now to be described.

Edgar

Edgar was a short, somewhat underdeveloped, infantile-appearing youngster of thirteen years, who was brought to my attention following failure of his fifth foster home placement, during which he had assaulted his foster siblings, physically attacked his foster parents and damaged their home furnishings, abjectly refused the services of a home-bound special education teacher, experienced repeated nightmares and multiple phobias, was nocturnally enuretic, and had attempted to strangle several stray cats and dogs.

Following his birth, Edgar had been abandoned by his unmarried mother, herself in middle adolescence; the whereabouts of his parents were unknown, and he had been made a state ward with the usual round of well-meaning and sanguine foster-care placements and boarding home assignments. In each, Edgar had managed to behave well for several months, only then to lapse into his usual sequence of increasingly disruptive actions, necessitating removal and relocation. By age eleven, Edgar had been seen by no less than ten diagnostic-consultative professionals and agencies, with a variety of diagnoses, abortive attempts at outpatient treatment (including one recommendation for "play therapy"), and eventual failure of all efforts to help him.

During the preadmission interview, Edgar presented a pitiable, waiflike appearance and exuded a clinging winsomeness, which covered his intense underlying fearfulness and rage. He fidgeted, cocked his head at a wry angle, lacked any capacity for sustained attentiveness and concentration, and emitted frequent belches and squeaking vocalizations. He was greatly interested in the examiner's desk implements, "I could burn up the whole place with this here lighter!" He admitted to auditory, visual and tactile hallucinations and somatic delusions, stating, "I have a poopie in my head and it goes 'click, click' on and off!" He was the picture of diffuse anxiety, with an inner world filled with monsters and space beings he feared would eat him. His cognitive skills were retarded, evidenced by his WISC VIQ of 72, PIQ of 78, and FSIQ of 76. The projective and thematic tests amply underscored the clinical picture of a severely and chronically disorganized youngster with profoundly impaired object relations, gross failure of ego development, and intense immersion in an autistic pseudo-community filled with numerous "internal persecutors." Edgar's thought processes were tattered, with no evidence that categorical ideation had ever developed.

Unlike Helen, Edgar had never developed any sort of infantile maternal tie from which he could even begin to separate-individuate. His early infantile abandonment had led to numerous unsuccessful placements with an array of well-intentioned people who, in response to the child's initial capacity to evoke pity, took him in, only later to discover that Edgar had almost literally to consume, to fuse with, and then, from mounting terror, to attempt to destroy them as well as to batter his competition for them to pieces. Clinging desperately to the only "world" he knew—his terrifying autistic pseudocommunity—he would eventually perceive his would-be helpers as murderers, destructive robbers, and dimly differentiated feeding objects, whose offerings to him were ultimately poisoned and lethal. Patient analysis of Edgar's bizarre inner world during his course of prolonged residential treatment revealed it to represent the tattered fragments of an idealized pseudofamily, fused in Edgar's fantasies with his own internal organs and bodily products.

Edgar's diagnosis was schizophrenia of childhood. The clinical syndrome he presented could be termed a *presymbiotic psychosis of adolescence.*

It will be clear from the foregoing discussion that the developmental phenomenon basic for an understanding of adolescent schizophrenia, not to mention its preadolescent and adult forms, is the mother-infant symbiosis, which attains its peak at four to five months postnatally (Mahler 1968). The concept of symbiosis developed by Mahler in a series of classic studies (Mahler 1952, 1965a, 1965b, 1967, 1968, 1972, Mahler and Gosliner 1955, Mahler, Ross, and DeFries 1949, Mahler, Furer, and Settlage 1959) complements the work of Kanner (1943, 1949, 1965) and Spitz (1955, 1957, 1959, 1965) on the foundations of early object relations and the processes by which their formation goes awry, the latter resulting in either of the two major psychoses (schizophrenias) of childhood—the presymbiotic (autistic-presymbiotic) and the symbiotic.

The application of this dyadic nosology to the major psychopathological syndromes of adolescence has several advantages. First, it presents for both the presymbiotic and the symbiotic cases an inclusive and comprehensive classification, subsumed within which are a wide variety of autoplastic and alloplastic syndromes that are usually accorded a similar variety of traditional diagnoses. Second, it applies the concepts of autism and symbiosis and the pivotal, interrelated developmental processes of symbiotization-desymbiotization and separation-individuation (Mahler 1968, Masterson 1971b, 1972b) to the sphere of adolescent psycho-pathology, the latter viewed as the end result of antecedent developmental failure. Third, it thereby conceptualizes adolescent psychopathology as the outcome of long-standing failure in the development of object relations, extending back in time through latency, prelatency and infancy. Fourth, it reinforces the view that the major psychopathological syndromes of adolescence represent caricatures of otherwise normal adolescent emancipatory strivings and hence of the preadolescent child's earlier efforts to work through those nuclear conflicts that center upon the process of separation-individuation. From this it follows that the adolescent who experiences serious difficulties with emancipation and identity formation has long harbored the residuals of failure of separation-individuation, and thus of object relations dating from the period of infancy.

PRESYMBIOTIC (AUTISTIC-PRESYMBIOTIC) PSYCHOSIS OF ADOLESCENCE

The inclusive term, presymbiotic psychosis of adolescence, refers to a congeries of schizophrenic disorders traditionally called *process or nuclear* (chapters 8, 9, 10, Rinsley 1971a). The major determinant of adolescent presymbiotic psychosis is the *persistence of part-object relations,* based in turn on failure to have achieved the normal mother-infant symbiosis during the first two trimesters of the first postnatal year (Mahler 1968). The sweeping coping and developmental arrests that result from the failure of normal infantile imprinting in these adolescents give rise, in turn, to a relatively high frequency of somatic and physical-developmental signs and symptoms, as described by Bender (pseudodefective schizophrenia) (1947, 1956) and by Goldfarb (childhood schizophrenia, organic group) (1961). Thus, these adolescents often present a variety of "soft" neurological signs (problems associated with gait, station, equilibrium, articulation, visual-motor integration, neuromuscular coordination, and the like) and developmental anomalies and asymmetries, particularly of ectodermally derived structures, whereas some suffer from diagnosable central neural pathology or are primarily retarded, superimposed on which are what amount to psychotic coping mechanisms (propfschizophrenia). Included in the presymbiotic group are the more classical examples of early infantile autism (Kanner's syndrome) (Kanner 1943, 1949, 1965), the etiology of which is thought by some to lie in an organically based failure of development of the capacity for abstraction (Scheerer, Rothman, and Goldstein 1958) or in anomalous functioning of the brainstem reticular system (Koegler and Colbert 1959, Rimland 1964). Certain of the adolescents classifiable in the presymbiotic group also represent examples of youngsters now diagnosable as having suffered from infantile psychosis (Kolvin et al. 1971, Reiser 1963) or "atypicality" (Rank 1949, Reiser 1963), who have entered the period of chronological adolescence.

Irrespective of etiology, presymbiotic adolescents present evidence of the earliest and profoundest failure of ego development, predicated in turn upon failure to have experienced a need-satisfying mother-infant symbiosis. The effects of symbiotic failure include the following:

1. Various degrees of eye-mouth-hand incoordination, based upon failure to have experienced consistent gratification from the infantile feeding (face-breast-kneading) interaction (Spitz 1971).
2. Arrest at the autoerotic stage of development, the infantile preobject of Spitz (1971), in which erogenous zones pursue independent pleasure gain bereft of any developed degree of psychic organization (Fliess 1961, Freud 1905, 1914).
3. A resulting inhibition of primary identification with consequent impairment of development of the infantile stimulus barrier and persistent reliance upon splitting defenses, including introjection-projection, scotomatization (negative hallucination), denial, and on transitivism (Rinsley 1968a, 1971b).

4. A related buildup and persistence of an extensive autistic pseudocommunity containing a welter of reintrojected "persecutors" (M. Klein 1935, 1940, 1946), which are representative of reinternalized remnants of the infant's oral sadism directed toward the ambivalently proffered and perceived feeding part-object.

5. Diffuse identification of one's own bodily parts and products with the ambivalently perceived, persecutory internal mental representations in which the infant's omnipotence comes to be invested. These bodily parts and products come thus to be endowed with enormous power, possess an essentially "negative" (raw aggressive) valence (Rinsley 1968a, Kernberg 1966), and are retained or expelled in accordance with the child's need to "protect" others from them or to "eliminate" others by means of them.

6. Failure of development of object permanency and object constancy (Mahler 1968), with associated persistence of sensorimotor cognitive operations and reliance upon magic-hallucination (Ferenczi 1913). Thus, the "comings and goings" of the feeding part-object are never worked through, with the result that "comings" signify fusion and engulfment while "goings" signify perceptual extinguishment, both of which are experienced as catastrophic. The classical schizophrenic approach-avoidance conflict is a result.

7. Persistence of predepressive anxiety (M. Klein 1935, 1940, 1946), with associated failure of normal internalization and structuralization. Thus, archaic superego introjects never undergo "metabolization" or "assimilation" (Kernberg 1966), and hence are not incorporated into the early ego's defensive and perceptual functions (Rinsley 1968a).

8. Resulting failure of mastery, deficiency of neutralization of "raw" drives, and inhibition of development of repression and hence of later efforts toward sublimation and secondary autonomy (Hartmann 1955).

A fifteen-year-old girl, a presymbiotic inpatient, told her therapist that she greatly feared menstruating "because I was afraid to lose my family." Deserted in early infancy by her unmarried parents, she had desperately clung to a congeries of archaic parental mental representations that had become fused with her cloacal products—particularly her genital secretions and her menstrual effluvium, the latter having been almost totally suppressed throughout her early adolescence.

A fourteen-year-old presymbiotic inpatient boy of measured borderline intelligence was discovered to harbor an extensive and elaborate preoccupation with ancient Egyptian deities, mummies, sarcophagi, and burial crypts for which he had a horrified fascination. Although he had not known his natural parents, themselves seriously disorganized personalities, he had been told that his father was Jewish, and over the ensuing years the boy had malabsorbed the Biblical legend of the Diaspora. His autistic preoccupation with ancient Egyptian objects and icons in part symbolized his fragmented attempts to work through his early loss of the condensed mother-father figure for whose "banishment" (murder) he had long felt responsible, various bits and pieces of whom, in the form of pharaonic items, regularly returned to plague and persecute him.

9. In the great majority of cases, cognitive-intellectual developmental arrest or failure, with measured IQs in the borderline-mildly retarded range or below, with associated educational retardation or failure (chapter 8).

From a historical-anamnestic standpoint, presymbiotic adolescents very commonly demonstrate the following:

1. There may be a history of adaptive-developmental problems dating from early in the first postnatal year, including a variety of antenatal, paranatal, and postnatal difficulties. Careful familial case study often reveals a maternal history of efforts at massive or total "abolishment" (Fliess 1961) or "inanimate depersonification" (chapter 10) of the new baby extending throughout infancy and childhood; in some cases, what appears to have comprised a

substantial deficiency in the infant's "sending power" *ab initio* apparently precipitated the mother's persistent efforts to appersonate or depersonify the infant (chapter 10).

2. A high frequency of familial "disasters," including child neglect, abuse, and desertion, may be associated with presymbiotic adolescents. There is often a multiplicity of boarding and foster-home placements and histories of parental separation and divorce associated with violent and criminal actions. Major psychopathology in one or both parents is invariable, and the adolescent's families have been fragmented and disorganized (pseudofamilies), replete with egregious generational, age, gender, and role obfuscations, confusions, and reversals (chapter 10, Lidz, Fleck, and Cornelison 1965, Wynne 1972, Zentner and Aponte 1970).

3. In many cases, particularly if the child has had foster placement, there is a history of from one to several pediatric and psychiatric consultations with a variety of ensuing diagnoses, often of brain damage, mental retardation, or nonspecific encephalopathy. Many presymbiotic children reach adolescence as inmates of institutions for the retarded, in the most "enlightened" of which efforts have usually been made at corrective or remedial treatment with varying degrees of success.

Symptomatically, presymbiotic adolescents display a high frequency of hebephrenic and catatonic signs, and hallucinate frequently or continuously in visual, auditory, and tactile spheres. Their most definitive feature, however, is the presence of severe and obvious classical schizophrenic thought disorder.

SYMBIOTIC PSYCHOSIS OF ADOLESCENCE

The inclusive term, symbiotic psychosis of adolescence (chapters 8 and 9, Rinsley 1971b), has reference to a heterogeneous group of clinical syndromes with notably variable symptomatology, common to which is the presence of classical thought disorder, whether overt or latent.[1] They are further grouped together on the basis of one etiologic common denominator—failure of separation-individuation—which has its origin at four to five months of age (the so-called *differentiation* subphase of Mahler), and proceeds through the ensuing subphases or *practicing* (ten to fifteen months), *rapprochement* (fifteen to twenty-two months), and *object constancy* (twenty-four to thirty-six months) (Mahler 1968, Masterson 1971b, 1972b). The basis for failure of separation-individuation is found in the peculiarities of the hypersymbiotic (Fliess 1961) mother-infant bond, wherein continuance of necessary narcissistic supplies is made absolutely conditional on the infant's failure to begin to achieve autonomy apart from the mother.

The persistence of what Mahler has termed the "omnipotent symbiotic dual unity" of mother and child, as represented within the latter's self-perceptions, leads to serious psychic disorganization when the "incontrovertible fact" of separateness becomes evident to the child. In the classic cases of symbiotic psychosis of childhood, such disorganization appears between the ages of three and five years. In numerous other cases, including the adolescents presently under discussion, the highly ambivalently perceived breast-mother introject is retained behind a protean symptomatic and defensive facade, which may persist throughout the individual's life course. When such is the case, the individual is notably vulnerable to real and fantasied object losses and separations, which symbolize the loss of desperately needed supplies as well as of auxiliary ego functions—stimulus barrier (Inhelder and Piaget 1958, Spitz 1955, 1957)—representative of the functions of the retained idealized breast-mother introject. The result is a personality that is at once basically grandiose and suspicious, lacking in basic trust, subject to overwhelming depressive anxiety (Koegler and Colbert 1959) in circumstances in which the idealized introject comes under the threat of exposure (hence loss), and characterized by the pervasive ambivalence typical for failure to have made the transition from part-object to whole-object relations (M. Klein 1935, 1940, 1946).

Thus, failure to have worked through the expected process of separation-individuation results in a variety of clinical syndromes that both express symptomatically and conceal from the patient's conscious awareness the underlying need to maintain the primal symbiotic tie with the idealized maternal introject.[2] Such individuals may justifiably be termed *unseparated personalities.*

ADOLESCENT SYMBIOTIC SYNDROMES

As noted before, the clinical manifestations of symbiotic psychosis of adolescence are numerous and variable. In some cases, there is a history of occurrence of a classical symbiotic psychosis of childhood (Mahler 1952, 1965a, b, 1967, 1968, 1972, and Gosliner 1955, Mahler, Ross, and DeFries 1949, Mahler, Furer, and Settlage 1959) from which the child has appeared to make a semblance of recovery. Some symbiotic psychotic adolescents have a chronic history of childhood maladaptation, with prior diagnoses such as hyperactivity or minimal brain damage, schizoid personality, late onset psychosis (Kolvin et al. 1971) and childhood schizophrenia, nonorganic group (Goldfarb 1961). Again, one often finds prior or current diagnoses of reactive schizophrenia, or of pseudoneurotic or pseudopsychopathic schizophrenia (Bender 1959). Of great significance is the serious extent to which these adolescents are underdiagnosed as suffering from psychoneurosis, personality or characterologic disorder, and "adolescent adjustment reaction" (chapters 8 and 9, Rinsley 1971b, Masterson 1967b, 1968, Masterson and Washburne 1966); the latter two in particular representative of holdovers from the turmoil school of adolescence. As summarized in chapter 8:

> Some of these adolescents are overtly psychotic, whereas others present their psychopathology in the form of hyperactive, impulsive, megalomanic, destructive, asocial, or antisocial (pseudopsychopathic) behavior or through a wide range of anxiety-laden, phobic, hysteriform, and obsessive-compulsive (pseudoneurotic) symptomatology. . . . Whatever the symptomatic facade may show, careful study reveals that these symbiotic youngsters rely heavily on an autistically organized inner world, the content of which centers on mother-child fusion and reunion fantasies which must at all

costs be protected from the scrutiny of others. Within this category are found some adolescents labeled as "brilliant but crazy," including the odd or strange "model student" and occasional examples of the "childhood genius" whose purported genius reflects massive pseudointellectual overcompensation rather than genuine originality and creativity.

. . . the [symbiotic] adolescent is . . . frequently misdiagnosed as psychoneurotic or as suffering from some sort of phase-specific "adjustment reaction" or "turmoil state" supposedly confined to adolescents. . . . The postadmission WISC Full Scale IQs of [these] adolescents range from borderline through superior scores. Some are intellectually gifted but have achieved below their educational potential because of the inroads of their illness, whereas others have achieved brilliantly in academic work at the expense of otherwise healthy peer-group and wider social and interpersonal relationships. Sudden or insidious decompensation occurs in these adolescents, as it often does in younger primary school children, when the requirements of both the school and the wider social environments threaten to overwhelm the youngster's precarious, guarded autistic personality organization.

The studies of Masterson, Tucker, and Berk (1963, 1966) on "symptomatic" adolescents seen at the Payne Whitney Psychiatric Clinic delineated five symptom clusters:

1. *Thought disorder syndrome,* characterized by thought disorder, inappropriate affect, delusions, hallucinations, bizarre ideation and motor behavior, confusion, ideas of reference, mutism, and habit disorganization.
2. *Psychoneurotic syndrome,* characterized by anxiety, psychomotor hyperactivity, hypochondriacal preoccupations and complaints, and objective or situational fear.
3. *Acting-out syndrome,* characterized by stealing, school rebellion, negativism, temper outbursts, hostility and physical aggression toward others, delinquency, pathological lying, and lack of impulse control.

4. *Depression syndrome,* characterized by depressive affect, crying, suicidal preoccupations or attempts, pathological guilt, and self-depreciation.
5. *Hysterical personality disorder syndrome,* characterized by erotic and histrionic behavior, dramatic attention seeking, marked sexual consciousness, and provocativeness.

Excluding those adolescents who present the *thought disorder syndrome* (considered schizophrenic or "psychotic"), Masterson (1971b, 1972b) has since applied the term, *borderline syndrome,* to the remainder, typical for whom are the following:

1. Some degree of acting out, which may begin on a minor scale and progress to major and dramatic degrees.
2. A history of environmental separation from a parent, relative or other key person.
3. Historical-clinical evidence of an orally fixated character structure.
4. Symbiotically fixated (borderline) parents, who were themselves denied adequate parenting.
5. Disturbed families, replete with confusion, blurring, and denial of normal family roles — the so-called amorphous family nexus of Zentner and Aponte (1970) — resulting in a variety of mutual intrafamilial depersonifications or appersonations (chapter 10).

It is instructive, now, to compare Easson's categories of "severely disturbed" adolescents (1969), who require inpatient or residential treatment, with Masterson's classification of his "symptomatic" group. Easson groups his patients as follows:

1. The severely handicapped neurotic adolescent.
2. The disturbed adolescent with ego defects and developmental arrest.
3. The disturbed adolescent with severe conscience defects.
4. The psychotic adolescent, further subdivided into
   a. The process psychotic (nuclear schizophrenic) adolescent
   b. The reactive psychotic adolescent.

Careful review of Easson's and Masterson's writings suggests a considerable diagnostic and symptomatic overlap among Easson's first three groups and Masterson's latter four syndromes; indeed, it is probable that Masterson would diagnose Easson's "neurotic," "ego defect," and "conscience defect" adolescents as suffering from the borderline syndrome of adolescence. By the same token, Easson's "process psychotic" and "reactive psychotic" patients would appear to fall into Masterson's category of thought disorder syndrome. Furthermore, it is highly likely that some of Masterson's adolescents with thought disorder syndrome would correspond with Easson's "process psychotic" group, whereas others would correspond with Easson's "reactive psychotic" group. Thus, some of Masterson's patients with thought disorder syndrome (grouped by Easson as process psychotic or nuclear schizophrenic) would correspond, in turn, with those adolescents here diagnosed as suffering from *presymbiotic psychosis of adolescence,* whereas others (grouped by Easson as reactive psychotic) would correspond in turn with those adolescents here diagnosed as suffering from *symbiotic psychosis of adolescence.*

It remains, now, to consider those symptomatic or severely disturbed adolescents whom Masterson would diagnose as suffering from borderline syndrome and whom Easson would group as neurotic, ego-defective or conscience-defective. It is this clinically heterogeneous population of admittedly seriously disturbed adolescents who are most subject to euphemistic underdiagnosis; the vast majority of them, on careful diagnostic study, will be found to present various degrees of latent or overt classical thought disorder, which establishes a schizophrenic diagnosis; numerous of their waking and unconscious fantasies center upon the vicissitudes of their desperately retained idealized maternal introject, which lead them, in turn, into affect-dominated ideation and actions at gross variance with the demands of reality; and they are the adolescents who emerge, in later life, as borderline and narcissistic personalities or who later develop major cyclic illness, frank psychosis, involutional disturbances, or even less than severely disabling "neurotic" illness, indicative of failure to have effected a degree of secondary autonomy and hence of self-objectification that would otherwise signify the ultimate resolution of the symbiotic mother-infant bond. Under circumstances of stress, especially where real or fantasied object-loss threatens, various degrees of regression ensue which lead to periods of what is often termed episodic psychotic thinking, feeling, and acting. Or, the individual may live out his life in a chronically parasitic, exploitive fashion with few if any episodes of frank regression or disorganization. These are, indeed, the adolescents who do not "grow out of it"; the persistently symbiotic nature of their illness guarantees the persistence of a basically autistic personality organization. They therefore conform to the diagnoses, pseudo-neurotic and pseudopsychopathic schizophrenia, and thus our criteria for the diagnosis, symbiotic psychosis of adolescence. The criteria for this diagnosis may be stated as follows:

1. Established evidence of failure of separation-individuation, as outlined by Masterson (1971b, 1972b).
2. Presence of thought disorder, whether overt or latent.
3. Need for residential (inpatient) treatment, as outlined by Easson (1969). The third criterion is in line with our own long-term observation (chapter 6) that adolescents with lesser degrees of psychopathology are rarely if ever brought, by whatever route, for inpatient treatment, irre-spective of the specifics of their clinical symptomatology.[3]

It is tempting to view the symptomatic manifestations of sym-biotic psychosis of adolescence as evidence of developmental derailment at once of the individuative way stations along the indi-vidual's life course, at any of which he may reach a point of crisis and hence come to psychological grief. For the developing individ-ual, each thrust toward separation-individuation and thus toward enhanced autonomy may awaken afresh whatever fixations remain as echoes from the dim infantile past when, between five and thirty months of age, the child embarked upon the journey toward self-actualization as a being separate from the maternal succoring object. The crisis may occur at any of the acknowledged nodal points of psychosexual development: at birth itself; at weaning; at the end of the first infantile year when walking and talking assume signal importance for the skills of physical separation and communication; at two and a half to four years, when object constancy should have occurred and when an outbreak of classical symbiotic psychosis is likely; upon entrance into school when separation crisis in the form of school phobia is common; at adolescence; upon entrance into college or graduation from secondary school; at marriage; with the arrival of one's own children, who begin at once to recapitulate in their unique fashion the individuative struggles of their parents; at middle age; at senescence; and distributed along the entire life course, in the endless and varied familial, sibling, parental, and peer-group separations, geographical removals, divorces, and demises.

A wide range of individual and social phenomena are understandable in part in terms of the problems associated with desymbiotization and separation-individuation. Examples are the academically successful but psychologically unseparated graduate student who undergoes a temporally circumscribed depressive-depersonalizing crisis and who may eventuate as an endless university hanger-on who never does complete the doctoral dissertation; the middle-aged corporation executive who undergoes a severe depression upon the prospect of promotion to a high administrative position; the late adolescent who drops out to a "hippy" lifestyle in pursuit of a schizoid pseudomutuality as reflective of unexpressed rage at the hands of parents who failed to parent in a family governed by relationships of pseudomutuality and pseudo-hostility (Wynne 1972); the fiftyish housewife whose involutional disorder reflects the emergence of long-repressed rage at her mother as the tangible if (for her) specious sign of her autonomous womanhood (the menses) terminates; the manic-depressive whose cyclic bouts are triggered by fantasied narcissistic wounds or losses symbolic of the primal separation-individuation he had never worked through; the paranoid who battles with external persecutors as he clings to the few "good" objects he yet feels he possesses; the militant devotee of "women's liberation," who displaces to men her long-suppressed rage at her mother for not having had a phallus and hence for not having "given" one to her daughter;

the alcoholic who nourishes himself with bottles of poisoned milk; the religious ascetic for whom "Mother Church" is too obvious a symbol; and the politician whose narcissism finds expression in the pursuit of power over others, as symbolic of his profound grandiosity, in turn a cover for feelings of emptiness and inadequacy.

IMPLICATIONS FOR TREATMENT

In the final analysis, the operational definition and validity of any diagnostic nosology are its therapeutic applicability. In the case of the adolescent with symbiotic psychosis of adolescence, the goal of treatment is to promote desymbiotization, which means to rekindle those processes of separation-individuation which became blighted during the latter half of the patient's first postnatal year. The goal of desymbiotization is best accomplished within the full-time, intensive residential therapeutic process, the course and dynamics of which have been outlined elsewhere (chapters 5, 7, 8, 9, Rinsley 1971b). Masterson's definitive presentation of the treatment of those adolescents he terms borderline (1972b) describes the natural history of this work in fine detail, including the flowering and resolution of the symbiotic transference.

In the case of the adolescent with presymbiotic psychosis of adolescence, the major therapeutic goal is from the beginning biphasic—that is, intensive efforts to promote symbiotization followed by efforts to promote desymbiotization. The complexities and arduous nature of this work beggar description, as they mirror the inception and fruition of those most fundamental preverbal mother-infant affiliations and subsequent psychological separations from which whole-object constancy ultimately develops.

Of notable importance are those residential adolescent patients whom Masterson designates as suffering from thought disorder syndrome. Some of these adolescents conform to the diagnosis, presymbiotic psychosis of adolescence (process, nuclear, or unremitting psychosis), for whom a desymbiotizing program is in the highest sense premature and thus fraught with potential disaster. Others represent more regressive examples of the symbiotic psychotic

Table 1. Classification of Adolescent Psychosis (Schizophrenia) and Kindred Syndromes

Author's Terminology chapters 8 and 9, 1971b)	Masterson's Terminology (1963, 1966)	Easson's Terminology (1969)	Equivalent or Approximate Synonyms for the Syndrome or its Precursors
Presymbiotic psychosis of adolescence	Thought disorder syndrome (some cases)	Process schizophrenia Nuclear schizophrenia	Early infantile autism (Kanner's syndrome 1943, 1949) Nonremitting schizophrenia (Wynne 1972) Pseudodefective schizophrenia (Bender 1947, 1956) Infantile psychosis (Kolvin et al. 1971, Reiser 1963) Childhood schizophrenia, organic group (Goldfarb 1961)
Symbiotic psychosis of adolescence	*Borderline syndrome of adolescence* (1971b, 1972b)* Psychoneurotic syndrome Depression syndrome Acting out syndrome Hysterical personality Disorder syndrome Thought disorder syndrome (some cases)	Reactive schizophrenia Severely handicapped neurotic Ego defects and developmental arrest Severe conscience defects	Symbiotic psychosis of childhood (Mahler 1968) Remitting schizophrenia (Wynne 1972) Pseudoneurotic schizophrenia (Bender 1947, 1956) Pseudopsychopathic schizophrenia (Bender 1959) Late onset psychosis of childhood (Kolvin et al. 1971) Childhood schizophrenia, nonorganic group (Goldfarb 1961) Various "personality" disorders: schizoid, infantile, narcissistic, hysterical, obsessive-compulsive, etc.

*Notably candidates for intensive residential or inpatient treatment.

adolescent, whose overt thought disorder and more bizarre general symptomatology represent much more heroic defenses against the working through (introject work) elsewhere described by Masterson (1971b, 1972b) and Rinsley (chapters 5 and 9, 1971b). The most careful differential diagnosis of these more overtly psychotic adolescents is required, particularly in view of the fact that the latter (symbiotic) group will respond most favorably to a desymbiotizing program, despite often herculean initial difficulties, whereas the former (presymbiotic) will not.

The role of the intensive residential (inpatient) milieu in the treatment of these adolescents cannot be overemphasized. In those cases in which symbiotizing work comprises the first phase of treatment of the presymbiotic patient, the latter's mounting terror in the face of failure of splitting defenses and the threat of impending whole-object relations require the most comprehensive and carefully titrated external controls against periods of massive ego collapse, self-destructive and homicidal acting out, and escape from the milieu. In those cases in which desymbiotization with concomitant exposure and analysis of the primitive breast-mother introject are the order of the day, similar external controls are required, as well as intensive ongoing work with staff countertransference in the wake of the adolescent's massive if temporary regressions as heroic devices by which to ward off the threat of loss of internal object-representations.

Notes

1. The term *overt* is here employed to refer to autistic (dereistic) ideation that appears spontaneously during the clinical interview; the term *latent* refers to disordered categorical ideation which appears rarely if at all during clinical interview but which is evoked upon application of more refined tests of concept formation, such as the Wechsler Similarities Subtest, the various sorting tests and the like.

2. The term *introject* is here used for the sake of brevity. More precisely, maternal introject has reference to a complex self- and object-representation comprised, in turn, of the qualities of part-object (breast) and whole-object (mother) representations (Jacobson 1964, pp. 170–193).

3. Masterson's extensive clinical experience with those adolescents he diagnoses as suffering from borderline syndrome of adolescence leads him to differentiate them from the group here designated as suffering from symbiotic psychosis of adolescence. He bases his distinction in part on the following: (1) The borderline adolescent does not display classical thought disorder; (2) the major anxiety of the borderline adolescent concerns loss of love, whereas that of the symbiotic psychotic adolescent concerns loss of the object; (3) although both the borderline and the symbiotic psychotic adolescent represent failure of separation-individuation, the former, unlike the latter, regresses to the use of essentially psychotic mechanisms of defense only under circumstances of major separation threat. Thus, Masterson allows for a continuum with the borderline adolescent at one end and the symbiotic psychotic adolescent at the other, and his borderline adolescent appears to closely resemble adult borderline personalities both symptomatically and defensively (personal communication). It is possible that a difference in patient populations underlies the reported difference in diagnostic classification, including in particular the differential emphasis placed on less overt degrees of classical schizophrenic thought disorder. The nosology here proposed, while including *most* adolescents with borderline syndrome in the group suffering from symbiotic psychosis of adolescence, places particular emphasis on those adolescents who require full-time inpatient or residential treatment to reestablish the previously blighted process of separation-individuation. In any case, Masterson's and my own therapeutic approaches to the severe developmental pathology displayed by these adolescents are remarkably similar (chapters 5, 8, 9, Rinsley 1971b, Masterson 1971b, 1972b).

12

The Etiology
of Borderline Personality

BY JAMES F. MASTERSON, M.D.
AND DONALD B. RINSLEY, M.D.

The psychoanalytic literature is equivocal concerning the extent of the mother's role in the etiology of the developmental arrest peculiar to the borderline patient. Kernberg (1966, 1967, 1968, 1970a, b, 1971a, b, 1972a) minimizes the role of the mother and emphasizes constitutional factors. Mahler (1953, 1963, 1965b, 1968, 1971, 1972), Mahler and Furer (1963), Mahler and LaPerriere (1965), Mahler and McDevitt (1968) and Mahler, Pine and Bergman (1970) stress the vital contribution of the mother's libidinal availability to normal ego development. Although she urges caution in drawing inferences concerning adult psychopathology based upon observations of childhood developmental phenomena, Mahler (1972) notes that there is considerable clinical evidence in support of the inference that the ego fixation of the borderline individual occurs during the rapprochement subphase (sixteen to twenty-five months) of separation-individuation, and in a case illustration she has pointed out the central theme of the patient's search for reunion with the "good symbiotic mother."

Chapter 12 describes the role of the mother's faulty libidinal availability in the development of the borderline syndrome. It describes in terms of object relations theory the effects of alternating maternal libidinal availability and withdrawal, at the time of separation-individuation (rapprochement subphase), upon the development of the psychic structure of the borderline patient — the *split ego* and the *split object-relations unit* (Fairbairn 1954, Guntrip 1961, 1969, M. Klein 1935, 1946, Parens and Saul 1971, Rinsley, chapter 11, 1968a, 1971a, b). It then demonstrates how these find expression and proceed to function in the therapeutic alliance, and in transference and resistance.

KERNBERG'S CONTRIBUTIONS

The Object-Relations Theory of Normal Development

Object-relations theory may be defined as the psychoanalytic approach to the internalization of interpersonal relations (Kernberg 1971a). Kernberg (1972a) postulates four stages in the development of normal internalized object relations. The earliest stage of development, roughly coincident with the first postnatal month of life, precedes the establishment of the primary, undifferentiated self-object constellation built up in the infant under the influence of his pleasurable, gratifying experiences in his interactions with the mother (Jacobson 1964). The second stage, roughly occupying the first to the third postnatal months, comprises the establishment and consolidation of an undifferentiated self-object image or representation (Jacobson 1964) of a libidinally gratifying or rewarding ("good") type under the organizing influence of gratifying experiences within the context of the mother-child unit; concomitantly, a separate primitive intrapsychic structure, comprising an undifferentiated "bad" self-object representation, is built up under the influence of frustrating and painful (that is, traumatogenic) psychophysiological states. Thus two sets of opposite primitive self-object-affect complexes are built up and fixed by memory traces as polar opposite intrapsychic structures. The third stage is reached when the self-image and the object-image have become differentiated within the core "good" self-object representation; the differentiation of self-image from object-image within the core "bad" self-object-representation occurs later and is complicated by early forms of projection—that is, intrapsychic mechanisms that attempt to externalize the "bad" self-object constellation (Kernberg 1966, Rinsley 1968a, Spitz and Wolf 1946). This stage is said to occupy the period between the fourth postnatal month and the end of the first year. The fourth stage has its inception at some point between the end of the first year of life and the second half of the second year and continues to evolve throughout the remainder of childhood. During this stage, "good" and "bad" self-images coalesce into an integrated self-concept. In other words, self-images establish coherence and continuity under the impact of polar opposite emotional-interpersonal experiences; affects become integrated, toned down and undergo further differentiation, and the child's self-concept and his actual presentation of behavior in the social field become closer. At the same time, "good" and "bad" object-images also coalesce such that the "good" and the "bad" images of mother become integrated into a whole-object maternal concept which closely approaches the actuality or reality of the mother in the child's perceptual-interpersonal field.

Kernberg (1972a) emphasizes the progressively integrative aspects of these stages for both ego and superego development, for the establishment of ego identity, and for the development of the capacity for deep and consistent relationships with other persons.

The Ego Fixation of the Borderline Syndrome

Kernberg theorizes that the fixation peculiar to the borderline syndrome takes place during the third stage of this developmental scheme, when there yet remains a dissociation of libidinally determined ("good") from aggressively determined ("bad") self- and object-representations—that is, "good" self- and object-representations and "bad" self- and object-representations are perceived as separate and unrelated.[1] He then outlines the structural consequences of this fixation, which determine the clinical manifestations of the borderline (Kernberg 1967, 1968): pathological persistence of the primitive defense of splitting; failure of development of an integrated self-concept; chronic overdependence upon external objects; development of contradictory character traits in relation to contradictory ego states, resulting in chaotic interpersonal relationships. Superego integration suffers as a result of failure of the guiding function of an integrated ego identity, with persistent contradiction between exaggerated "ideal" object-images and extremely sadistic "all-bad" superego forerunners. Failure of development of an integrated object representation inhibits and ultimately limits development of the capacity for understanding of, and empathy for, other persons.[2] Ego strength depends in particular upon the neutralization of "raw" energies which occurs in intimate connection with the process of integration of libidinally derived ("good") and aggressively derived ("bad") self- and object-images, and it is precisely this integration that fails to occur in future borderline personalities. Failure of neutralization in turn compromises specific aspects of ego strength, including anxiety tolerance, control of impulses, and the potential for true sublimations (Rinsley 1968a).

Kernberg's view of the etiology of this failure places predominant emphasis upon constitutional factors—an excess of oral aggression, a deficiency in the capacity to neutralize aggression, or a lack of anxiety tolerance (Kernberg 1966):

> More characteristic for the borderline personality organization may be a failure related to a constitutionally determined lack of anxiety tolerance interfering with the phase of synthesis of introjections of opposite valences. The most important cause of failure in the borderline pathology is probably a quantitative predominance of negative introjections. Excessive negative introjections may stem both from a constitutionally determined intensity of aggressive derive derivatives and from severe early frustration.

A predominantly heredocongenital view of etiology of the developmental failure peculiar to the borderline personality would emphasize the infant's *a priori* propensity to form preponderantly negative introjections, which Mahler (1968) considers to be typical in infantile psychosis. Although, as Weil (1970) has recently stated, there is considerable evidence for a wide range of "basic core" variation; predominantly heredoconstitutional views can readily lead to underestimation of the importance of the mother's libidinal availability to the infant during the developmentally critical period of separation-individuation, which occupies the period from six to thirty months postnatally.

MAHLER'S VIEWS

Genesis of the Fixation of the Borderline:
Nature-Nurture or Constitution-Experience

In discussing this often polemical issue with respect to infantile psychosis, Mahler (1968) suggests the complementary relationship between nature and nurture:

> If, during the most vulnerable autistic and symbiotic phase, very severe, accumulated, and staggering traumatization occurs in a constitutionally fairly sturdy infant, psychosis may ensue. . . . On the other hand, in constitutionally greatly predisposed, oversensitive or vulnerable infants, normal mothering does not suffice to counteract the innate defect in the catalytic, buffering, and polarizing utilization of the human love object or mothering agency in the outside world for intrapsychic evolution and differentiation. [p. 48]

Mahler clearly avers that, in her view, constitutional defect serves as the basis for infantile psychosis, the victims of which she describes as lacking or failing to acquire the capacity to internalize the representation of the mothering object as a guide for the differentiation of inner from external stimulation.

The presence of excessive oral aggression in the borderline leads Kernberg to favor a constitutional etiology for the borderline syndrome. Although undue degrees of oral aggression do indeed characterize the borderline individual, their presence does not per se justify a purely or predominantly constitutional view of borderline psychopathology, and Kernberg adduces no other evidence in support of his view. There is, to be sure, a parallel deficiency of libidinal cathexis of both self- and object-representations that could as likely lead to a theory of deficiency of libidinal energy— constitutional or otherwise—a view originally put forward by Federn (1952). The issue becomes largely academic, however, in view of incontrovertible clinical evidence, drawn from reconstructive analytic psychotherapy and from intensive residential treatment, that both adolescent and adult borderlines demonstrate a full capacity for internalization once their abandonment depression has been worked through (chapters 5, 9, 10, Rinsley 1971b, Masterson 1971a, b, 1972a, b).

Our contention is that the determining cause of the fixation of the borderline individual is to be found in the mother's withdrawal of her libidinal availability (that is, of her libidinal supplies) as the child makes efforts towards separation-individuation during the rapprochement subphase; and further that the fixation comes into existence at exactly that time because the child's individuation constitutes a major threat to the mother's defensive need to cling to her infant and, as a consequence, drives her toward removal of her libidinal availability.

The twin themes (reward and withdrawal) of this interaction are subsequently introjected by the child, become the leitmotif of his psychic structure, and reappear in his pathologic split self- and object-representations as these are recapitulated within the therapeutic transference.

In view of these considerations, it may be argued that the child's excessive oral aggression becomes entrenched in consequence of the mother's withdrawal of supplies in the wake of the child's efforts toward separation-individuation, further aggravated by the latter's inability to integrate positive and negative self- and object-representations because such integration would require further separation-individuation, which in turn would provoke further withdrawal of maternal libidinal supplies. There thus comes about a situation in which aggression is repetitively provoked without any constructive means conducive to its neutralization.

The Role of the Libidinal Availability
of the Mother in the Development
of Normal Object Relations

Mahler's work is replete with references to the fundamental importance of the mother's libidinal availability for the development of normal object relations. In discussing Hartmann's view that infantile psychosis results from a defect in the ego's capacity for drive neutralization with ensuing interference with the development of other ego functions and of object relations, Mahler (1968) states,

> My view places special emphasis, however, on the interaction of both these factors with the circular processes between infant and mother, in which the mother serves as a beacon of orientation and living buffer for the infant, in reference to both external reality and his internal milieu. [p. 229]

She continues,

> During the course of the normal separation-individuation process, the predominance of pleasure in separate functioning, in an atmosphere in which the mother is emotionally available, enables the child to overcome that measure of separation anxiety that makes its appearance at that point of the separation-individuation phase at which a differentiated object representation, separate from the self, gradually enters conscious awareness. [pp. 220–221]

> In a quasi-closed system or unit, the mother executes vitally important ministrations, without which the human young could not survive. The intrauterine, parasite-host relationship within the mother organism . . . must be replaced in the postnatal period by the infant's being enveloped, as it were, in the extrauterine matrix of the mother's nursing care, a kind of *social symbiosis.* . . . The mutual cueing between infant and

mother is the most important requisite for normal symbiosis . . . (p. 34).

It is the mother's love of the toddler and her acceptance of his ambivalence that enable the toddler to cathect his self-representation with neutralized energy. [p. 222]

The question concerning the manner in which the mother's libidinal availability determines the development of the child's intrapsychic structure is answerable in terms of the child's internalization of his interactions with her to form self- and object-representations, the nature of which will have profound consequences for ego integration (Jacobson 1964, Kernberg 1972a, Mahler 1968). Functioning according to the pleasure principle, which both comprises and determines his initial orientation in the extrauterine field, the infant will draw away or will attempt to expel or eliminate in the face of painful or unpleasurable interactions with the mother. Of critical importance, especially in early infancy, is the equation, "good" *equals* pleasurable *equals* minimally stimulating, as well as the equation, "bad" *equals* unpleasurable (painful) *equals* overstimulating (traumatogenic), as they apply to the quality of the mother-infant interactions. These interactions are introjected to form scattered "good" and "bad" memory islands that proceed to integrate into the progressively differentiated self- and object-images that Kernberg (1966) has described.[3]

Mahler articulates the mother's role as follows (1968):

It is the specific unconscious need of the mother that activates, out of the infant's infinite potentialities, those in particular that create for each mother "the child" who reflects her own *unique* and individual needs. This process takes place, of course, within the range of the child's innate endowments.

Mutual cueing during the symbiotic phase creates that indelibly imprinted configuration—that complex pattern— that becomes *the leitmotif for "the infant's becoming the child of his particular mother."* . . .

In other words, the mother conveys—in innumerable ways—

a kind of "mirroring frame of reference," to which the primitive self of the infant automatically adjusts. [p. 19]

Mahler suggests the possible developmental consequences of the mother's libidinal unavailability to the infant. She asserts that in instances in which the mother in fantasy or in actuality fails of acceptance of the infant, the latter experiences a deficit in self-esteem and a consequent narcissistic vulnerability. She goes on to say,

> If the mother's "primary preoccupation" with her infant — *her* mirroring function during earlier infancy — is unpredictable, unstable, anxiety-ridden, or hostile; if her confidence in herself as a mother is shaky, then the individuating child has to do without a reliable frame of reference for checking back, perceptually and emotionally, to the symbiotic partner. . . . The result will then be a disturbance in the primitive "self-feeling." . . . [1968, p. 19]

On the other hand, while emphasizing the importance of the mother's libidinal availability for optimal infantile ego development, Mahler also points out the normal infant's striking capacity to extract supplies from any available human contact. In support of this view, she cites Spitz's (1945, 1946, 1965) investigation of the infants who experienced the loss of a symbiotic love object during the second half of the first year; although the infants perished if a substitute object was not found, they recovered when one was.

Mahler also cites studies of children who spent their first year of life in a concentration camp (A. Freud and Dann 1951). She states: "While these experiences left their traces on these children's object relationships, the children developed strong ties to each other and none of them suffered from a childhood psychosis" (1968, p. 50). She further cites Goldfarb's studies of children placed in foster homes (1945) who

> . . . amidst the most trying circumstances . . . were able to extract, as it were, substitutions for the actual loss of mothering.

Although they may have paid the price for this object loss with neurotic disorders, character distortions, or psychopathic difficulties later in life, they *never* severed their ties with reality. [1968, pp. 50–51]

Mahler's cited evidence may be adduced in support of her argument for a constitutional etiology for infantile psychosis, since the children studied did not develop such severe psychopathology despite having been subjected to severe stress, particularly as a result of having been deprived of their mothers. On the other hand, her evidence may indeed be taken as favorable to the concept of an environmental etiology of the borderline, particularly in view of her suggestion that these same children might well have later developed neurotic-characterological disorders typical for borderline personalities.

It is, in fact, impossible to compare the children reported on in these cited studies (A. Freud and Dann 1951, Goldfarb 1945, Spitz 1946, 1965) with borderline children. The former had lost their mothers at an early age and were subsequently able to "find" substitutes for them. On the other hand, the borderline child has a mother with whom there is a unique and uninterrupted interaction with a specific relational focus — reward for regression and withdrawal for separation-individuation. As we shall attempt to show in what follows, the unique "push-pull" quality of this sort of mother-infant interaction becomes powerfully introjected and forms the basis for the progressive development of the borderline syndrome.

THE ROLE OF THE MOTHER'S LIBIDINAL AVAILABILITY

The Development of the Psychic Structure of the Borderline

The mother's withdrawal of her libidinal availability in the face of her child's efforts toward separation-individuation creates the leitmotif of the borderline child, with the result that the child becomes the unique child of the borderline mother. The borderline mother, herself suffering from a borderline syndrome, experiences significant gratification during her child's symbiotic phase. The crisis supervenes at the time of separation-individuation, specifically during the rapprochement subphase, when she finds herself unable to tolerate her toddler's ambivalence, curiosity and assertiveness; the mutual cueing and communicative matching to these essential characteristics of individuation fail to develop. The mother is available if the child clings and behaves regressively, but withdraws if he attempts to separate and individuate. The child needs the mother's supplies in order to grow; if he grows, however, they are withdrawn from him (Masterson 1971a, b, 1972a, b). The images of these two mothers are, as it were, powerfully introjected by the child as part-object representations together with their associated affects and self-representations. Thus is generated the *split object-relations unit,* which forms so important a part of the intrapsychic structure of the borderline case.

The evidence in support of this formulation and of what follows in greater detail is derived from several sources (chapters 5, 7, 9, 10, 15, Rinsley 1971b, Masterson 1971a, b): *observation* — (1) casework-family therapy on a once- or twice-weekly basis, for as long as four years, of the parents of inpatient and outpatient borderline adolescents; (2) treatment of borderline mothers in private office practice; (3) detailed observation and study of borderline mothers in conjoint interviews with their borderline adolescent children; and (4) long-term, intensive residential psychiatric treatment of borderline adolescents; and *reconstruction* — the memories and associated affective responses of borderline adolescents in intensive psychotherapy as they worked through their underlying abandonment depression.

Intrapsychic Structure of the Borderline

As noted before, the terms split ego and split object-relations unit are employed to define and describe the intrapsychic structure typical for the borderline personality. These terms require further definition.

Splitting (Kernberg 1967). Splitting is a mechanism of defense, the function of which is to keep contradictory primitive affective states separated from each other; the contradictory states remain in consciousness but do not mutually influence each other. Splitting also keeps apart the internalized self- and object-representations mutually linked with these affective states. Used normally by the immature ego, splitting ordinarily becomes replaced or supplanted by repression. The ego of the borderline, however, retains splitting as its principal mechanism of defense, whereas the capacity for normal repression remains underdeveloped.

Split ego (Kernberg 1967). Along with its reliance upon the splitting defense, the ego of the borderline is itself split into two parts—one of which functions according to the pleasure principle, and the other according to the reality principle.

Split object-relations unit (Kernberg 1972a). The object-relations unit is derived from internalization of the infant's interactions with the mothering object. The unit comprises a self-representation, an object-representation, and an affective component that links them together.[4] The object-relations unit of the borderline turns out to be split into two part-units, each of which in turn comprises a part-self representation and a part-object representation, together with their respective associated affects.

The Split Object-Relations Unit

In the case of the borderline, the object-relations unit remains split into two separate part-units, each of which comprises as it were a part-self-representation, a part-object-representation, and an affective component which links the former two together. These two part-units are derived from internalization of the two principal themes of interaction with the borderline mother: The mother responds to the child's regressive behavior by maintaining her libidinal availability and to the child's efforts toward separation-individuation by its withdrawal. Thus, the two aforementioned part-units, which may be termed the *withdrawing part-unit* and the *rewarding part-unit,* are produced; each has its own component part-self-representation, part-object-representation and predominant linking affect; the withdrawing part-unit is cathected predominantly with aggressive energy, the rewarding part-unit with libidinal energy, and both remain separated from each other through the mechanism of the splitting defense. It will be recalled that this situation comes about through fixation at Kernberg's Stage 3, with ensuing failure of integration of "good" (positive, libidinal) and "bad" (negative, aggressive) self- and object-representations into whole (positive plus negative) self-representations and object-representations, which would otherwise be expected to have occurred during Stage 4.

The borderline split object-relations unit is summarized in Table 1.[5]

Table 1.
Summary of the borderline split object-relations unit

WITHDRAWING OR AGGRESSIVE PART-UNIT

Part-object-representation	*Affect*	*Part-self-representation*
A maternal part-object that is attacking, critical, hostile, angry, withdrawing supplies and approval in the face of assertive-ness or other efforts toward separation-individuation	Chronic anger, frustration, feeling thwarted, which cover profound underlying abandonment depression	A part-self-representation of being inadequate, bad, helpless, guilty, ugly, empty, etc.

REWARDING OR LIBIDINAL PART-UNIT

Part-object-representation	*Affect*	*Part-self-representation*
A maternal part-object that offers approval, support and supplies for regressive and clinging behavior	Feeling good, being fed, gratification of the wish for reunion	A part-self-representation of being the good, passive, compliant child

The Split Ego

Freud (1911) originally emphasized that in the beginning the child's behavior, under the domination of the primary process, is motivated by the pleasure principle—that is, to seek pleasure and to avoid pain. Governed "by the peremptory demands of internal needs" the child originally made use of hallucination to provide for their satisfaction. Freud added, however, that

> It was only the non-occurrence of the expected satisfaction, the disappointment experienced, that led to the abandonment of this attempt at satisfaction by means of hallucination. Instead of it, the psychical apparatus had to decide to form a conception of the real alteration in them. A new principle of mental functioning was thus introduced; what was presented in the mind was no longer what was agreeable but what was real, even if it happened to be disagreeable. This setting-up of the *reality principle* proved to be a momentous step.

Freud proceeds to trace the development of the use of the sense organs, perception, memory, consciousness and thought as agencies of the developing ego's capacity for reality testing. He goes on to say, "Just as the pleasure-ego can do nothing but *wish,* work for a yield of pleasure, and avoid unpleasure, so the reality-ego need do nothing but strive for what is *useful* and guard itself against damage." Of central importance is Freud's emphasis upon the gradual transformation of the pleasure ego into the reality ego in the wake of the child's increasing experience with the failure of hallucinatory wish-fulfillment.

In the case of the borderline individual, the term *split ego* has reference to a persistent stunting of ego development such that a substantial part of the pleasure ego fails to undergo the expected transformation into the reality ego, with resultant pathological persistence of the former; thus, a large part of the ego of the borderline continues under the domination of the pleasure principle. It should be emphasized that in the case of the borderline, the concept of ego splitting implies not that a previously formed structure had undergone regressive splitting, but rather that a coherently functioning ego, operating in accordance with the reality principle, had failed to develop. Thus, that part of the ego Freud termed the pleasure ego could, in the case of the borderline individual, be termed the *pathological ego,* whereas the "remainder" could be termed the *reality* or *healthy* ego.

It is necessary now to inquire into the basis for the persistence of the pathological (pleasure) ego in these cases. To begin with, the future borderline child finds himself caught between his genetically determined drive toward separation-individuation and the perceived threat of withdrawal of maternal supplies in the face of it. As the child's self-representation begins to differentiate from the object-representation of the mother—as the child begins to separate—he now experiences the abandonment depression[6] in the wake of the threat of loss or withdrawal of supplies; at the same time, the mother continues to encourage and to reward those aspects of her child's behavior—passivity and regressiveness—which enable her to continue to cling to him.

Thus the mother encourages and rewards in the child the pathological ego's key defense mechanism of denial of the reality of separation, which in turn allows the persistence of the wish for reunion, which later emerges as a defense against the abandonment depression. Thus, part of the ego fails to undergo the necessary transformation from reliance upon the pleasure principle to reliance upon the reality principle, for to do so would mean acceptance of the reality of separation, which would bring on the abandonment depression.

The mother's clinging and withdrawing and the patient's acting out of his wish for reunion promote the failure of one part of the ego to develop, resulting in an ego structure split into a pathological (pleasure) ego and reality ego—the former pursuing relief from the feeling of abandonment, and the latter the reality principle. The pathological ego denies the reality of the separation, which permits the persistence of fantasies of reunion with the mother, which are then acted out through clinging and regressive behavior, thus defending against the abandonment regression and causing the patient to "feel good." Extensive fantasies of reunion are elaborated, projected onto the environment, and acted out, accompanied by increasing denial of reality. The two, operating in concert, create an ever-widening chasm between the patient's feelings and the reality of his functioning as he gradually emerges from the developmental years into adulthood.

Again, it should be emphasized that such an arrest of ego development in all likelihood reflects not a sudden or acute occurrence at the time of separation-individuation, but rather a persistent, ongoing developmental failure, dating possibly from the mother's ambivalence toward the infant's earliest moves toward differentiation at about four to five months postnatally.

THE RELATIONSHIP BETWEEN THE SPLIT OBJECT-RELATIONS UNIT AND THE SPLIT EGO

As already noted, the splitting defense keeps separate the rewarding and the withdrawing object relations part-units, including their associated affects. Although both the rewarding and the withdrawing maternal part-objects are pathological, the borderline experiences the rewarding part-unit as increasingly ego-syntonic, as it relieves the feelings of abandonment associated with the withdrawing part-unit, with the result that the individual "feels good." The affective state associated with the rewarding part-unit is that of gratification at being fed, hence "loved." The ensuing denial of reality is, in the last analysis, but a small price to pay for this affective state.

An alliance is now seen to develop between the child's rewarding maternal part-image (rewarding part-unit) and his pathological (pleasure) ego, the primary purpose of which is to promote the "good" feeling and to defend against the feeling of abandonment associated with the withdrawing part-unit. This ultimately powerful alliance further promotes the denial of separateness and potentiates the child's acting out of his reunion fantasies. The alliance has as an important secondary function the discharge of aggression, which is associated with and directed toward the withdrawing part-unit by means of symptoms, inhibitions, and various kinds of destructive acts. The aggression, which gains access to motility through the agency of the pathological (pleasure) ego, remains un-neutralized and hence unavailable for the further development of endopsychic structure (Rinsley 1968a).[7]

The withdrawing part-unit (part-self-representation, part-object-representation, and feelings of abandonment) becomes activated by actual experiences of separation (or of loss), as a result of the individual's efforts toward psychosocial growth and by moves toward separation-individuation within the therapeutic process, all of which *inter se alia* symbolize earlier life experiences which provoked the mother's withdrawal of supplies.

The alliance between the rewarding part-unit and the patho-logical (pleasure) ego is in turn activated by the resurgence of the withdrawing part-unit. The purpose of this operation, as it were, is defensive, to restore the wish for reunion and thereby to relieve the feeling of abandonment. The rewarding part-unit thus becomes the borderline's principal defense against the painful affective state associated with the withdrawing part-unit. *In terms of reality, however, both part-units are pathological; it is as if the patient has but two alternatives — either to feel bad and abandoned (withdraw-ing part-unit) or to feel good (rewarding part-unit), at the cost of denial of reality and self-destructive acting out.*

THERAPEUTIC CONSIDERATIONS

It is necessary now to consider the impact that this intrapsychic structure exerts upon therapeutic transference and resistance. In brief, the transference which the borderline develops results from the operation of the split object-relations unit — the rewarding part-unit and the withdrawing part-unit — each of which the patient proceeds alternatively to project onto the therapist. During those periods in which the patient projects the withdrawing part-unit (with its part-object-representation of the withdrawing mother) on to the therapist, he perceives therapy as necessarily leading to feel-ings of abandonment, denies the reality of therapeutic benefit, and activates the rewarding part-unit as a resistance. When projecting the rewarding part-unit (with its reunion fantasy) onto the therapist, the patient "feels good" but, under the sway of the pathological (pleasure) ego, is usually found to be acting in a self-destructive manner.

The Therapeutic Alliance

The patient begins therapy feeling that the behavior motivated by the alliance between his rewarding part-unit and his pathological (pleasure) ego is ego-syntonic; it makes him feel good. He is furthermore unaware of the cost to him, as it were, which is incurred through his denial of the reality of his self-destructive (and, of course, destructive) behavior.

The initial objective of the therapist is to render the functioning of this alliance ego-alien by means of confrontative clarification of its destructiveness. Insofar as this therapeutic maneuver promotes control of the behavior, the withdrawing part-unit becomes activated, which in turn reactivates the rewarding part-unit with the appearance of further resistance. There results a circular process, sequentially including resistance, reality clarification, working through of the feelings of abandonment (withdrawing part-unit), further resistance (rewarding part-unit), and further reality clarification, which leads in turn to further working through.

In those cases in which the circular working-through process proves successful, an alliance is next seen to develop between the therapist's healthy ego and the patient's embattled reality ego; this therapeutic alliance, formed through the patient's having internalized the therapist as a positive external object, proceeds to function counter to the alliance between the patient's rewarding part-unit and his pathological (pleasure) ego, battling with the latter for ultimate control of the patient's motivations and actions.

The structural realignments that ensue in the wake of the working-through process may now be described. The repetitive projection of his rewarding and withdrawing part-units (with their component maternal part-object-representations) onto the therapist, together with the latter's interpretative confrontation thereof, gradually draws to the patient's conscious awareness the presence of these part-units within himself. Concomitantly, the developing alliance between the therapist's healthy ego and the patient's reality ego brings into existence, through introjection, a new object-relations unit: the therapist as a positive (libidinal) object-representation who approves of separation-individuation plus a self-representation as a capable, developing person plus a "good" feeling (affect) that ensues from the exercise of constructive coping and mastery rather than regressive behavior.

The working through of the encapsulated rage and depression associated with the withdrawing part-unit in turn frees its component part-self- and part-object-representations from their intensely negative, aggressively valent affects. As a result, the new object-relations unit (constructive self plus "good" therapist plus "good" affect) linked with the reality ego becomes integrated into an overall "good" self-representation, whereas the split object-relations unit linked with the pathological (pleasure) ego becomes integrated into an overall "bad" self-representation; both are now accessible to the patient's conscious awareness as are their counterparts within the person of the therapist. At this point, the patient has begun in earnest the work of differentiating good and bad self-representations from good and bad object-representations as prefatory to the next step, in which good and bad self-representations coalesce, as do good and bad object-representations. The stage is now set for the inception of whole-object relations, which marks the patient's entrance into Stage 4 (Kernberg 1972a).

The delinking of "raw" instinctual energies from the rewarding and withdrawing part-units renders these energies increasingly available to the synthetic function associated with the patient's expanding reality ego and hence available for progressive neutralization. With this, and concomitant with the progressive coalescence of good-bad self- and object-representations, splitting becomes replaced by normal repression, with progressive effacement of the personified or "unmetabolized" images associated with the disappearing split object-relations unit (Kernberg 1966). The patient is now able to complete the work of mourning for these "lost" images, which characterize his final work of separation from the mother.

Clinical Examples

The following clinical examples illustrate the foregoing considerations, particularly the operation of the rewarding and withdrawing object relations part-units, the pathological (pleasure) ego and the therapeutic alliance.

A twenty-seven-year-old married woman, a college graduate with a successful career as a television actress, came to treatment with a depression against which she had been defending herself through drinking, abuse of drugs, and having an affair. She complained that her husband did not care for her because he spent too much time at his work.

The patient's history included an alcoholic mother, who spent most of her time sitting at home drinking and who rewarded the patient, at least verbally, for passivity, inactivity, and regressive behavior but who withdrew whenever her daughter demonstrated any form of constructive behavior. For example, when the patient, as an adolescent, cooked a meal, the mother would withdraw and assume a critical attitude; the same ensued whenever the patient attractively decorated her room or had success at school.

(In what follows the patient clearly describes the withdrawing maternal part-image — that is, the mother's withdrawal from the girl's assertiveness, activity or need to grow up, with the associated feelings of abandonment and the accompanying part-self-representation of being bad, ugly, inadequate, and unworthy. She also clearly reports the rewarding part-unit: a rewarding maternal part-image, feeling "good" and the self-image of a child who is taken care of. The mother's commands and the patient's behavior are thus linked together as the basis for the alliance between the rewarding part-unit and the pathological [pleasure] ego.)

Therapeutic progress had activated the withdrawing part-unit, which in turn activated the rewarding part-unit as a defense, with the patient's behavior coming under the control of the pathological (pleasure) ego, that is, passivity, drinking, and the affair. As the patient improved, as if despite herself, every step symbolized separation-individuation and proceeded to activate the withdrawing part-unit with its feelings of abandonment. She experienced her improvement as a loss, a frustration of the wish for reunion; and each time she improved she became resistant and hostile, projecting her anger at the mother's withdrawal on to the therapist and the therapeutic situation.

After a year of individual therapy three times a week, during which she had gained control over the behavior motivated by the alliance between the rewarding part-unit and the pathological (pleasure) ego, she reported, "This week I pulled myself more into reality. . . . I felt you had left me but told myself it wasn't true and the feelings went away. . . ." (*Note in what follows, however, the activation of the withdrawing part-unit and attendant resistance.*) "Yet today I don't want to tell you . . . I'd like to report that I was fucked up all weekend . . . I guess I felt healthy over the weekend. Last night I made a big drink but threw it out rather than drink it." (*Note that the improvement brings on further resistance.*) "I woke up angry at you this morning . . . . I recognize I'm doing better and I'm afraid you'll leave me. When my work went well one side of me was pleased." (*Note rewarding part-unit.*) ". . . the other side said why did I do that and I wanted to drink. I don't think I can maintain a mature way of living . . . when I have to do something responsible one side of me says no and wants to go out and get drunk." (*Note wish for reunion.*) "The better I do the more I want to hang on to the fantasies of lovers and drink." (*Note withdrawing part-unit.*) "If I'm grown up, independent, on my own, I'll be all alone and abandoned."

A little later the patient reports that, in effect, the alliance between the rewarding part-unit and the pathological (pleasure) ego has become ego-alien: "I had a fight with my bad side—the baby. . . ." (*Note the rewarding part-unit and the pathologic [pleasure] ego.*) ". . . I was enjoying myself reading and it was as if I heard a little voice saying have a drink. I could feel myself turn off feeling, then I took a drink. The bad side is my mother's commands . . . I'm ten years old and I can't decide myself . . . I have to follow the command but as I become aware of the command I can now disregard it and decide for myself."

In the next interview the patient reports, "I had two successes—each time it was as if I heard my mother's voice get started but each time I overcame it and went ahead." (*Again, however, control of the rewarding part-unit activates the withdrawing part-unit, which is then projected onto the therapist as a resistance maneuver.*) "I wasn't going to tell you today as you'd think I was better and act like my parents. If I get better you'll leave me. I worry about this, especially when you go on vacation. I feel you're leaving me because I'm doing better. My image of myself is of a person who drinks and has affairs, or of a young little girl who has to be taken care of."

As another example of how improvement had activated the withdrawing part-unit and produced resistance, the patient stated, "I didn't want to come today. I saw my old boyfriend. The baby side of me made me feel angry that I didn't want those old satisfactions. I don't want you to think I'm doing too well or I'll want to leave you . . . as if I want to get back at you . . . angry at you, you're doing this, making me better to get rid of me . . . I'm losing you. The baby side of me is angry that you think I can handle myself. Whenever I have five good days the baby side of me gets angry at you, but I can't verbalize it or you'll leave me for sure! I like to sit here and say nothing just to piss you off! I see getting better as your withdrawing affection. Last night as I saw I had fixed up my apartment nicely I got furious at you. Mother used to resent any creativity in me . . . . I never imagined verbalizing this anger at mother . . . fantasies and the feeling were all action—hitting, stabbing, killing her!"

As illustrated by this case, the alliance between the rewarding part-unit (rewarding maternal part-object-representation) and the pathological (pleasure) ego had as its objective the restoration of the wish for reunion and the relief of feelings of abandonment (separation anxiety and resultant rage), the latter being acted out and hence discharged in behavior. Thus, aggression otherwise available to build intrapsychic structure gains access to motility via self-destructive behavior.

The second case example concerns a twenty-year-old man who had dropped out of college because of severe depression and a work inhibition; he reported that he felt unable to perform, study, or even think. The patient's frankly paranoid mother had openly attacked him throughout childhood, both verbally and physically, for any assertion or expression of individuality; the father, rather than come to his son's aid, demanded that the boy submit to the mother's assaults as the price for the father's approval.

Analysis of the patient's withdrawing part-unit revealed the following structure: a part-object-representation consisting of a condensed image which included elements of the attacking mother and the withdrawing father; the predominant affect was, as expected, that of abandonment; the part-self-representation was that of a person who had caused the abandonment, who had leprosy, was no good, inadequate, "crazy" and "bad." The rewarding part-unit included the affect of feeling "good" and the part-self-representation of an obedient child, both dependent upon the pathological (pleasure) ego's use of avoidance, inhibition, and passivity, with denial of reality in pursuit of the wish for reunion. The patient's efforts to assert himself, to study and to learn activated the withdrawing part-unit, which in turn activated the rewarding part-unit, leading to the defensive use of avoidance, inhibition, and passivity.

As the patient improved in treatment and attempted to resume studying he would block; however, he was now able to report the maternal part-image, the part-self-image, and the abandonment feelings (the withdrawing part-unit) as well as the results of activation of the rewarding part-unit—that is, inhibition, avoidance, passivity, and blocking. He stated, "When I sit there trying to study I feel hurt, stepped on, crushed, and I want to give up. I never felt any support or connection with my mother. It's a feeling of complete loss, helplessness, inability to cope with reality . . . I feel adrift, alone . . . mother has no love for me. My image of mother's face is one of an expression of disgust like despising, criticizing, mocking me. I want her to love me but she hates me, and she acts as if I did something against her, and she wants to get back, and she attacks me. I haven't done anything for her to hate me . . . she used to discourage my interest in girls or in my taking any activity in the home or outside. When I appealed to my father for help he was never home and he would tell me to cut it out because I was upsetting his relationship with my mother.

"When they left me alone they took part of me with them. They take something with them that leaves me empty. They doublecross me . . . no feeling of worth or meaning . . . the feeling of being deserted kills me. I can't handle the aftermath of asserting myself or speaking out, studying or learning. I feel it's wrong to be myself and I can almost hear my father's voice telling me to cut it out, that if I don't he will leave me. Mother told me that father didn't care about me . . . she was the only one who cared . . . if I didn't stay with her she'd leave me.

"Trying to learn is tempting fate, risky, treacherous. It brings them down on me . . . I can almost hear their voices . . . I can't break their hold . . . I feel I'm dying. I can't think and not feel hurt so I give up. I feel they don't care and they're laughing at me. I can't fight them every second. I have to block out. When I sit down to study it's as if I hear my father saying, 'Don't you see the anguish you're causing me?'

"I feel completely abandoned and I yell, 'Help me out! Where is everybody?' And they say, 'He's crazy!' Father tells me it's my fault . . . the way I see things is all wrong. They feel sorry for me. I say, 'Please forgive me for having leprosy.' I can't scream or beg any more because they think I'm crazy. I'm so afraid if they don't protect me I'll die!"

As the just-described communicative sequence reveals, the activation of the withdrawing part-unit in the wake of the patient's efforts toward self-assertiveness leads the patient into a condition of abandonment that brings him close to experiencing delusions, somatic delusions, and auditory hallucinations. The untrammelled operation of his split object-relations unit could be seen to have brought him close, at times, to regression into Stage 2, with consequent blurring of the distinction between self-representations and object-representations.

The third case example concerns an unmarried, nineteen-year-old girl, a freshman in college who had been an outstanding high-school student and who had subsequently dropped out of college because of depression and "panic."

The patient's father, a manic-depressive professional man, had had an explosive temper. Throughout the patient's childhood the father had behaved as a dependent child in his relationship with the mother, had openly attacked the patient for her "childhood inadequacies," but had envied her achievements. The major role obfuscations within the family found the mother playing the role of the father's mother and demanding that the patient not only submit to the father's attacks but also serve in the role of her own (the mother's) mother (chapters 10 and 15, Rinsley 1971a).

The patient's withdrawing maternal part-image was that of a mother who exploited her and who was deliberately cruel and enjoyed the patient's helplessness and dependency; the associated affect included abandonment depression and the fear of engulfment; the part-self-image was that of being inadequate, worthless, guilty, an insect, and a bug. The patient harbored cannibalistic fantasies and fears throughout childhood, relieved during that time by masturbation; in the fantasies, she was at times the victim and at other times the cannibal. The rewarding maternal part-image was that of a strong, idealized ("all-good") mother who would save her from death; the associated affect was that of feeling "good" and the part-self-image was that of a helpless, clinging child.

After some five months of treatment, the patient had begun to separate, with emergence of the withdrawing part-self-image (withdrawing part-unit), which precipitated her into near-panic. She reported, "I feel everybody's angry at me. I'm about to be attacked. I feel like an insect, a bug. It's all because I don't want to be like my mother, I don't want to hold on to her. The role she puts me in fit her needs but also gave me security. She would love me no matter how bad I was. I want her and I want to be taken care of and I can't breathe without her. I don't have a separate existence and I feel guilty if I try. I can't stop wanting my mother like a baby. I can't seem to make a life of my own."

Whenever the withdrawing part-unit was activated as a result of a move toward separation-individuation, the patient projected her resultant anger at the withdrawing maternal part-image and became resistant to treatment, which she then viewed as conducive to abandonment. Thus she expressed her wish to kill the therapist, her mother and herself: "Over the weekend I felt completely independent but cut off. I talked about my job very self-confidently, then I got frightened and went into a rage. I wanted to tear myself apart, rip my mother apart or you apart and I felt terribly depressed. I realized I'm getting better and I don't want to admit it. I don't need my mother. I lost my motivation, my desire to go on. I feel humiliated, defeated, dead, and cold. I hate you! I don't think you can help me and I want revenge on my mother and you!"

This patient's pathological (pleasure) ego, shaped by her mother's "rewarding" responses, comprised regressive-defensive behavior, such as acting helplessly, clinging, a variety of somatic symptoms and carrying out the mother's assigned role of an inadequate, hysterical child.

The fourth case example concerns a twenty-two-year-old unmarried college graduate who lived alone. She complained of anxiety, depression and hysteriform fears that her legs "might not work" and that she might be unable to eat or swallow; she had, in addition, experienced several episodes of impaired consciousness. There were also feelings of helplessness and inability to cope, and she almost constantly contacted her mother for reassurance.

The mother had idealized the family unit and had rewarded infantile-compliant behavior, which she viewed as a religious virtue; conversely, she vigorously attacked her child's efforts toward self-assertiveness or originality, an example of which had been her refusal to attend the patient's high school graduation exercises when she had learned that the girl had participated in a demonstration against the war in Vietnam. The mother had particularly attacked heterosexual relations as "the work of the Devil." The father, an emotionally distant man, served in the role of the mother's figurehead.

The patient's withdrawing maternal part-image was that of an angry, punitive, and vengeful mother who would kill her; the associated affect was a compound of fear and abandonment depression;

the part-self-image was that of being guilty, worthless, and despicably bad. The rewarding maternal part-image was that of an omnipotent, god-like mother; the associated affect was relief from anxiety and feeling "good"; the part-self-image was that of a helpless, compliant child. The pathological (pleasure) ego, which functioned to maintain the wish for reunion, abetted the fulfillment of the mother's wishes by being helpless, dependent, unassertive, clinging, and asexual. Again, therapeutic progress activated the withdrawing part-unit, which then triggered off the rewarding part-unit with ensuing helpless clinging, passivity and phobic and hysteriform symptomatology.

Following resolution of the patient's initial resistances, she reported, "I think I'm destined to die because I'm growing up. I can envisage no life outside my mother or family. I'm made up of two parts—one me, one her. The part that she has worked on, taken care of and given to me . . . if I move away from her the part of her that's in me would turn against me . . . mother will make it turn against me and it will punish me. I don't feel strong enough to battle in spite of myself. Mother insists that I remain helpless and not grow up."

The patient continues, "I'm afraid if I grow up I'll lose her. I will take away her reason for living. I carry out what mother says—I'm an empty shell. Mother puts in the values, otherwise I will be nothing. I'm empty except for her. Mother sees me as a tool for herself. She instructed me in the one thing I can't do—grow up and leave her—or I'll be punished for it."

The patient experienced intense guilt over her hostility toward the mother, "I feel dirty and disgusting! Mother equates growing up with stealing and murder. Defying her is like defying God—you feel guilty and frightened. I've been frightened into believing that growing up is wrong. If I do anything that mother doesn't approve of, like have sex or smoke grass, I'm throwing myself to the winds and anything can happen to me. Mother suggested that sexual intercourse before marriage would make me mentally ill. If I smoke or have intercourse I'm violating the bargain I made with her not to leave her. I'm afraid she will leave me.

"When I assert myself rather than complying I feel nasty and impudent and that everybody will be angry with me. I'm just beginning to realize the extent to which I carry out mother's wishes. If I don't do what she says it's wrong . . . if I reject one thing it's like rejecting all. In other words, having sex is like lying, stealing or rejecting my mother. She would rather I die than go out and do something she didn't want. Mother wanted me in order, just like she wanted the nice, clean bathroom in order. When I go and do something that is not in order she goes into a rage and would like to kill me."

In this case the alliance between the rewarding part-unit and the pathological (pleasure) ego engendered the patient's feeling of panic over anticipated punishment if she attempted to grow; the punishment she expected would take the form of her "going crazy," and of paralysis of walking, talking, and swallowing. In her case the pathological (pleasure) ego discharged aggression by means of autoplastic symptom-formation.

CONCLUSION

Chapter 12 described the contribution of maternal libidinal availability and withdrawal to the etiology of the borderline syndrome. It underscored Mahler's emphasis upon the mother's vital contribution to normal ego development and related the effects of deficiency in that contribution to the development of the intrapsychic structure of the borderline: the split ego and the split object-relations unit. The latter, which develops from internalization of the two major themes of interaction with the mother, produces the leitmotif of the borderline's intrapsychic structure: the rewarding and withdrawing object-relations part-units. The rewarding part-unit becomes allied, as it were, with the pathological (pleasure) ego to defend against the withdrawing part-unit, but at the cost of failure to cope with reality. The relationship of these borderline intrapsychic structures to each other and to the therapist's intrapsychic structures, as developed in the therapeutic transference and resistance, was described and illustrated by means of clinical case examples.

Notes

1. It will be evident that Kernberg's and Mahler's timing of the occurrence of the fixation underlying borderline personality development differs significantly, the former citing the period of four to twelve months and the latter the period of the "rapprochement subphase," coinciding with sixteen to twenty-five months postnatally. No attempt will be made here to choose between these two differing schedules, although the preponderance of evidence would appear to be more favorable to Mahler's timing.

2. Associated failure to develop an integrated self-representation and an integrated object-representation, normally accomplished during Stage 4, may be viewed in terms of failure of development of whole-object relations from antecedent part-object relations. It may be noted that developmental fixation at Stage 3 corresponds with fixation at Fairbairn's late oral stage of infantile dependence (Fairbairn 1954), during which the (maternal) whole-object is characteristically perceived and treated as part-object (breast). The borderline's cathexis of whole-objects as if they were part-objects leads in turn to a welter of later interpersonal depersonifications and appersonations elsewhere described (chapter 11).

3. It should be noted here that, with reference to mother-infant interactions during the first postnatal year, and in particular during its first half, the term "mother" in fact has reference to the maternal part-object (breast); thus the term mother is used here in this connection for convenience and simplicity.

4. The object-relations unit, with its triadic representational-affective structure (Kernberg 1966) has been elsewhere defined as an ego state (Rinsley 1968a).

5. The reader will immediately discern the similarity of the split object-relations unit to Fairbairn's split internalized bad object, and Fairbairn deserves full prior credit for having perceived its basic structure in his analysands. Thus the withdrawing part-unit may be seen to correspond with Fairbairn's rejecting object (R.O.) whereas the rewarding part-unit may be seen to correspond with his exciting object (E.O.).

6. As here employed, the term *abandonment depression* refers to the core affect structurally linked to the part-self and part-object-representations which together comprise the withdrawing (aggressive) part-unit. The subjective state conveyed by the term includes a core anxiety component and a more differentiated component.

The former is of an instinctual quality and corresponds with the primal experience of impending loss of the maternal stimulus barrier against endopsychic and external stimulation, with ensuing gross ego trauma. The latter, more structuralized, conveys the feeling of guilt which signifies the ego's anxiety over impending "abandonment" or sadistic assault by the superego, also perceived as a threatened loss or withdrawal of supplies. The basic feelings common to the state of abandonment depression thus comprise a profound sense of emptiness and, as an aspect of estrangement, a sense of the meaninglessness of the external world.

7. Again, the reader will discern the similarity of these formulations to those of Fairbairn. Fairbairn originally postulated a splitting within the infantile ego in correspondence with the split internalized "bad" object and, in effect, postulated an alliance between their parts. He postulated, on the one hand, an alliance between the exciting object (E.O.) and what he termed the libidinal ego (L.E.) and another between the rejecting object (R.O.) and what he termed the antilibidinal ego (anti-L.E.). The exciting object–libidinal ego alliance fairly directly corresponds with that, here presented, between the rewarding part-unit and the pathological (pleasure) ego. For Fairbairn, the antilibidinal ego came to represent the punitive, sadistic aspect of the superego, allied with the rejecting object as a split mental structure.

13

Individual Psychotherapy in Residential Treatment: The Case of Sheryl

At the time of her admission into full-time residential treatment, Sheryl was a twelve-and-a-half-year-old, Caucasian, Protestant, sixth-grader from a nearby small town, the fourth of six living siblings born to a truck driver and his wife; siblings included an eldest unmarried sister, age twenty-one; an older brother who would have been nineteen but who died at two months of age following meningitis; another older brother, sixteen years old, with a lengthy history of delinquency, truancy, and antisociality; and two younger siblings, a sister of eleven and a brother of nine years, both in elementary school. Sheryl's father, who had had an eighth-grade education, was thirty years old at the time of her birth; he had had a lengthy history of emotional instability, and following overseas Army service in the Pacific Theater of Operations in World War II, developed multiple psychosomatic symptoms and increasingly displayed ideas of reference, profound suspiciousness, frank persecutory delusions, and pathological jealousy of his wife, Sheryl's mother, whom he repeatedly accused of marital infidelity. Sheryl's mother, one of the offspring of a rural barber and his wife, had a history of mild mental retardation; she impetuously eloped with Sheryl's father when she was fifteen and when he was nineteen, during the latter's leave from Army duty.

The marriage proved to be exceedingly stormy from the outset, with paternal drunkenness, wife beating, violent arguments, and rages; the father repeatedly castigated the mother in the presence of the children, and the mother was reportedly in dire and chronic fear of her life at the father's hands. Sheryl was born of a normal, full-term gestation and delivery, weighed six pounds and six and a half ounces at birth and developed normally until struck by acute anterior poliomyelitis at five months of age, leaving her with marked scoliosis and moderate atrophy of both lower extremities. There ensued, between age seven years and her admission, numerous orthopedic operations, including several spinal fusions, tendon transplants, and heel-lengthening procedures to both feet, and between ages ten and eleven years, application of a whole-body cast for spinal curvature for six months. Three months before her admission, Sheryl underwent an appendectomy, and a month before admission, she underwent the last of her numerous surgical procedures, a triple arthrodesis of her left foot; hence, she was wearing a cast at the time she entered residence.

In the years following Sheryl's father's discharge from the Service after World War II, he became increasingly disturbed, necessitating several brief periods of hospitalization for paranoid schizophrenic illness at a local Veterans' Administration hospital. He became increasingly preoccupied with violence, repeatedly threatened his wife's life, and suffered fits of depression and bouts of jealous rage. On December 7, 1956, the anniversary of the Japanese attack on Pearl Harbor, following a dispute with his wife over the disposition of a VA check, he abruptly shot her to death with a blast from the family shotgun, in full view of Sheryl, then aged five, the only other person present in the home at the time. Sheryl's terror and confusion at these events did not obscure her later recall of them; she remembered her mother, struck full in the chest by the shotgun blast, her lungs laid bare, jerking and moaning in her death throes as blood and gore gushed from her wound and her mouth — with Sheryl clasping the dying woman to her body on the floor, crying, "Mommie, don't die!" This graphic and tragic scene — together with multiple antecedent precursors, including Sheryl's poliomyelitis residuals — was to set the stage for the long-standing illness, exacerbation of which predetermined her later hospitalization and the dramatic course of her ensuing treatment.

Immediately following the killing, the father rushed out of the house with the shotgun, intent upon murdering his wife's parents as well, only to be apprehended by the State Highway Patrol and remanded to jail pending formal criminal charges. An exceedingly important event occurred during the ensuing police action: Sheryl, the only witness to her mother's murder, was promised that she would be allowed to see her father if she told all she had seen; the little girl was reluctant, but believing the police interrogator, she told the story. The promise was never fulfilled, leaving the child with a lasting hatred toward authority figures. The father was subsequently declared mentally incompetent to stand trial, and was hospitalized in the Criminally Insane Unit of a state mental hospital pending his restoration to competency. He finally came to trial eight years later, some one and a quarter years after Sheryl's hospitalization; the original charges were then dropped owing to a lack of witnesses, and he entered a local VA facility from which he was finally discharged a year later to return to his hometown, where he later remarried; his further history is not relevant to what follows.

Meanwhile, various siblings had been farmed out to relatives, with Sheryl, her older sister, and her brother coming to live with the divorced and remarried maternal grandmother. The latter, who had divorced a man described as a drunken wastrel years before, had next married a man whose personality so closely resembled that of Sheryl's father as to cast her into a lifelong terror of him; he proved a brutal, sadistic man, fond of his small arms collection, dwelling in a past life which, as he liked to relate it, resembled the existence of a Theodore Roosevelt Rough Rider. Throughout her latency years, Sheryl became a stoical, seclusive, negativistic, and passively hostile youngster; she was quick to collect injustices, prone to masochistic self-effacement, and became progressively withdrawn into an autistic world populated by the events of her mother's assassination, impotent rage at a world she felt had deprived and rejected her, and unremittent pathological mourning for the lost maternal object. Despite her numerous operations, the actions of the sadistic stepgrandfather, the ambivalent and emotionally infantile grandmother, and numerous sexual advances by her older brother (particularly during periods when she had been physically immobilized), Sheryl managed to maintain low-passing schoolwork with periods of regular attendance and homebound instruction when required. Her episodes of recalcitrance, intransigence toward authority (especially the grandmother), and stubborn negativism that Sheryl actually and not incorrectly rationalized to herself as, in effect, the necessary defensive equipment of a deprived, miserable child who had to battle for everything she got and against the many family members and age-peers whose taunts and jibes over her obvious physical deformities both cast her into despair and provoked in her a passive-looking, tooth-gritting, stoical rage.

Throughout Sheryl's latency years, scant if any attention had been paid to her evident and deepening emotional difficulties by her family and by the battery of orthopedists who went on with multiple surgical procedures as if she were devoid of sensitivity, indeed even of sensibility. Three months prior to admission, following her appendectomy, she became increasingly depressed and negativistic. Her triple arthrodesis two months later was followed by a deepening of these symptoms; in addition, she became phobic of adult males, slept more and more, withdrew increasingly from family interactions, and developed persecutory delusions centering on her school principal (a man) and mounting terror of her stepgrandfather. A few days before admission, she abruptly cut her forearms lightly with broken glass while consuming numerous buffered aspirin tablets, accompanied by thoughts of "ending it all." She was next seen at the hospital's outpatient clinic and was referred for admission with the diagnosis of schizophrenia, catatonic type, characterized by catalepsy, bizarre affect, classical thought disorder, withdrawal, impoverishment of thought, episodic mutism, paranoid ideation, negativism, and suicidal preoccupation.

FIRST CLOSED-WARD PHASE

The opening phase of Sheryl's residential treatment found her in residence in a closed girls' ward. For several months following her admission, she proved underspontaneous and undercommunicative to the point of periods of muteness; she shunned peer and staff contact, appeared preoccupied and self-absorbed, and went about assigned ward duties desultorily. Her ankle cast was removed six weeks after her admission and she was slowly started in a limited off-ward program of occupational therapy and academic school classes. Her behavior now proceeded to change from that of a seemingly detached, alienated-appearing girl to that of an amazingly subtle injustice-collector, whose charismatic qualities of quiet, behind-the-scenes leadership and manipulativeness reflected her emergence as a narcissistic, controlling figure, who repeatedly involved her ward peers in serving her and doing her bidding, including acting out against each other by proxy. When it became clear that Sheryl was evolving as a potentially powerful ward leader, her privileges were curtailed, and direct interpretations were made by the ward team of her behavior and evident, narcissistic motivations. We saw, in effect, that Sheryl was attempting to recapitulate on the ward her angry, narcissistic position at home, utilizing in the transference the same defenses she had long employed with her grandparents and siblings. Her ability to sow discord among her peers was viewed as an externalization of archaic splitting defenses, which had to be interrupted and brought to a halt as quickly as possible.

As a result of these maneuvers by the staff, Sheryl began to show a variety of somatic symptoms. She repeatedly injured herself by "accidental" cuts, bruises, and falls, and, most significantly, she developed a classic hyperventilation syndrome when frustrated, characterized by crescendo hyperpnea, pallor, weakness, and syncope, followed by rapid, stertorous respiration, head-rolling, and hip motions typical for a grand hysterical seizure; her overbreathing proceeded to induce a respiratory alkalosis, with classical tetany, carpopedal spasm, and positive Chvostek and Trousseau signs. It was evident in these seizures that Sheryl was reenacting the death throes of her murdered mother through the mechanism available to her at that tragic time — restitutive introjective identification; it was likewise evident that she utilized a classical splitting defense, such that the mother's death was at once affirmed and acted out while it was denied in deed. No attempt was made, at this point, to interpret these matters to her, and her "fits" were met with minimal overt concern and a matter-of-fact attitude by the staff. The secondary gain served by her seizures was notably expressed through her ward peers, who would become guilt-ridden and would attempt, unless prevented, to rush to her aid and succor her.

There followed, until the end of her first year of treatment, a gradual lessening of these seizures and what appeared to be a slow emergence of Sheryl from her alienated, solitary condition, such that she appeared to be forming better relations with staff and peers; she became less negativistic, actually began to smile, and indeed began to compete with the peers in feats of physical prowess, obviously to show herself and them that her deformities did not hinder her. At the end of a year's time, the staff concluded that Sheryl had progressed sufficiently to be transferred to a semiopen ward and she was accordingly moved there fourteen months after her admission.

Of great importance, but unknown to the staff at the time, was Sheryl's response to the sudden death by myocardial infarction of her grandmother a few weeks prior to the transfer. She became depressed, preoccupied with the idea that her "badness" had killed the old woman, viewed her transfer as a cold rejection from a secure environment and, indeed, as it later turned out, perceived the transfer in direct transferential terms as a recapitulation of her mother's rejection of her through the former's cruel demise. It was at this time that Sheryl made her first approaches to me for individual psychotherapy, based upon an effort to identify herself with my own slight but evident poliomyelitis residual (right leg) and expecting that I could understand her problems better than others could. She also expressed the opinion that I could control her should she be tempted to act up in her new ward, and one could sense beneath these a counterphobic maneuver toward an otherwise frightening adult male figure.

Shortly following these approaches to me, as if to motivate me toward her, Sheryl began to cause increasing difficulties in her new ward. The old negativism returned as did the hyperventilation syncopes; she became overtly hostile and demanding, attempted to form liaisons with older males from the hospital's adult psychiatric service, was caught sneaking contraband (cigarettes, sloe gin) onto the ward, and began to openly defy the ward staff. Her school and activity therapeutic work became erratic, she began to refuse to attend classes, and for the first time she began to verbalize homicidal wishes toward the staff and suicidal wishes. Concomitantly, Sheryl began to verbally abuse her older sister openly, now her legal guardian, during the latter's visits, and to alienate the sister by demanding gifts, clothing, cosmetics, and notions, which the sister could not afford to purchase for her.

Less than a month following her transfer, Sheryl was started in twice-weekly psychotherapy. From the beginning, she attempted to play off the psychotherapist against the ward psychiatrist and the rest of the ward team, another manifestation of her splitting defense, and considerable coordinated work was required to preclude her successful misuse of both modalities. When, five months after starting psychotherapy, I became her ward psychiatrist for administrative reasons, her terror of closure mounted. She openly stated that she felt she could no longer "fool" her two doctors as they had now become condensed in the figure of one, and her defiance, negativism, manipulativeness, and rebelliousness increased as she stubbornly defended herself against the expressed fear that I would attack, even kill her. Events reached a climax nine months after her transfer, when she abruptly broke and literally chewed up and swallowed shards of a glass perfume bottle along with a dilute bleaching solution used for ward laundry purposes. With this, Sheryl was transferred back to the closed ward in seclusion; she was openly suicidal, terrified, resistive, and pervasively depressed.

OPENING PHASE OF PSYCHOTHERAPY

I consider the opening phase of Sheryl's psychotherapy to have extended from its inception roughly a month after her transfer from the closed to the semiopen ward to the point at which she was returned to the closed ward, a period of approximately nine months. During the first five months of this period, Sheryl's ward psychiatrist and her psychotherapist were, of course, different individuals; this period was marked by Sheryl's growing yet tolerable level of anxiety on the ward and by a fairly productive series of therapeutic hours with me. During the latter she alternated between hours of mutism and passive defiance of me and hours during which she verbalized fairly freely and coherently. During the latter, Sheryl addressed herself to several matters of concern to her. She communicated her pervasive self-view of a deformed, monstrous being with "bad legs" and strange somatic-delusional ideas about her pelvic and abdominal viscera, which she perceived as distorted, "out of place," and full of "bad" matter. She claimed to be infertile and sexually unattractive, in part by which themes she was obviously asking me how I too viewed her and whether I would hurt or assault her. Sheryl next began, via metaphor, to hint at the strength of her sexual urge and its fusion with aggression, and during her twelfth hour she fell into a hyperventilatory syncope, requiring my physical intervention to prevent her from injuring herself. During the height of this attack she screamed, "Mommy, mommy . . . don't die!" and, repeatedly, "You're gonna rape me and I'll kill you first!" Both communications served in large part to explain the basis for the attack — to relive the mother's murder and to both invite and ward off the fantasied murderous assault by me, her paternal transference object. In succeeding hours, Sheryl seemed to have been relieved by her hour-long attack, and she was able to reveal the long-standing sexual abuse at the hands of her older brother and, gradually, her enormously paranoid world-view in which she viewed other people as dangerous, untrustworthy persecutory objects, bent upon wresting her "goodies" (good objects) from her, communicating therewith her fear that I, her therapist, would so rob (rape) her.

The acquittal of her father, at last brought to trial a month after psychotherapy had begun, awakened in Sheryl proxy-maternal fantasies of succoring and nurturing him, followed by communications that all her relatives were bad, crazy, and dangerous and that she, like them, was similarly dangerous, intractable, and unchangeable. These various messages built up in crescendo fashion until the dramatic events surrounding her retransfer to the closed ward. (Sheryl much later confided that during this period she was terrified that I, her ward psychiatrist during the latter four months of her semiopen residence, would "put together" enough information about her as to become powerfully able to control and, ultimately if I wished, destroy her; many of her "messages" both in the ward and the therapy hours amounted to efforts to convey this. In addition, as it turned out, she had viewed the semi-open ward as a seduction by the staff for her to act out, and she had concluded that her transfer there following the death of her grandmother as "punishment" for her "responsibility" for the grandmother's demise, a sort of forcible expulsion from the womb or, in her later words, the Garden of Eden—a traumatic and frightening rebirth from which she had to retreat and the effects of which she had to fight.)

The nine months of this phase of Sheryl's psychotherapy witnessed her direct projection of fused aggressive and libidinal wishes, in the form of transference onto me. The transference psychosis comprised, in part, efforts to provoke me to assault and kill her and to recapitulate both the events of the traumatic death of her mother and the chronic frustrations and aggressions deeply associated with the long-standing effects of her poliomyelitis residuals and the abuses to which her multiple periods of physical immobility had repeatedly exposed her. Her need to reconstitute and resymbiotize with the "lost" maternal object found ultimate expression in her success in getting herself returned to the security of the closed ward and, because of her intensely self-injurious actions, confined further in seclusion.

SECOND CLOSED-WARD PHASE

The second closed-ward phase of Sheryl's treatment occupied a total period of twenty-one months. The first two months of these came at the end of the service period of an older, warm, kindly resident physician as her ward psychiatrist, toward whom Sheryl had become rather attached and under whose guidance she had become a bit more comfortable. Her initial responses to her return to the closed ward included moderate depression ("I've lost all I gained") and, once more within the security of the highly structured setting, the reappearance of her former quiescent, "adaptive" adjustment to the ward. The arrival on the scene of a new ward psychiatrist — an aggressive, driving, obsessional young resident — witnessed the outbreak of Sheryl's mounting terror of him; she now proceeded to attempt to split off the new doctor and me, with my becoming her "good" doctor and his becoming an evil, frightening potential attacker, and she now increasingly threatened to kill herself. At times, Sheryl became openly combative toward the ward staff and punched and pounded her own body and banged her head against the floor and walls of her room, requiring increased dosages of oral and parenteral psychotropic medication and the application of four-limb restraints. Along with these events, she abjectly refused to attend school and occupational therapy classes, began to experience auditory and visual hallucinations, and required around-the-clock one-to-one supervision.

Six months after her return to the closed ward, during the fourth month of her new ward psychiatrist's tenure on the ward, Sheryl managed one day to break free of her one-to-one supervised toilet activities, grabbed a large open safety pin, and swallowed it; the pin lodged open-ended in the prepyloric outlet area of her stomach, and she was accordingly transferred to the hospital's Medical and Surgical Unit where a gastrotomy was performed under general anesthesia and the pin removed.

It could justifiably be said that this time represented the nadir of Sheryl's overall course of treatment. On the Medical and Surgical Unit she proved resistive in the extreme, attempted to tear at her bandages and sutures, repeatedly expressed the wish to die, asked to be killed, had to be tube-fed, and taxed the Unit staff to the utmost. Upon her return to her home ward, she broke out in acne-form pustules over her face and trunk, and screamed repeatedly, "All the bad things are coming out of me!" She required full-time one-to-one specialing, four-limb restraints, went through brief periods of urinary and fecal retention, expressed the fear that the staff would rob her of her "insides," and had to be bathed under protest. Staff countertransference reached its expectable peak during those weeks, and numerous team and staff conferences were devoted to understanding and explaining her regressive symptomatology and to exploration of further ways in which to help her through this period of crisis.

Six months following her return to the closed ward, Sheryl presented the following picture: her gastrotomy had healed; she was in seclusion with twenty-four-hour one-to-one special coverage; she was receiving high daily doses of phenothiazine medication; she often required brief periods of four-limb restraints, lest she lash out at the staff members attending her; she required, and responded well to, spoon-feeding; she went through periods of urinary and fecal retention necessitating enemas and catheterizations; her facial and truncal skin was spotted with acneform pustules; and she was hallucinating in visual, auditory, and tactile spheres, presented classical schizophrenic thought disorder, and experienced waves of depersonalization and periods of oneiric dissociation. When not enraged, she often displayed fetal posturing, echopraxia, and waxy flexibility.

Eight months following Sheryl's return to the closed ward, the greatly feared ward psychiatrist was reassigned and, again for administrative purposes, I became her ward psychiatrist while continuing to be her individual psychotherapist. Her initial response to this situation was to shout, "God, I'm glad I've got him back . . . now I won't be able to get away with it any more!" My return to take up duties on her ward signaled a gradual upward trend in Sheryl's clinical condition, and from that point until thirteen months later, when she was returned to the semiopen ward for the second and last time, she underwent sustained and accelerating clinical improvement. During this period, Sheryl gradually moved from seclusion to open-door room status, then to limited dayhall privileges, then to one-to-one on- and off-ward through gradually expanded intermediary privilege statuses until ten months later she had reached maximum privileges for a closed ward, had reentered academic, occupational, and recreational classes, and had developed strong affectionate ties with several of her wardmates. Each progressive step was fraught with great fear for her, as each symbolically represented dispossession from the ambivalently perceived uterine state of maximal security, and, likewise, each step required careful working through before she could take it. As matters progressed, Sheryl became increasingly outgoing, took part in group activities, displayed vastly improved affect, and improved in her relationship with her older sister. The defensive aspects of her negativism became progressively trans-formed into a spunky individualism, including insistence upon being allowed to "think things through" and, in her words, a shift in her "suspiciousness" toward what she could call "a healthy respect for others."

SECOND PHASE OF PSYCHOTHERAPY

The second phase of Sheryl's psychotherapy coincided with the second closed-ward phase of her residential treatment. During this twenty-one-month period, therapy continued on a twice- to thrice-weekly formal basis, although as both her therapist and ward physician, I made myself available to her almost on demand. Initially and during the first several months, I saw Sheryl in her seclusion room. Her status at that time was such that she could do little more than hurl imprecations at the staff, if rather fewer of them at me. Indeed, her behavior during therapeutic hours came to suggest that she was desperately trying to retain something, to conceal it from me. Gradually, the nature of this "hidden" material became clear, and Sheryl revealed it to comprise an exten-sive autistic pseudocommunity. Within it, Sheryl had meticulously reconstituted an idealized family with herself as proxy mother; she had held herself responsible for her mother's death and had counterphobically identified herself with *both* the lost mother and the terrifying father, thereby reinforcing her archaic splitting defense and sundering her self- and sexual identities. When this pseudocommunity was approached interpretively, Sheryl regressed deeply: she mumbled, displayed magic-symbolic and transitivistic thinking, tried to retain her bodily products, and attempted to banish me by outright visual scotomatization and by developing a microptic illusion of me as a lilliputian figure imprisoned in several bottles on her room floor. She was terrified lest the coalescence of her split-off part-self- and part-object-representations would agglomerate enough aggression to destroy her, expressed in part through loudly uttered world-destruction fantasies. I stimulated her process of internalization in each hour by bringing her some candy that we both ate, and I refused to catheterize her myself but left this to the nurse, much to Sheryl's relief. She again spoke of her visceral distortions and of her "torn-up" (mutilated) genital. At times both of us entered her autistic world, sharing symbolic primary-process talk and symbolically fusing.

Initial evidence that our program was at last making inroads into her basic splitting defense was Sheryl's gradual awareness that she could never reconstitute her dead mother. She began to accept the fact that her family was "scattered to the four winds," and she slowly began to emerge from her intensely autistic mode of thinking and to reinitiate relationships with "outside" objects. Of great significance was her communication, during the two-hundredth hour of therapy, that she could no longer remember many of the early childhood events for which she had long been hypermnestic, thereby signaling the inception of normal repression and of depressive working through. Concomitantly, Sheryl began to masturbate with growing pleasure, during which she felt increasingly free to fantasize physical intimacy with me and with a growing number of male peers, something she later could admit she could never have allowed herself to do. There next ensued a powerful positive transference, which I felt could now provide the fulcrum of her subsequent treatment and the content of which conveyed her ability to internalize me as *both* a maternal and a paternal figure; she began to imitate my style of speech and expressive gestural mannerisms and to strengthen her "inner controls." A revealing interchange took place during her two-hundred-and-twenty-third hour:

Sheryl: You know, sometimes when you and I were "talking crazy" together, I was afraid you were as crazy as I was.
Therapist: Yes, I know that. What's the difference now?
Sheryl: Well, you could always stop acting crazy, but I couldn't . . . you could turn it off. . . .
Therapist: And now . . . ?
Sheryl: Now *I* can turn it off too . . . I've got control of it. . . .

Sheryl was now able to increasingly tolerate more and more responsibility for herself. As noted before, each step away from seclusion temporarily frightened her and required careful working through, in her case by intensive examination of the meaning and possible consequences of her stepwise "liberation." Six months before her final return to the semiopen ward, Sheryl had attained maximum privileges. She had successfully worked through her feelings upon her initial transfer to the semiopen ward and was getting ready, now, to return to it.

By this time, Sheryl had dealt effectively with the following: (1) her split-off yet fused "good" and "bad" self-object-representations; (2) her rage at the "lost" maternal object; (3) the reinforcing effect that her prolonged childhood immobility and surgical assaults had had upon her defensive clinging to an idealized "good" feeding object; (4) her counterphobic identification with her murderous father; and (5) her infantile-omnipotence, oral sadism, and persistent transitivistic (symbioticlike) world view. In addition, Sheryl had begun to correspond with her father, now close to discharge from his final hospitalization. She could recognize from his letters that he continued to be mentally ill and began to "forgive" him for robbing the family of their mother as well as of himself, their father. The gradual giving up of her infantile-omnipotence signaled, of course, a concomitant growth of her capacity to sense and test reality, to come to a realistic awareness of her physical limitations, and to begin to plan for the future.

FINAL PHASE OF TREATMENT

The final phase of Sheryl's residential treatment may be said to have begun with her return to the semiopen ward, some forty-three months after her admission and thirty months following her initial transfer to it. Progress from that point was sustained. One after another, the sources of her negativism proceeded to emerge, each to be meticulously worked through as before. With each minor, temporary "setback" in this work, as she called them, such as "little" physical injuries, losses of temper, or short bouts of solitariness, Sheryl would proceed to "analyze" her behavior, relate it to past events, and attempt to grasp the connections — much of this on her own. She delighted in my approval of this work, as well as in her sustained improvement in her academic school work. She progressively emerged as a "benevolent" leader of her ward peers, no longer attempting to press them into her narcissistic service as much as before, and she began to make some good friendships. The masochistic injustice-collecting and pity-gathering behavior fell away. Her relations with her older sister had now become essentially amicable, as with her father; in each case, she could recognize the limitations inherent in the relationship and guide her expectations and conduct accordingly.

Increasingly, Sheryl's communications during her therapy hours began to center on her future — her continued need for individual psychotherapy following her discharge from residential care, where she would live, her future relations with boys, and other such concerns. There continued to be no doubt that much of her sustained improvement rested upon her transferential relationship with me, which increasingly assumed the quality of a genuine transference neurosis, most notably during the three postdischarge years of my continued work with her.

Limitations of time have precluded the inclusion of considerable information that would further illuminate the foregoing material. To mention a few, evidence of seriously disturbed mothering dating almost from the time of Sheryl's birth; her deeply buried identification with Jesus Christ, connected with her postparalytic immobility and surgery (crucifixion and immolation); her passive seduction of her assaultive brother, thereby to be "fed" by his breast-phallus; and her cloacal fantasies, including her syncretic perception of her urogenital and fecal products as items of food.

From the beginning, there was no doubt regarding Sheryl's psychotic illness, which her postadmission studies and the subsequent course of her residential treatment proved to be of the "mixed" presymbiotic-symbiotic form. There was also little doubt that individual psychotherapy was the critical factor in assisting Sheryl to use the residential environment nor that the psychotherapy, by further exposing her splitting defenses as the latter were systematically frustrated in the ward environment, precipitated the crisis-laden regressions basic for the extrusion of her "bad" self-object-representations and hence for the beginning of her therapeutic internal reorganization.

EPILOGUE

Reasons of confidentiality and propriety preclude more than a relatively broad outline of Sheryl's subsequent life course. It can be said that she made excellent use of her postdischarge individual treatment and is no longer psychotic. Although her extramural life often proved difficult, with progressively damped-down but nonetheless upsetting "realistic" and recapitulative near-crises, she survived these, in part by means of the sort of gritty determination and self-sensitivity she had earlier demonstrated during the final phase of her residential experience. She has found a mate, has become a successful mother, and has successfully pursued a career in a technical field of work. I correspond with her from time to time, and her writings convey her ability to have worked through her separation-individuation from me, to be, as she has put it, "my own person."

14

The Developmental Etiology of Borderline and Narcissistic Disorders

The following discussion of the developmental etiology of borderline and narcissistic disorders takes its departure from the contributions of Mahler and her colleagues (Mahler, Pine, and Bergman 1975) and the formulations of Kernberg (1972a, 1975), based in turn upon object-relations theory.

Mahler postulates a sequence of three "phases" of infantile development, pointed ultimately toward the child's attainment of a sense of self and of separateness distinct from the mother. The *phase of absolute autism* — the period of William James's "blooming, buzzing confusion" — occupies the first postnatal month and is characterized by the operation of basic, life-sustaining reflex activities and responses essentially devoid of mental representations. During this period, the infant's kaleidoscopic world is organized around a primitive "good-bad" dichotomy of perceptions in accordance with the pleasure principle, which dictates that whatever reduces drive tension is "good" and whatever increases or fails to reduce it is "bad."

During the ensuing phase of symbiosis, which occupies the period from the second through the sixth postnatal months, the infant's "good-bad" perceptual dichotomy undergoes organization in relation to the figure or person of the mother, thus generating two fused or undifferentiated, polar opposite self-and-object (S-O) internal images or representations. During this period the infant makes essentially no distinction between his nascent sense of self (self-representation) and his dim awareness of the maternal feeding object (maternal object-representation experienced as a breast). It will be seen that the phases of absolute autism and symbiosis coincide with the classical early oral (oral-receptive, oral-incorporative) stage of psychosexual development.

At about six months the infant enters Mahler's third phase, that of *separation-individuation*; indeed, the infant has begun to "hatch," as it were, from the mother-infant "symbiotic dual unity," to manifest sustained attentiveness to his environment, to begin hesitantly to assert his individuality, to crawl away from and back to mother. During the following ten months, the infant's sensory-perceptual and motor-coordinative skills develop with amazing rapidity under the watchful eye of his healthy mother, who appropriately encourages his need to explore himself and the world apart from her, but who also serves as his safe harbor or haven when the going gets rough. During this (roughly) ten-month period, the infant's "all good–all bad" world continues to be organized in accordance with undifferentiated internal self-object representations, albeit in decreasing degree as the period sixteen-twenty-six months approaches, termed by Mahler the *rapprochement subphase* of separation-individuation.

The *rapprochement subphase* witnesses the emergence of a variety of ambivalent, often regressive behaviors indicative of the child's growing awareness that he is indeed a being separate and distinct from his mother. As the period of the "terrible twos" is ushered in, the major conflict over *dependence versus independence* evokes waves of separation anxiety and depression and the child responds to and displays these with provocativeness; negativism; phobic, hysteriform, and obsessional symptoms; and even with terror-stricken perceptual aberrations of a more regressive nature—all of which constitute the so-called *rapprochement crisis*. The child's world continues to be organized in accordance with the "all good-all bad" dichotomy and the pleasure principle, but within the core "all good" and "all bad" self-object representations, self-representations (S) and object-representations (O) have begun to differentiate, a major step in separation-individuation. Thus, the developing child's core conflict between his ineluctable drive toward separation-individuation and his persistent anaclitic need to persevere within the undifferentiated state of symbiosis reaches its peak during this period. With optimal mutual cuing and communicative matching between mother and child throughout this period (i.e., with what Winnicott [1951, 1960] has termed "good enough mothering"), the child will negotiate the rapprochement subphase successfully and will proceed into the next subphase, that of *object constancy.* During this period the self- and object-representations become fully differentiated and the child's inner images of himself, his parents, and others undergo consolidation, hence become stabilized and reliable. At the same time, the "all good–all bad" dichotomy becomes internalized so that the progressively differentiating self- and object-representations contain, respectively, both "good" (G) and "bad" (B) components. In more technical terms, the self-representations and object-representations become invested or "cathected" with *both* libidinal and aggressive drive energies, thereby providing impetus for their progressive neutralization or sublimation. Now, increasingly becoming his own person, the developing child proceeds to replace the primitive splitting defense (with its manifestations in various forms of projection and introjection, denial, and magic-hallucination) with normal repression and, as a consequence, to view himself and the world around him increasingly realistically. On the average, these interrelated self-building processes should be well under way by the end of the third postnatal year, by which time the child has "traversed" the classical anal stage of psychosexual development and has entered the oedipal (phallic-incestuous) stage.

Masterson and I (chapter 12) have traced the etiology of borderline personality disorder to a particular pattern of mother-infant interaction originating in the early separation-individuation phase and reaching its peak during the rapprochement subphase. We have postulated that the mother of the future borderline child and adult, herself borderline, rewards (provides libidinal supplies and gratification to) her infant when he behaves in a dependent, clinging manner toward her, but threatens to reject or abandon (withdraw libidinal supplies and gratification from) him when he makes efforts toward being independent of her, that is, toward separation-individuation. Thus, the infant (later the borderline individual) comes to perceive that independence, growth, and autonomy lead only to abandonment, while remaining symbiotically dependent guarantees the flow and acquisition of necessary support and supplies, albeit at the ultimate and disastrous expense of healthy independence and autonomy. Thus, the borderline individual's double bind: to remain infantile is to retain the mother and her love, to grow is to lose them (the ultimate meaning of the term *loser*).

As Masterson and I have shown (chapter 12, Rinsley 1977, 1978a), the developmental arrest that results from such a pattern of mother-infant interaction accounts very well for the symptomatology of the borderline individual. Self- and object-world remain partly undifferentiated ("Who am I? Who are you?"); the ego remains infantile, pleasure-oriented, deficient in frustration tolerance, hence action-oriented; everybody and everything, including one's self, are either "all good" or "all bad," hence people are perceived and valued in terms of whether they give, please, and reward ("entitlement"), or take and withhold.

The "bad" part of the self continues to be perceived, alternatively, as evil, ugly, dangerous, diseased, and empty, threatened with rejection and abandonment and suffused with the rage and depression which ensue in the wake of frustration, or as passive, obedient, and compliant, hence accepted, valued, and loved for incompetency and ineffectuality. The "raw" instincts associated with these split "bad" self-images remain essentially unsublimated: thus the borderline individual's difficulties with secondary process thinking and the ability to sense and test reality, hence with fore-planning and consistent and sustained achievement. The "good" part of the split self covertly pursues growth but to little avail in view of the continued impact of the split-off "bad" part. Persistent reliance on the primitive splitting defense thus precludes the transition from part-object relations to whole-object relations, with ensuing failure of development of the capacity for empathy; instead there remains an exquisitely sensitive, paranoid-style scanning or reconnoitering perceptual function which causes the borderline individual to appear amazingly aware of the unexpressed intent and motives of others, the aim of which is to detect quickly and ward off any impending or potential rejection or abandonment which threatens disaster (Carter and Rinsley 1977, Rinsley 1977, 1978a).

The borderline individual's partly fused and undifferentiated self-percepts remain subject to the infantile pleasure-ego's reliance upon primitive introjective and projective defenses; hence Kohut calls them *unstable archaic self-objects* (Ornstein 1974). It is this reliance upon such pristine defenses that appears to differentiate the borderline personality from its close relative and subtype, the narcissistic personality.

In accordance with the view of narcissistic personality as a sub-type of borderline personality (Kernberg 1977), it may be postulated that the basic, pathogenic, doubly binding pattern of mother-infant interaction that is etiologic for borderline personality is likewise etiologic for narcissistic personality. Clinical experience indeed bears this out. In narcissistic cases, however, the mother rewards or provides reinforcement and approval for the child's growth toward separation-individuation, *but only* and *ultimately in relation to herself,* thereby fixating the developing child's infantile-grandiosity in relation to achievements which center upon the still partly fused self- and object-images. Kohut calls these *stable archaic self-objects,* and they are, indeed, stable ("unfragmented"), because they are much less subject to introjective-projective mechanisms than are the self-objects of the borderline individual. Put another way, the narcissist's self-object boundary is, as it were, firmer than that of the borderline, albeit still subject to regressive fragmentation at the prospect or in the wake of narcissistic injury (Ornstein 1974). Again, Adler (1979) contrasts the borderline personality's deficient object constancy, conveyed in impaired evocative memory, with the relatively well-preserved object constancy of the narcissistic personality. Thus, the latter appears more internally coherent and capable of sustained, genuine achievement than does his more primitive brother, the borderline, albeit on the basis of a still partly fused, undifferentiated, mother-infant self-object which robs him of any real capacity to invest himself significantly in, and relate meaningfully to, others.

CONCLUSION: THE DEVELOPMENTAL CONTINUUM

Based upon and utilizing a combined developmental and object-relations approach (Rinsley 1979), the concept of major personality or characterologic pathology developed here permits the elaboration of a phasic-chronologic continuum of the major diagnostic syndromes (see Figure 1) and allows the following inferences and conclusions:

1. The correlation of later clinical syndromes with Mahler's phasic view of separation-individuation bears a significant relationship to their similar, earlier correlation with Freud's and Abraham's classical "stages" of psychosexual development (Fenichel 1945), based originally upon the psychoanalytic treatment of adult cases.

2. Considered developmentally, borderline pathology is noted to be more closely related to the primary affective than to the schizophrenic disorders.

3. The continuum accounts for the occurrence of so-called atypical schizophreniform and schizoaffective syndromes.

4. The continuum also allows for an explanation of the more traditional analyzability of narcissistic personalities (Kohut 1971) as contrasted with the need for a combined exploratory-supportive technique with borderline personalities (Kernberg 1972b, Masterson 1976, Rinsley 1978a) in terms of the differences in the degree of stability of their respective internalized self-objects.

5. Finally, the continuum allows for the prediction of the therapeutic value of antidepressant or combined antidepressant and antipsychotic medication in the treatment of borderline cases (D. F. Klein 1977).

FIGURE 1

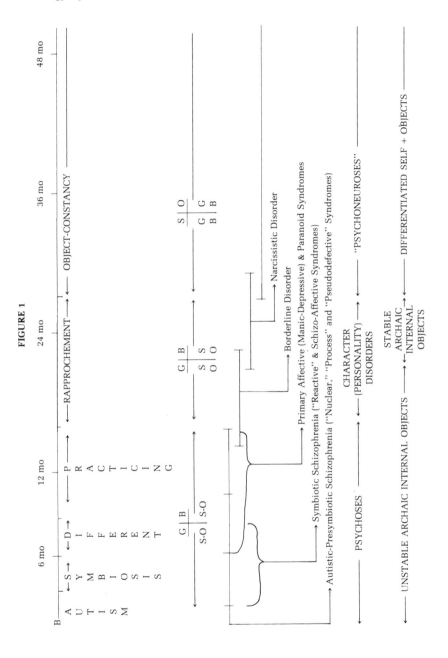

15

Diagnosis and Treatment of Borderline and Narcissistic Children and Adolescents

> In Sigmund Freud's day . . . most of the patients Freud saw were suffering from unresolved Oedipal conflicts developed within the tight-knit and emotionally charged Victorian family. Those children who failed to resolve normal tensions between their own libidinal drives and the needs and prohibitions of their parents grew up to be guilt-ridden and neurotically inhibited adults.
>
> Today . . . more and more psychiatric patients suffer from "disorders of the self" arising from the absence of normal Oedipal conflicts . . . . In today's families, where . . . parents are frequently remote from their children, a different pathology emerges. [Woodward and Mark 1978, p. 70]

This quotation, based largely upon Kohut's contributions (1971) to the psychopathology of the self, is taken from an article entitled "The New Narcissism," a phrase now widely used, particularly by students of the Western cultural scene (Nelson 1977, Lasch 1977, 1978). It reflects the pervasive and eruptive psychosocial and cultural events and changes of the 1960s, which left their indelible marks on that time and which, in gradually decreasing degree, continue to exert widespread social effects (Brende and Rinsley 1979, Rinsley 1978b). A brief consideration of these events and effects is a necessary preliminary to any discussion of the diagnosis and treatment of borderline and narcissistic disorders, particularly those from which increasing numbers of children and adolescents are found to suffer.

The decade of the 1950s, outwardly relatively untroubled and often characterized as a period of smugness, nonetheless served as the setting for the bomb scare ethos and, in this country, rampant if short-lived anticommunist witch-hunting. The ensuing 1960s witnessed the rapid emergence of sweeping changes which bespoke the "demythologization" of traditional religiocultural and familial values: indeed, "future shock" had seemed to have arrived; mental illness was declared a myth; the task of the public schools was to prepare students for "life" and not to bore them with the discipline of learning literate cognitive skills; everyone was to enjoy "equal opportunity"; any and all forms of sexual conduct were normal and healthy, and the "pill" and easy abortions would free the populace of responsibility in favor of an "anything goes" attitude toward sexual relations; "women's liberation" and the so-called unisex and feminist movements at last would free the distaff population from the shackles of a stifling patriarchalism, and women would swell the ranks of the breadwinning work force. Indeed, the decline of the traditional family (Lasch 1977, Voth 1974) and the mutual alienation of parents and children typified increasing numbers of middle-class households, in which parents seemed perplexed over how to deal with their offspring and each other; thus, divorce, illegitimate birth, and juvenile crime rates and the attachment of alienated youth to ear-splitting "rock" cacophonies, mind-altering drugs, and arcane, oriental-styled and culture-alien quasi-religious cults burgeoned (Pruyser 1977).

The changes in traditional family structure reflective of these psychosocial phenomena become more evident when "traditional" and "evolving contemporary" patterns of family life are compared and contrasted.

Traditional Pattern	*Evolving Contemporary Pattern*
1. Sexual intercourse is legitimized only within the marital relationship and in accepted if not inevitable relationship to the birth and rearing of children.	1. Because sexual intercourse (or, for that matter, any form of sexual behavior) is basically if not merely another variety of human communication and since almost all forms of sexual behavior are completely private and equally normal or healthy, sexual activity bears no fundamental or ultimate relationship to child rearing or family building.
2. The family's basic task is the intergenerational transmission of traditional, wider, sociocultural values and norms, thereby providing for the socialization of the next generation's members.	2. The family cannot serve as transmitter of wider sociocultural norms and values since these are subjective and situational.
3. Children are not merely little adults. Their progressive and effectual socialization requires careful, nurturant, parental attention to their age-graded developmental needs and capabilities throughout childhood and adolescence. Such nurturant attention is predominantly supplied by the mother.	3. Because children cannot be expected to conform their thought and behavior to such norms and values, the basic parent-child relationship is essentially symmetric; as a corollary, children shall enjoy the same constitutional and civil rights as adults.
4. The basic task of childhood is separation-individuation from the infant's early symbiotic tie to the mother, the significant	4. The nurturing of children may be equally shared or delegated between the father and the mother and parental roles are

implementation of which is performed by the father, whose basic familial role is that of nest-protector, breadwinner, administrator, and planner.

largely if not fully interchangeable.

5. The basic parent-child relationship, later expressed in the teacher-student relationship, is therefore asymmetric. In decreasing degree as the child matures and progressively socializes, he submits to the parents' benevolent but firm authority and support, and "rewards" the parents by identification with and acceptance of their standards of conduct and belief and by successful performance of the child's "occupation," namely, successful use of the school. The parents' responsibilities to the child include successful promotion of the latter's emancipation and assumption of independence, the last in turn expressed through the child's own marriage and family building. The parents' grandparenting of their children's children serves as metaphor for the ultimate success of their child-rearing efforts.

5. The parents' laissez-faire attitude toward their children, reflected in the symmetric parent-child relationship, seeks no "rewards" in terms of the child's ultimate separation-individuation and eventual emancipation, in turn expressed in marriage and child rearing. The parents' grandparental role vis-à-vis their children's children no longer legitimizes or justifies the parents' parenthood. How the child eventuates is his or her own affair and no business of the parents.

The latter "evolving contemporary" pattern may be taken to indicate a significant degree of identity diffusion among parents whose families reflect notable degrees of schism and skew (Lidz,

Fleck, and Cornelison 1965, Lidz et al. 1968); gender, role, and intergenerational blurring and obfuscation; and communicative mismatch and incoherence (Bateson 1972, Bateson et al. 1968, Singer and Wynne 1965a, b, Wynne 1961, Wynne and Singer 1963a, b). Such families are at significant risk for the "production" of schizophrenic, borderline, and narcissistically fixated children, some of the etiology of which I will now examine.

ETIOLOGIC CONSIDERATIONS

Although a considerable literature has developed regarding borderline disorder (Kernberg 1966, 1970a, 1971b, 1972a, 1975), of particular interest has been the concept of its etiology in terms of early mother-infant interaction (chapter 12, Carter and Rinsley 1977, Masterson 1972b, 1976, Rinsley 1977, 1978a, 1979). Succinctly stated, borderline psychopathology is held to result from a specific developmental arrest or fixation which occurs during the later practicing and rapprochement subphases of separation-individuation (Mahler, Pine, and Bergman 1975), that is, from ten through twenty-six months postnatally as a consequence of a particular mode of mother-infant interaction during that period. Within that mode of interaction, the mother relates to her infant in such fashion as to reward or reinforce his dependency on her, including all forms of behavior which reflect anaclitic-clinging needs, and to threaten withdrawal of her libidinal supplies (rejection, abandonment) in the wake of his normal, oftentimes aggressive efforts toward separation-individuation. These twin themes — reward for dependent clinging, and abandonment in the face of efforts toward separation — reflect the mother's own interactive experience with *her* mother; the mother of the future borderline child projects them onto her infant, as it were, who in turn introjects them, whence they proceed to function as the basis of what Masterson and I have termed the *split object-relations unit* (SORU) of the borderline personality. This powerfully introjected SORU is analogous with the so-called "split internalized bad object," first described by Fairbairn (1944), and is the basis for the ensuing symptomatology of the borderline individual.

Considered developmentally, the borderline personality's separation-individuation failure reflects an incomplete resolution of the otherwise normal mother-infant symbiosis, which occupies the second through the fifth postnatal months. Considered in terms of object relations, the borderline individual has only partly succeeded in differentiating self (self-images, self-representations) from others (object-images, object-representations), with ensuing failure to achieve object constancy (Fraiberg 1969) and a stable self-identity.

The particular pattern of mother-infant interaction that underlies the development of borderline disorder represents but one of a variety of forms of failure of Winnicott's "good enough mothering" (1949, 1960) or "holding environment" (Shapiro et al. 1975). Where such failure exists, the maternal figure is discovered to perceive and respond to the child as someone or something other than what the child really is, a pathogenic process termed *appersonation* or *depersonification*. (chapter 10, Rinsley 1971a). Depersonification reflects a breakdown of an otherwise finely tuned mutual cueing and communicative matching (Mahler, Pine, and Bergman 1975) between mother and infant that is essential for the latter's healthy development. Rather than traversing the normal course of ego development, the depersonified infant proceeds to develop what Winnicott calls a *false self*; this false self evolves as expression of the child's pathological, pseudocomplementary response, in terms of self-image and later self-identity, to the mother's misperception and mishandling of him; instead of a self-image reflective of increasing separation-individuation vis-à-vis the mother, the child proceeds to develop a self-image based upon the depersonifying mother's projections onto him and responds accordingly. Thus, what emerges as the growing child's self-identity actually reflects a pseudo-identity based upon and developing in relation to the mother's own pseudo-identity. As one borderline adolescent girl put it:

I never felt I was my own person . . . . I never knew myself . . . never got rid of feeling empty. . . .Mother always

always decided what was best for me and I stuck with that until it almost drove me crazy.

Another patient, an adolescent Jewish male, interestingly and almost typically said:

> My father told me that if I ever went with a shiksa [a non-Jewish girl] it would kill my mother . . . . That hit me real hard . . . . I was always aware that if I didn't do what my mother wanted it would somehow kill her . . . . I had to marry somebody like her . . . come to think of it I think she really wanted to screw me to keep me from ever getting away from her. God, what a thought!

Experience reveals a significant difference between the mothering patterns of schizophrenic children and adolescents and those of borderline and narcissistic children and adolescents. The mothers of future borderline individuals experienced and expressed gratification with their infants' dependency during most of the first postnatal year, but experienced mounting anxiety, frustration, and hostility toward the infant thereafter as the infant began to initiate significant efforts toward separation-individuation. By contrast, the mothers of future schizophrenic children found little or no gratification in motherhood (Rinsley 1978a); rather, they exhibited from the beginning what Goldfarb (1961) has termed *parental perplexity,* viewing their newborns as odd, strange, confusing, hence persecutory and dangerous almost from the time of delivery. As a consequence of these two differing mothering patterns, the child with borderline disorder develops a pseudo-complementary false self, whereas the schizophrenic child never develops a self at all, a conclusion consistent with the finding that the borderline child has indeed achieved some degree of self-object differentiation whereas the schizophrenic child has not.

Patterns of Depersonification

Analysis of the patterns of mother-child depersonification discovered in 100 adolescents in full-time residential treatment and their families (chapter 10, Rinsley 1971a) revealed the following forms of parental misperception of the growing child:

Psychotic and Severe Borderline Patterns:

1. *The child perceived as an inanimate object* (a "thing"), i.e., the child is perceived and dealt with as a doll, toy, or machine, or, in keeping with current science fiction motifs, may be perceived as a robot, android, even a clone (the last a fascinating and unusual manifestation of the Capgras phenomenon).

2. *The child perceived as a part or excrescence of one's own body, bodily organs, or organ systems.* In this pattern the child is pressed into symbolic use as the parent's eyes or ears, neuromuscular apparatus, phallic genital, excretory products and bodily secretions, etc.

3. *The child perceived as a subhuman animal or a monster,* i.e., the child is perceived in an illusory fashion as either a pet or a dangerous animal or being, such as a wolf, vampire, zombie, and the like.

4. *The child perceived as nonexistent ("abolished"* — Fliess 1961). This extreme pattern, not rarely observed in postpartum psychotic mothers, conveys the parent's need to scotomatize or negatively hallucinate the newborn and extends in less blatant fashion throughout childhood in other cases. It is analogous to the "Don't be!" message of transactional analysis.

Less Severe Borderline and Narcissistic Patterns:

1. *The child perceived as parental surrogate figure,* i.e., the child becomes, in effect, a conscience (superego) representation, a powerful figure who provides guidance, control, and limits for the parent. This pattern represents the classic parent-child reversal of roles.

2. *The child perceived as spouse,* i.e., the child is perceived as a parental surrogate with the fateful addition of a notable degree of sexualization which renders the parent-child tie into a covertly or overtly incestuous relationship.

3. *The child perceived as sibling,* i.e., the child is perceived as a brother or sister and the parent-child tie assumes the features of peer or sibling rivalry and competition, often of a mutually highly destructive nature. Laissez-faire approaches to parenting and child rearing and to classroom educational practice reflect this form of depersonification.

4. *The child perceived as an endlessly infantile or dependent baby.* In contrast to 1 and 2 directly above, which represent varieties of adultomorphization, this pattern reflects the parent's more directly expressed need to keep the child from growing up.

The difference between the more perceptibly borderline and the more perceptibly narcissistic patterns of depersonification is of particular significance. In the former, the parent's "message" is "If you grow up I will abandon you"; in the latter, the parent's message is "You may grow up but only if you never leave me" or "but only if everything you do is ultimately in relation to and centers on me" (Rinsley 1980).

As already noted, the families which "produce" persons with borderline and narcissistic conditions almost invariably harbor considerable parental psychopathology; indeed, their family structure and dynamics often resemble closely those which "produce" one or more schizophrenic children (Bateson et al. 1968, Lidz, Fleck, and Cornelison 1965, Lidz et al. 1968). The salient features of these pathogenic or dysfunctional families include: various degrees of disarticulation from the extrafamilial world; absence of clear-cut lines of authority; confusion of parental executive and nurturing roles; and confusion or obfuscation of parental self- and gender identity and of age and intergenerational roles and functions. Particularly significant in such families is the intergenerational transmission of irrational forms of thinking and relating

(Singer and Wynne 1965a, b, Wynne and Singer 1963a, b), characteristics strikingly similar to the "microscopic evidence of ego
weakness" which Knight (1953) originally found to typify his
borderline patients.[1]

Scapegoating and the "Identified Patient"

In modern parlance, a scapegoat is a person who is made to bear
the blame for the evil, misdeeds, or sins of others. The etymology
of the term is of more than passing interest: "scape" is of Hebrew
origin, originally denoting a demon (*azazel*), later rendered as *oz
azel,* meaning a goat which departs, symbolic of the Yom Kippur
ceremony in which a he-goat, upon whose head are placed the sins
and guilt of the people, is sent into the wilderness. Recall also that
the Devil is often personified as a goat in the literature of medieval
witchcraft. Thus, in its original sense and in accordance with its
latter-day meaning, the scapegoat serves as an expiatory object in
whom are reposed enormous demonic powers, as the bearer of the
individual and collective sins of others who could indeed reverse
the situation and wreak havoc upon the scapegoaters.

The concept of the family scapegoat received important application by Healy and Bronner (1936) in their work on delinquent
youth. Their view found further expression in the contributions of
Johnson (1949, 1959) and Johnson and Szurek (1952) who saw in
the "superego lacunae" of delinquents the expression of parents'
unconscious need to "act out" through their children their own disowned and unexpressed aggressive and sexual needs.

The particular symptomatology which the scapegoated child
(the "identified patient") exhibits will depend upon the particular pattern or patterns of his depersonification. His pseudo-
complementary false self, hence his later distorted self-identity,
will have evolved in intimate relation to those of his depersonifying
parent in whom he cannot repose his otherwise healthy infantile-
megalomania, hence whom he cannot basically trust. Thus, in
significant measure unseparated and unindividuated, the child
feels inadequate, impotent, and empty; as the scapegoat, he paradoxically feels evil and powerful, yet rejected and abandoned.

These characteristics of the borderline child (later, adult) in turn reflect his commitment to not growing up. For example:

> After nearly two years of therapy, an eleven-year-old borderline boy could relate how his mother would come to his bed during his late preschool years and repeatedly read to him excerpts from *The Wizard of Oz*; indeed, she called him "my little wizard," one who would ultimately rescue her ("Dorothy") and allow her to grow up.

> A fourteen-year-old girl in intensive residential treatment put it differently: "My favorite person is Peter Pan. He never grew up . . . he never got old and he lived forever, flying around the big castle" (the castle proved to be symbolic of her mother, from whom she had never individuated, viewing herself as a satellite forever trapped in her mother's field of influence). The girl's mother provided the "complementary message": "I knew right away when I had her she was just like me. Even when she was a little baby she fought me all the way . . . she just wore me out." The mother continued, "She never wanted to grow up . . . just like me!"

The Three "Basic Tasks" of Childhood

To paraphrase Erikson (1963), the three "basic tasks" of the preschool child comprise three metaphors which convey the child's mode of self-experience, viz., "I am" (oral), "I can" (anal), and "I am a boy (girl)" (oedipal). The "I am" metaphor develops as the child successfully differentiates from the mothering figure with the further evolution of a sense of self which signifies the child's separateness per se. The "I can" metaphor conveys the child's awareness of his capacity for mastery and control and to communicate with and have impact upon others and the world generally. The "I am a boy (girl)" metaphor conveys the task that is undertaken in earnest in the latter half of the preschool years and largely completed upon entrance into young adulthood; it signifies the consolidation of the child's gender identity, of the boy's sense of maleness and masculinity and the girl's sense of femaleness and femininity, with all they imply for future object relations, productivity, and creativity.

Because the borderline child (later, adult) has never adequately completed the first of these tasks, he has never completed the ensuing two. He complains, whether directly or through symptomatic behavior, that he does not know who he is. He is bored, feels empty (Kumin 1978) and alienated, is gripped with labile emotions he cannot comprehend or fathom; he says he is "phony," "fake," that he has a "facade," and he senses himself as unreal. And, by the convenient use of projection, he perceives others in the same way. Thus, "Nothing makes sense," "I can't figure myself out," "It's all crap," etc., comprise the statements of the person who is an enigma to himself.

The borderline individual's failure to attain a coherent sense of self leads to the ensuing failure to attain a sense of mastery: thus, "I can't do anything," "I'm a mess," "I never get anything done," "Whatever I do turns out bad," "I have no friends," etc. The task sequence necessary to attain a coherent gender identity likewise is not completed. The gender defect finds expression in a variety of ways that reflect the use of sex and sexuality to assuage more primitive and regressive needs, leading to enduring patterns of infantile polymorphous-perverse sexual expression and behavior which become consolidated during adolescence.

That these self-perceptions of emptiness, powerlessness, and meaninglessness coexist with equally powerful charges of infantile omnipotence and grandiosity constitutes the dynamic and symptomatic paradox of borderline children, adolescents, and adults. They are alternatively or concomitantly demanding, egocentric, presumptuous, importuning, and intimidating as they attempt to extract from a world they perceive as empty and hostile the very supplies they are convinced it lacks or else destructively withholds from them. The paradox, however, yields to the understanding that these patients' mutually conflicting and contradictory perceptions, affects, and actions reflect the endopsychic structure of children between six months and three years of age.

Résumé of Etiology

Disorders of the self, including the major psychoses and the borderline and narcissistic personality or character disorders, represent expressions of developmental arrest or defect. Such arrest or defect in turn mirrors the effects of those social and familial determinants that have brought about an upsurge of narcissistic lifestyles and interpersonal relationships. These considerations must become a major focus for anyone undertaking the diagnosis and treatment of borderline and narcissistic children and their families.

DIAGNOSIS

As noted elsewhere (Rinsley 1977), the literature is often equivocal regarding the differential diagnosis of childhood psychosis and borderline disorder. The nosology presented here views borderline and narcissistic disorders of both children and adults as manifestations of personality or character pathology intermediate, as it were, between the psychoneuroses and the psychoses (Ornstein 1974, Rinsley 1977, 1978a). Thus, object-relations theory allows a gradation of the more severe psychopathological syndromes along a continuum based upon degree of impairment of self-object differentiation and of proneness to regression (Rinsley 1979). In the psychoses, self- and object-representations remain partial and fragmented, hence pervasively undifferentiated, and the degree of regression is correspondingly most profound. In the borderline conditions, some degree of differentiation of self- and object-representations has come about, while they yet remain partial ("part-images" or "part-representations") and prone to regressive fragmentation with associated descent into psychotic modes of perception, cognition, and experience. In the narcissistic conditions, the partially differentiated self- and object-representations are relatively stable, hence more resistant to regressive fragmentation; in such conditions, emergent oedipal themes, significant reliance on repression, an overly strict superego with ensuing obsessional manifestations, and the attainment of some degree of whole-object relations convey a neurotic-like picture (Mahler and Kaplan 1977). Nevertheless, common to all three conditions is the inability to work through real and fantasied separations and losses ("narcissistic injuries") with resultant persistence of vulnerability to the underlying abandonment depression (chapter 12; see also Frankel 1977).

Creak (1963) listed "nine points" that characterize psychotic children: (1) inability to relate normally to people; (2) apparent unawareness of personal identity; (3) preoccupation with inanimate objects; (4) sustained resistance to change; (5) abnormal responses to sensory experience; (6) a tendency to disintegrate into utter confusion; (7) speech disorders, including mutism, echolalia, and noncommunicative verbalizations and vocalizations; (8) various motor disturbances; (9) isolated instances of fantastic prowess against a general background of poor achievement. These characteristics are similar to those Chiland and Lebovici (1977) cited as being characteristic of borderline or prepsychotic children: *preschool child*—irritability, manic hyperactivity, early and intense insomnia, anorexia, poor emotional contact; *early latency child*—school phobia (school refusal), agitation in class, poor impulse control, insensitivity to discipline, negativism, explosive rage, extrafamilial mutism, dysphasia and dyspraxia, bizarre phobias, "psychopathic" traits including extreme cruelty. Engel's psychological test study of "borderline psychotic" children (1963) led her to characterize them as follows: (1) an overwhelming preoccupation with basic survival; (2) intense struggles to maintain, and notable waxing and waning of, reality contact; (3) a view of the environment as making insurmountable demands; (4) the significant use of distance devices, including bizarre fantasy, to ward off others; (5) notable vulnerability to inner and outer stimuli, a characteristic of borderline children which Ekstein (1966) also emphasized. Later (1972) Engel stated:

> As the name implies, borderline children are not as sick as psychotic youngsters. Their alienation from reality is not complete; they struggle to maintain themselves in the face of pathology. Because psychotic and neurotic aspects of their

personality coexist and alternate . . . their treatment offers particular challenges and problems. [p. 138fn]

Until Masterson's pioneering work (1972b, 1973, 1974, 1975), the diagnosis of the borderline adolescent was likewise beset with difficulty. Adolescents recognized as borderline were diagnosed variously as suffering from "severe neurosis," "ego defect and developmental arrest," and "superego defect" (Easson 1969); character disorder or character neurosis; pseudopsychopathic schizophrenia (Bender 1959); "adjustment reaction of adolescence"; "delinquency"; and sundry "conduct" and "behavior" disorders. Masterson's catalog (1972b) of the borderline adolescent's presenting symptomatology included: boredom, restlessness, difficulty in concentration, hypochondriasis, and excessive physical and sexual activity, these often progressing into stealing, drinking, drug abuse, promiscuity, running away, slovenly dress, and dyssocial peer affiliation.

Goldstein and Jones (1977) delineated four major behavioral-symptomatic groups of adolescents with borderline disorder:

Group I. Aggressive-Antisocial
. . . characterized by poorly controlled, impulsive, acting-out behavior. Some degree of inner tension or subjective distress . . . subordinate to the aggressive patterns which appear in many areas of functioning, i.e., family, school, peer relations, the law.

Group II. Active Family Conflict
. . . characterized by a defiant, disrespectful stance toward their parents and belligerence and antagonism in the family setting. They often exhibit signs of inner distress and turmoil, such as tension, anxiety, and somatic complaints. Few manifestations of aggression or rebelliousness appear outside the family.

Group III. Passive-Negative
. . . characterized by negativism, sullenness, and indirect forms of hostility or defiance toward parents and other

authorities. In contrast to Group II, overt defiance and temper outbursts are infrequent and there is superficial compliance to adults' wishes. School difficulties are frequent, typically described as underachievement, although there is little evidence of (overtly aggressive or) disruptive behavior.

Group IV. Withdrawn–Socially Isolated
    . . . characterized by marked isolation, general uncommunicativeness, few, if any, friends, and excessive dependence on one or both parents. Gross fears or signs of marked anxiety and tension are often present. Much of their unstructured time is spent in solitary pursuits. [pp. 215–216]

Clinical experience with these adolescent patients attests to the borderline early adolescent's symptomatic similarity to the borderline latency child, hence to the latter's more protean, psychotic-like clinical appearance. As the borderline adolescent traverses middle and late adolescence, the clinical picture in many cases comes increasingly to resemble that of the borderline adult, including the four borderline "types" originally described by Grinker, Werble, and Drye (1968) and later by Grinker and Werble (1977).

TREATMENT

The literature devoted to the treatment of children with borderline and narcissistic disorders is, to say the least, scanty. A few salient exceptions include Ekstein's classic work involving pre-adolescents and adolescents (1966), Masterson's contributions (1971a, b, 1972a, b, 1973, 1974, 1975) to the treatment of adolescents with borderline syndrome (Rinsley 1974), and a brief review chapter by Fuchs and vanderSchraaf (1979). One reason for this state of affairs is the yet unsettled nature of the diagnostic nosology of borderline and narcissistic disorders. Another related reason is that vast numbers of children with borderline disorder are labeled as suffering from one or another variety of "hyperkinetic syndrome" or "minimal brain damage," and hence are treated largely or exclusively with drugs. Further compounding the problem is the trend away from the use of long-term intensive psychotherapies. Finally, there is the significant trend away from what has pejoratively come to be termed the "institutionalization" of children and adolescents, with its concomitant headlong rush toward "community-based" treatment accompanied by legislation and judicial decrees which complicate the residential or inpatient placement and treatment of seriously disturbed children and youth.[2]

The treatment of children with borderline and narcissistic conditions, as with all seriously troubled or disturbed young people, ideally pursues the following goals:

1. Establishing and maintaining a stable, predictable ("average expectable") environment within which individualized understanding and resolution of psychopathology may be developed and carried out, and providing appropriate opportunities for otherwise healthy growth and development.
2. Controlling untoward symptomatic behavior.
3. Working with the young patient's family with a view toward unraveling the complex strands of mutually depersonifying communications and interactions from which the "identified patient's" psychopathology has emerged and become manifest.
4. Reestablishing the patient's blighted processes of separation-individuation and identity-formation.

The Residential or Inpatient Setting

Residential or inpatient treatment, whether part- or full-time, is reserved for those children and adolescents whose symptomatology precludes the effective use of outpatient therapy, and seeks to provide the stable, predictable milieu which many borderline and severely narcissistic youngsters lack. The criteria for home removal and admission into therapeutic residence were laid down as long ago as 1934 by Potter (1934a, b), and more recently by Easson (1969), Rinsley (1971b, 1974, 1980), and Wardle (1974). I have condensed and restated these criteria as follows:

1. Those cases in which the symptomatology, behavior, or conduct is seriously disruptive or bizarre, hence,
2. In which the youngster's ability to utilize home, school, church, and other growth-supportive adults and institutions is severely or profoundly compromised.
3. Those cases in which progressive psychosocial deterioration is in evidence despite all efforts, short of hospitalization or residential admission, to arrest or remit it.
4. Those cases in which parental-familial pathology necessitates removal of the youngster from a clearly dysfunctional, pathogenic family nexus.

It should be emphasized that the admission of a child or adolescent into full-time residential or inpatient treatment must be a highly selective procedure based upon thorough knowledge of the child's preadmission situation and of the family and the wider social environment (Szurek et al. 1971). Because these youngsters traditionally express their inner suffering by "acting out," that is, bizarre, antisocial, and not rarely destructive and self-destructive behavior, an early, ongoing feature of the residential or inpatient setting is to control such behavior for the purpose of assisting the patient to translate it, as it were, into communication that can be mutually understood or consensually validated.[3]

Outpatient Treatment

Not all children and adolescents with borderline and narcissistic personality disorders require full-time residential or inpatient treatment. In contrast with those who do, the candidate for outpatient treatment will meet the following criteria:

1. Symptomatology devoid of such strangeness, bizarreness, or disruptiveness and destructiveness as would cause social ostracism or danger to life.
2. A reasonable degree of age-appropriate academic achievement.
3. A family setting which, despite its pathogenic features, is nonetheless able to provide the elements of ongoing support for

individual and group change and growth. Such support includes parental recognition of their child's need for treatment and adequate voluntary acceptance of and cooperation with its requirements, including their and their child's prompt attendance at therapeutic sessions, payment of the requisite fees, and the like.

Specific Therapeutic Modalities

Individual psychotherapy. Whether provided within the residential or inpatient setting or on an outpatient basis, dynamically oriented individual psychotherapy is a sine qua non for the adequate treatment of borderline and narcissistic children and adolescents. Its course traverses three stages: (1) a resistance (testing) stage; (2) an introjective or definitive (working-through) stage; and (3) a resolution (separation) stage (Masterson 1972b, Rinsley 1974). All three stages must have appeared and the resolution stage have been on the way toward completion before the therapy can be considered successful.[4]

During the resistance or testing stage, the young patient's rapidly developing "psychotic transference" appears in a wide range of maneuvers directed toward keeping his autistic pseudocommunity (often involving pervasive and delusional fantasy) in concealment. Because neither the substantive content nor the defensive nature of the pseudocommunity can be interpreted before the therapist understands it, the basic task of the resistance stage becomes the generation of mutual trust between patient and therapist, essential to which is the patient's growing awareness that his intimate revelations will not provoke the therapist's rejection or abandonment or a variety of other fantasied disasters to himself, his parents, and his family. As this proceeds, and both therapist and patient come to a mutual awareness of the content of the patient's bizarre inner world, its use by the patient as a means of coping with the family's dysfunctional pattern of depersonifying communications gradually becomes evident and therefore interpretable. For example,

A late-latency boy with borderline disorder required over a year of therapy before he could reveal his fantasy that his mother had placed a terrifying dragon in his penis during his delivery, thus rendering that organ into an awful engine of destruction. The fantasy could in part be understood as the boy's defense against a mother who viewed him essentially as a phallic extension of herself and whose intense phallic envy found expression in her hostile and destructive fantasies toward male genitalia. The dragon fantasy also served as a defensive warning to the mother not to attempt to appropriate the penis under penalty of her own destruction. [5]

A six-year-old borderline girl in full-time residential treatment was able to share with her therapist, after some six months of therapy, her fantasy that she had been magically impregnated with millions of unborn babies ("fee-fees") whom she had at all costs to keep inside her body lest, being born, they would perish in a cruel outside world. Her fantasy in part expressed her continued reliance on a massive splitting defense ("millions of 'fee-fees'") through introjective identification with marked anal-retentive overlay (". . . got to keep them in me") to ward off the danger of her own birth into a hostile, persecutory, ungiving world (failure of separation-individuation). The mutual clinging between the patient and her depressed mother who also suffered from borderline syndrome was viewed as a manifestation of the little girl's fear that growing up would lead to her and her mother's death.

The task of the definitive (working-through) stage of therapy involves insightful exposure and interpretation of the patient's manic defenses (persistent infantile megalomania) and desperate need to cling and to remain dependent, hence not to grow up, etiologic for which is the basic splitting defense against the underlying abandonment depression and the associated wish for symbiotic reunion (chapter 12, Masterson 1975). As these defenses are revealed, understood, and interpreted within the therapeutic transference, the patient begins in earnest the previously blighted work of separation-individuation, i.e., completion of the work of the rapprochement subphase and beginning attainment of object constancy with its attendant sense of separateness and wholeness (Rinsley 1977, 1978a). This work is completed largely during the resolution or separation stage of therapy, when the eventual, successful termination process symbolizes the patient's own growing autonomy.

Family therapy. Only in a minority of cases can the therapy of the child or adolescent with borderline or narcissistic personality disorder proceed to a successful conclusion in the absence of a concomitant family therapy process. By the same token, family therapy is a necessary ingredient in the complex process by which the family's pathogenic nexus of depersonifying communications and relationships may be exposed, understood, interpreted, and eventually resolved (Zentner and Aponte 1970).[6]

Basic questions that the prospective family therapist poses in each case include: (1) Is the family's pathology of such nature and degree as will permit the surrogate figures, whether natural, adoptive, or foster parents, to support the "identified patient's" treatment, including their own participation in it as part of a group process? (2) If so, then what are the specifics of the particular family's depersonifying nexus of communications and interactions? (3) How do these provide insight into the family's particular pattern of confused, distorted, or obfuscated age, intergenerational, gender, administrative, and nurturant roles and practices? (4) Assuming that these may be identified, how capable is the family, including the "identified patient," of healthily altering them?

It is evident that the prospective family therapist will be called upon to decide both critical-ethical and psychodynamic-technical issues, the former in relation to the acknowledged "evolving contemporary pattern" of family life, which is in turn related to the increasing number of families whose dysfunctional *modus vivendi* reflects their alienation and anomie. In order to provide help to these families, the family therapist must be a healthily acculturated individual who is able to serve as a trustworthy identification object. In other words, a significant aspect of family therapy is the therapist's ability to re-parent the parents. Such re-parenting in effect provides the parents an opportunity to begin to resolve the pathology which arose from their own dysfunctional parenting and to begin to provide healthy parenting for their own children. Although a detailed account of the techniques for accomplishing this formidable task is beyond the scope of this chapter, it may be said that they amount to the means for resolving the individual and familial psychopathology common to no less than three successive generations.

Psychopharmacology. The more recent advances in understanding the etiology and dynamics of borderline and narcissistic disorders generally, and those of children and adolescents specifically, have not yet found their way into the standard child psychiatry texts, much less into those few works devoted to pediatric psychopharmacology. Major current texts (Gittelman-Klein 1975, Werry 1978, White 1977) take due note of the unsettled nature of child psychiatric diagnosis and nosology and tend to include those cases diagnosable as borderline according to our criteria under the rubrics of childhood psychosis or some form of "behavior disorder." The more purely narcissistic conditions, which may be considered to represent "higher level" borderline conditions (Ornstein 1974), fare even less well in the current literature. Gittelman-Klein et al. (1978) put it succinctly: "a close relationship between drug and diagnosis is . . . uncommon in pediatric psychopharmacology" (p. 139).

Many children and adolescents suffering from borderline and narcissistic disorders are accorded a variety of diagnoses, usually descriptive, in both the second and third editions of the *Diagnostic and Statistical Manual of Mental Disorders* (American Psychiatric Association 1968, 1980), including attention deficit disorders, pervasive developmental disorders, conduct disorders, eating disorders, anxiety disorders, and the like, and their treatment utilizing psychoactive agents is, with few exceptions, empirical. The following generalizations appear to be warranted:

1. Those children with borderline and narcissistic disorders who manifest what DSM-III labels as "attention deficit disorders" (that is, those suffering from "minimal brain dysfunction" or "hyperkinetic reaction") tend to respond to stimulant agents such as the amphetamines and methylphenidate. A minority are benefited by phenothiazines.

2. Those children with borderline disorders who manifest what DSM-III labels as "separation anxiety disorder" respond to imipramine.

3. Those children and adolescents with borderline disorders who manifest what DSM-III labels as "chronic motor tic disorder" (Gilles de la Tourette syndrome) benefit from haloperidol.

4. The remainder of children and adolescents in the poly-symptomatic group of borderline and narcissistic disorders respond differentially to the range of available antipsychotic and antidepressant medications, including the phenothiazines and haloperidol, the tricyclic antidepressants, and the monoamine oxidase inhibitors. The severely borderline adolescent who manifests episodes of grossly psychotic behavior expressed in alloplastic symptomatology responds best to antipsychotic agents, particularly thioridazine and chlorpromazine. In adolescent cases manifesting predominantly autoplastic symptomatology, including marked motor inhibition, lethargy, and withdrawal accompanied by psychotic thinking, the antipsychotic agents generally have a notably beneficial effect; in some of these cases, which some consider to represent manifestations of primary affective (psychotic depressive, manic-depressive) disorder appearing during adolescence, tricyclic antidepressants may prove beneficial. The role of lithium salts in the treatment of children and adolescents with borderline and narcissistic disorders has not been established.

Notes

1. L'Abate (1976) has reviewed in detail the major contributions to understanding pathogenic-dysfunctional families.

2. The prototypical case involving the mandate of "due process" in the legal commitment of minor children is *Bartley* v. *Kremens,* 402F. Supp., E.D. Pa., 1975, 96 S. Ct. 1457, 1976, which evolved into *Parham* v. *J.R.,* 99 S. Ct. 2493, 61L. Ed. 2d (U.S. 1979).

3. A more comprehensive discussion of the characteristics of the optimally therapeutic residential or inpatient milieu for these seriously disturbed children and adolescents is set forth elsewhere (Rinsley 1980).

4. The paradigm for this demanding and difficult work continues to be the contributions of Ekstein and his colleagues at the Menninger Foundation's Southard School and later at the Reiss-Davis Clinic in Los Angeles (1966, 1971), and the clinical contributions of Masterson (1972b, 1974). The role and significance of psychotherapy within the residential setting have been reviewed by Greenwood (1955), Robinson et al. (1957), and Hersov (1974).

5. Supervised case of Charles Staunton, M.D.

6. A recent review of this subject has been presented by Mandelbaum (1977).

References

Abend, S., Kachalsky, H., and Greenberg, H. R. (1968). Reactions of adolescents to short-term hospitalization. *American Journal of Psychiatry* 124: 949–954.

Abraham, K. (1927). *Selected Papers on Psycho-Analysis*. London: Hogarth.

Ackerman, N. W. (1958). *The Psychodynamics of Family Life*. New York: Basic Books.

————(1962). Adolescent problems: a symposium on family disorder. *Family Process* 1: 202–213.

Adler, G. (1979). The myth of the alliance with borderline patients. *American Journal of Psychiatry* 136 (5): 642–645.

Aichhorn, A. (1935). *Wayward Youth*. New York: Viking.

————(1964). *Delinquency and Child Guidance*. Collected Papers. Ed. D. Fleischmann. New York: International Universities Press.

Allport, G. W. (1968). *The Person in Psychology: Selected Essays*. Boston: Beacon.

American Psychiatric Association (1968). *Diagnostic and Statistical Manual of Mental Disorders*. 2nd ed. Washington, D.C.: American Psychiatric Association.

————(1980). *Diagnostic and Statistical Manual of Mental Disorders*. 3rd ed. Washington, D.C.: American Psychiatric Association.

Bateson, G. (1972). *Steps to an Ecology of Mind.* New York: Ballantine.

Bateson, G. et al. (1968). Toward a theory of schizophrenia. In *Communication, Family, and Marriage (Human Communication,* Vol. 1), ed. D. D. Jackson, pp. 31–54. Palo Alto: Science and Behavior Books.

Beavers, W. R. and Blumberg, S. (1968). A follow-up study of adolescents treated in an inpatient setting. *Diseases of the Nervous System* 29: 606–612.

Beckett, P. G. S. (1965). *Adolescents Out of Step: Their Treatment in a Psychiatric Hospital.* Detroit: Wayne State University Press.

Bender, L. (1947). Childhood schizophrenia: clinical study of 100 schizophrenic children. *American Journal of Orthopsychiatry* 17: 40–56.

———(1953). Childhood schizophrenia. *Psychiatric Quarterly* 27: 663–681.

———(1956). Schizophrenia in childhood: its recognition, description, and treatment. *American Journal of Orthopsychiatry* 26: 499–506.

———(1959). The concept of pseudopsychopathic schizophrenia in adolescents. *American Journal of Orthopsychiatry* 29: 491–512.

Benedek, T. (1952). Personality development. In *Dynamic Psychiatry,* ed. F. Alexander and H. Ross, pp. 63–113. Chicago: University of Chicago Press.

———(1956). Psychological aspects of mothering. *American Journal of Orthopsychiatry* 26: 272–278.

Beres, D. (1961). Character formation. In *Adolescents: Psychoanalytic Approach to Problems and Therapy,* ed. S. Lorand and H. I. Schneer, pp. 1–9. New York: Hoeber.

Berger, B. (1963). Adolescence and beyond. *Social Problems* 10: 394–408.

Bergman, P., and Escalona, S. (1949). Unusual sensitivities in very young children. *Psychoanalytic Study of the Child* 3/4: 333–352.

Berne, E. (1961). *Transactional Analysis in Psychotherapy.* New York: Grove.

———(1964a). *Games People Play: The Psychology of Human Relationships.* New York: Grove.

———(1964b). Principles of transactional analysis. *Current Psychiatric Therapies* 4: 35–45.

Beskind, H. (1962). Psychiatric inpatient treatment of adolescents: a review of clinical experience. *Comprehensive Psychiatry* 3: 354–369.

Bleuler, E. (1950). *Dementia Praecox, or the Group of Schizophrenias.* Trans. J. Zinkin. New York: International Universities Press.

Blos, P. (1941). *The Adolescent Personality*. New York: Appleton-Century-Crofts.

Bockoven, J. S. (1963). *Moral Treatment in American Psychiatry*. New York: Springer.

Boomer, L. W. (1969). The determination of the grade level for children in special education classes for the emotionally disturbed using the WISC, the WRAT, and previous grade placement. Unpublished Master's Thesis, Graduate School of Education, University of Kansas.

Bowlby, J. (1951). *Maternal Care and Mental Health*. Geneva: World Health Organization; New York: Columbia University Press.

———(1960a). Grief and mourning in infancy and early childhood. *Psychoanalytic Study of the Child* 15: 9–52.

———(1960b). Separation anxiety. *International Journal of Psycho-Analysis* 41: 89–113.

———(1961). Processes of mourning. *International Journal of Psycho-Analysis* 42: 317–340.

———(1962). Childhood bereavement and psychiatric illness. In *Aspects of Psychiatric Research,* ed. D. Richter et al., pp. 262–293. London: Oxford.

Brende, J. O., and Rinsley, D. B. (1979). Borderline disorder, altered states of consciousness, and glossolalia. *Journal of the American Academy of Psychoanalysis* 7(2): 165–188.

Bryan, W. A. (1936). *Administrative Psychiatry*. New York: Pageant.

Burnett, O. C. (1965). The dynamics of classroom grouping, curriculum, management and transfer of emotionally disturbed adolescents in a residential setting. Unpublished Master's Thesis, Graduate School of Education, University of Kansas.

Cameron, D. E. (1951). The day hospital: an approach to expanding hospital facilities. In *Mental Hospitals, 1950: Proceedings of the Second Mental Hospital Institute.* Washington, D.C.: American Psychiatric Association.

Cameron, N. (1947). *The Psychology of Behavior Disorders*. Boston: Houghton Mifflin.

Carter, L., and Rinsley, D. B. (1977). Vicissitudes of "empathy" in a borderline adolescent. *International Review of Psychoanalysis* 4(3): 317–326.

Charney, I. W. (1963). Regression and reorganization in the "isolation treatment" of children: a clinical contribution to sensory deprivation research. *Journal of Child Psychology and Psychiatry* 4: 47–60.

Chiland, C., and Lebovici, S. (1977). Borderline or prepsychotic conditions in childhood — a French point of view. In *Borderline Personality Disorders: The Concept, the Syndrome, the Patient,* ed. P. Hartocollis, pp. 143–154. New York: International Universities Press.

Cohen, R. L., Charney, I. W., and Lembke, P. (1960). Casework with parents of children in residential treatment. Paper read at the Annual Meeting of the American Orthopsychiatric Association, Chicago, February.

————(1961). Parental expectations as a force in treatment. *Archives of General Psychiatry* 4: 471–478.

Coleman, J. S. (1961). *The Adolescent Society.* New York: Free Press of Glencoe.

Conolly, J. (1856). *On the Treatment of the Insane Without Mechanical Restraints.* London: Smith-Elder and Company.

Coolidge, J. C. et al. (1962). Patterns of aggression in school phobia. *Psychoanalytic Study of the Child* 17: 319–333.

Creak, E. M. (1963). Childhood psychosis: a review of 100 cases. *British Journal of Psychiatry* 109(1): 84–89.

Deutsch, H. (1942). Some forms of emotional disturbance and their relationship to schizophrenia. In *Neuroses and Character Types: Clinical Psychoanalytic Studies,* pp. 262–281. New York: International Universities Press, 1965.

Devereux, G. (1956). *Therapeutic Education: Its Theoretical Bases and Practice.* New York: Harper.

Dollard, J., and Miller, N. E. (1950). *Personality and Psychotherapy.* New York: McGraw-Hill.

Douvan, E., and Adelson, J. (1966). *The Adolescent Experience.* New York: Wiley.

Dunn, L. M. (1963). *Exceptional Children in the Schools.* New York: Holt, Rinehart and Winston.

Easson, W. M. (1969). *The Severely Disturbed Adolescent: Inpatient, Residential, and Hospital Treatment.* New York: International Universities Press.

Eissler, K. R. (1958). Notes on problems of technique in the psychoanalytic treatment of adolescents. *Psychoanalytic Study of the Child* 13: 223–254.

Ekstein, R. (1966). *Children of Time and Space, Of Action and Impulse.* New York: Appleton-Century-Crofts. Reprinted 1974. New York: Jason Aronson.

————(1971). *The Challenge: Despair and Hope in the Conquest of Inner Space: Further Studies of the Psychoanalytic Treatment of Severely Disturbed Children.* New York: Brunner/Mazel.

Ekstein, R., Bryant, K., and Freedman, S. (1958). Childhood schizophrenia and allied conditions. In *Schizophrenia: A Review of the Syndrome,* ed. L. Bellak. New York: Logos.

Elkin, F., and Westley, W. A. (1955). The myth of adolescent culture. *American Sociological Review* 20: 680–684.

Engel, M. (1963). Psychological testing of borderline psychotic children. *Archives of General Psychiatry* 8(5): 426–434.

————(1972). *Psychopathology in Childhood: Social, Diagnostic, and Therapeutic Aspects.* New York: Harcourt Brace Jovanovich.

Erikson, E. H. (1956). The problem of ego identity. *Journal of the American Psychoanalytic Association* 4: 56–121.

————(1963). *Childhood and Society.* Revised Edition. New York: Norton.

Esman, A. H. (1962). Visual hallucinations in young children. *Psychoanalytic Study of the Child* 17: 334–343.

Fairbairn, W. R. D. (1944). Endopsychic structure considered in terms of object-relationships. In *Psychoanalytic Studies of the Personality,* pp. 82–136. London: Tavistock Publications, 1952; also in *An Object-Relations Theory of the Personality,* pp. 82–136. New York: Basic Books, 1954.

————(1954). *An Object-Relations Theory of the Personality.* New York: Basic Books. *(Psycho-Analytic Studies of the Personality.* Tavistock: London, 1952)

Federn, P. (1952). *Ego Psychology and the Psychoses.* Ed. E. Weiss. New York: Basic Books.

Felix, R. H. (1961). The psychiatric training of the medical student and the psychiatrist. *Bulletin of the Menninger Clinic* 25: 213–224.

Fenichel, O. (1945). *The Psychoanalytic Theory of Neurosis.* New York: Norton.

Ferenczi, S. (1913). Stages in the development of the sense of reality, pp. 181–203. In *Sex in Psychoanalysis.* New York: Dover, 1956.

Fliess, R. (1961). On the mother-child unit: its disturbances and their consequences for the ego of the neurotic adult. In *Ego and Body Ego: Contributions to Their Psychoanalytic Psychology,* pp. 21–76. New York: Schulte.

Fountain, G. (1961). Adolescent into adult: an inquiry. *Journal of the American Psychoanalytic Association* 9: 417–433.

Fraiberg, S. (1969). Libidinal object constancy and mental representation. *Psychoanalytic Study of the Child* 24: 9–47.

Frankel, S. A. (1977). The treatment of a narcissistic disturbance in childhood. *International Journal of Psychoanalytic Psychotherapy* 6: 165–186.

Freud, A. (1928). *Introduction to the Technique of Child Analysis.* Nervous and Mental Disease Monograph Series, no. 48. New York: Nervous and Mental Disease Publishing Company.

———(1935). *Introduction to Psychoanalysis for Teachers and Parents.* New York: Emerson.

———(1946). *The Ego and Mechanisms of Defence.* New York: International Universities Press.

———(1958). Adolescence. *Psychoanalytic Study of the Child* 13: 255–278.

Freud, A., and Dann, S. (1951). An experiment in group upbringing. *Psychoanalytic Study of the Child* 6: 127–168.

Freud, S. (1905). Three essays on the theory of sexuality. *Standard Edition* 7: 125–245.

———(1911). Formulations on the two principles of mental functioning. *Standard Edition* 12: 218–226.

———(1914). On narcissism: an introduction. *Standard Edition* 14: 69–102.

———(1917). A metapsychological supplement to the theory of dreams. *Standard Edition* 14: 219–235.

———(1927). Fetishism. *Standard Edition* 21: 152–157.

———(1940). Splitting of the ego in the process of defence. *Standard Edition* 23: 275–278.

Friedlander, K. (1947). *The Psycho-Analytical Approach to Juvenile Delinquency.* New York: International Universities Press.

———(1949). Latent delinquency and ego development. In *Searchlights on Delinquency: New Psychoanalytic Studies,* ed. K. Eissler, pp. 205–215. New York: International Universities Press.

Friedman, S. W. (1966). The diagnostic process during the evaluation of an adolescent girl. In *Children of Time and Space, Of Action and Impulse,* ed. R. Eckstein, pp. 15–62. New York: Appleton-Century-Crofts.

Fuchs, R. R., and vanderSchraaf, A. H. (1979). Borderline conditions. In *Clinician's Handbook of Childhood Psychopathology,* ed. M. M. Josephson and R. T. Porter, pp. 69–82. New York: Jason Aronson.

Geleerd, E. R. (1946). A contribution to the problem of psychoses in childhood. *Psychoanalytic Study of the Child* 2: 271–291.

———(1957). Some aspects of psychoanalytic technique in adolescence. *Psychoanalytic Study of the Child* 12: 263–283.

———(1958). Borderline states in childhood and adolescence. *Psychoanalytic Study of the Child* 13: 279–295.

———(1961). Some aspects of ego vicissitudes in adolescence. *Journal of the American Psychoanalytic Association* 9: 394–405.

Giovacchini, P. L. (1970). Effects of adaptive and disruptive aspects of early relationships upon later parental functioning. In *Parenthood: Its Psychology and Psychopathology,* ed. E. J. Anthony and T. Benedek, pp. 525–537. Boston: Little, Brown.

Gitelson, M. (1948). Character synthesis: the psychotherapeutic problem of adolescence. *American Journal of Orthopsychiatry* 18: 422–431.

Gittelman-Klein, R., ed. (1975). *Recent Advances in Child Psychopharmacology* (Child Psychiatry and Psychology Series). New York: Human Sciences Press.

Gittelman-Klein, R. et al. (1978). Diagnostic classifications and psychopharmacological indications. In *Pediatric Psychopharmacology: The Use of Behavior Modifying Drugs in Children,* ed. J. S. Werry, pp. 136–167. New York: Brunner/Mazel.

Glasser, W. (1965). *Reality Therapy.* New York: Harper.

Goldfarb, W. (1945). Psychological privation in infancy and subsequent adjustment. *American Journal of Orthopsychiatry* 15: 247–255.

———(1961). *Childhood Schizophrenia.* Cambridge: Harvard University Press.

Goldstein, K. (1939). *The Organism: A Holistic Approach to Biology.* New York: American Book Company.

———(1959a). Functional disturbances in brain damage. In *American Handbook of Psychiatry,* vol. 1, ed. S. Arieti, pp. 770–794. New York: Basic Books.

———(1959b). The organismic approach. In *American Handbook of Psychiatry,* vol. 2, ed. S. Arieti, pp. 1333–1347. New York: Basic Books.

Goldstein, M. J., and Jones, J. E. (1977). Adolescent and familial precursors of borderline and schizophrenic conditions. In *Borderline*

Personality Disorders: The Concept, the Syndrome, the Patient, ed. P. Hartocollis, pp. 213-229. New York: International Universities Press.

Gralnick, A. (1966). Psychoanalysis and treatment of adolescents in a private hospital. In *Science and Psychoanalysis,* ed. J. Masserman, vol. 9, pp. 102-108. New York: Grune and Stratton.

————(1969). *The Psychiatric Hospital as a Therapeutic Instrument.* New York: Brunner-Mazel.

Greaves, D. C., and Regan, P. F. (1957). Psychotherapy of adolescents at intensive hospital treatment levels. In *Psychotherapy of the Adolescent,* ed. B. H. Balser, pp. 130-143. New York: International Universities Press.

Greenwood, E. D. (1955). The role of psychotherapy in residential treatment. *American Journal of Orthopsychiatry* 25(4): 692-698.

Grinker, R. R., and Werble, B. (1977). *The Borderline Patient.* New York: Jason Aronson.

Grinker, R. R., Werble, B., and Drye, R. C. (1968). *The Borderline Syndrome: A Behavioral Study of Ego-Functions.* New York: Basic Books.

Guntrip, H. (1961). *Personality Structure and Human Interaction.* New York: International Universities Press.

————(1969). *Schizoid Phenomena, Object Relations, and the Self.* New York: International Universities Press.

Hamilton, G. (1950). *Psychotherapy in Child Guidance.* New York: Columbia University Press.

Harley, M. (1961). Some observations on the relationship between genitality and structural development in adolescence. *Journal of the American Psychoanalytic Association* 9: 434-460.

Hartmann, H. (1955). Notes on the theory of sublimation. In *Essays on Ego Psychology: Selected Problems in Psychoanalytic Theory,* pp. 215-240. New York: International Universities Press, 1964.

Healy, W., and Bronner, A. F. (1936). *New Light on Delinquency and Its Treatment.* New Haven: Yale University Press.

Healy, W., Bronner, A. F., and Bowers, A. M. (1930). *The Structure and Meaning of Psychoanalysis.* New York: Knopf.

Hendrickson, W. J. (1971). Training in adolescent psychiatry: the role of experience with inpatients. In *Teaching and Learning Adolescent Psychiatry,* ed. D. Offer and J. F. Masterson, pp. 21-38. Springfield, Illinois: Charles C Thomas.

Hendrickson, W. J., Holmes, D. J., and Waggoner, R. W. (1959). Psychotherapy with hospitalized adolescents. *American Journal of Psychiatry* 116: 527-532.

Hersov, L. A. (1974). Neurotic disorders with special reference to school refusal. In *The Residential Psychiatric Treatment of Children,* ed. P. A. Barker, pp. 105-141. New York: Wiley.

Hess, R. D., and Goldblatt, I. (1957). The status of adolescents in American society: a problem in social identity. *Child Development* 28: 459-468.

Hilgard, E. R. (1956). *Theories of Learning.* 2nd ed. New York: Appleton-Century-Crofts.

Hirschberg, J. C. (1953). The role of education in the treatment of emotionally disturbed children through planned ego development. *American Journal of Orthopsychiatry* 23: 684-690.

Holmes, D. J. (1964). *The Adolescent in Psychotherapy.* Boston: Little, Brown.

Inhelder, B., and Piaget, J. (1958). *The Growth of Logical Thinking from Childhood to Adolescence.* New York: Basic Books.

Jacobson, E. (1964). *The Self and the Object World.* New York: International Universities Press.

Johnson, A. M. (1949). Sanctions for superego lacunae of adolescents. In *Searchlights on Delinquency: New Psychoanalytic Studies,* ed. K. R. Eissler, pp. 225-245. New York: International Universities Press.

————(1959). Juvenile delinquency. In *American Handbook of Psychiatry,* vol. 1, 1st ed., ed. S. Arieti, pp. 840-856. New York: Basic Books.

Johnson, A. M., and Szurek, S. A. (1952). The genesis of antisocial acting out in children and adults. *Psychoanalytic Quarterly* 21: 323-343.

————(1954). Etiology of antisocial behavior in delinquents and psychopaths. *Journal of the American Medical Association* 154: 814-817.

Jones, M. (1953). *The Therapeutic Community: A New Treatment Method in Psychiatry.* New York: Basic Books.

Josselyn, I. M. (1952). *The Adolescent and His World.* New York: Family Service Association of America.

Kanner, L. (1943). Autistic disturbances of affective contact. *Nervous Child* 2: 217-250.

————(1949). Problems of nosology and dynamics of early infantile autism. *American Journal of Orthopsychiatry* 19: 416-426.

————(1961). American contributions to the development of child psychiatry. *Psychiatric Quarterly Supplement,* part 1, 35: 11-12.

————(1965). Infantile autism and the schizophrenias. *Behavioral Science* 10: 412-420.

Kasanin, J. S. (1946). *Language and Thought in Schizophrenia: Collected Papers.* Berkeley and Los Angeles: University of California Press.

Katan, A. (1951). The role of displacement in agoraphobia. *International Journal of Psycho-Analysis* 32: 41–50.

Keniston, K. (1965). *The Uncommitted: Alienated Youth in American Society.* New York: Harcourt Brace.

Kernberg, O. F. (1966). Structural derivatives of object relationships. *International Journal of Psycho-Analysis* 47: 236–253.

———(1967). Borderline personality organization. *Journal of the American Psychoanalytic Association* 15: 641–685.

———(1968). The treatment of patients with borderline personality organization. *International Journal of Psycho-Analysis* 49: 600–619.

———(1970a). A psychoanalytic classification of character pathology. *Journal of the American Psychoanalytic Association* 18: 800–822.

———(1970b). Factors in the psychoanalytic treatment of narcissistic personalities. *Journal of the American Psychoanalytic Association* 18: 51–85.

———(1971a). New developments in psychoanalytic object-relations theory. Paper read to the American Psychoanalytic Association, Washington, D.C.

———(1971b). Prognostic considerations regarding borderline personality organization. *Journal of the American Psychoanalytic Association* 19: 595–635.

———(1972a). Early ego integration and object relations. *Annals of the New York Academy of Science* 193: 233–247.

———(1972b). Summary and conclusions. *Bulletin of the Menninger Clinic* 36(1/2): 181–195.

———(1975). *Borderline Conditions and Pathological Narcissism.* New York: Jason Aronson.

———(1977). The structural diagnosis of borderline personality organization. In *Borderline Personality Disorders: The Concept, the Syndrome, the Patient,* ed. P. Hartocollis, pp. 87–122. New York: International Universities Press.

Kessler, J. W. (1966). *Psychopathology of Childhood.* Englewood Cliffs, New Jersey: Prentice-Hall, pp. 421–438.

Klein, D. F. (1977). Psychopharmacological treatment and delineation of borderline disorders. In *Borderline Personality Disorders: The*

Concept, the Syndrome, the Patient, ed. P. Hartocollis, pp. 365–383. New York: International Universities Press.

Klein, M. (1935). A contribution to the psychogenesis of manic-depressive states. In *Love, Guilt and Reparation and Other Works, 1921–1945,* pp. 262–289. New York: Delacorte, 1975.

———(1940). Mourning and its relation to manic depressive states. In *Love, Guilt and Reparation and Other Works, 1921–1945,* pp. 344–369. New York: Delacorte, 1975.

———(1946). Notes on some schizoid mechanisms. In *Envy and Gratitude and Other Works, 1946–1963,* pp. 1–24. New York: Delacorte, 1975.

———(1955). On identification. In *Envy and Gratitude and Other Works, 1946–1963,* pp. 141–175. New York: Delacorte, 1975.

———(1963). *Our Adult World.* New York: Basic Books.

Klineberg, O. (1954). *Social Psychology.* Revised ed. New York: Henry Holt.

Knight, R. P. (1953). Borderline states. *Bulletin of the Menninger Clinic* 17(1): 1–12.

Koegler, R. R., and Colbert, E. G. (1959). Childhood schizophrenia: role of the family physician. *Journal of the American Medical Association* 171: 1045–1050.

Kohut, H. (1971). *The Analysis of the Self: A Systematic Approach to the Psychoanalytic Treatment of Narcissistic Personality Disorders.* New York: International Universities Press.

Kolvin, I. et al. (1971). Studies in childhood psychoses, I-VI. *British Journal of Psychiatry* 118: 381–419.

Kraepelin, E. (1921). *Manic-Depressive Insanity and Paranoia.* Ed. G. M. Robertson, trans. R. M. Barclay. Edinburgh: Livingstone, 1921.

Kumin, I. M. (1978). Emptiness and its relation to schizoid ego structure. *International Review of Psycho-Analysis* 5(2): 207–216.

L'Abate, L. (1976). *Understanding and Helping the Individual in the Family.* New York: Grune and Stratton.

Lasch, C. (1977). *Haven in a Heartless World: The Family Besieged.* New York: Basic Books.

———(1978). *The Culture of Narcissism: American Life in an Age of Diminishing Expectations.* New York: Norton.

Levy, D. M. (1952). Critical evaluation of the present state of child psychiatry. *American Journal of Psychiatry* 108: 481–494.

Lewis, J. M. (1970). The development of an inpatient adolescent service. *Adolescence* 5: 303–312.

Lidz, T., Fleck, S., and Cornelison, A. (1965). *Schizophrenia and the Family.* New York: International Universities Press.

Lidz, T. et al. (1968). Schism and skew in the families of schizophrenics. In *A Modern Introduction to the Family,* ed. N. W. Bell and E. F. Vogel, pp. 650–662. New York: Free Press.

Lindemann, E. (1964). Adolescent behavior as a community concern. *American Journal of Psychotherapy* 18: 405–417.

Linn, L. (1959). Hospital psychiatry. In *American Handbook of Psychiatry,* vol. 2, ed. S. Arieti. New York: Basic Books.

Litin, E. M., Griffin, M. E., and Johnson, A. M. (1956). Parental influence in unusual sexual behavior in children. *Psychoanalytic Quarterly* 25: 37–55.

Lorand, S. (1961). Treatment of adolescents. In *Adolescents: Psychoanalytic Approach to Problems and Therapy,* ed. S. Lorand and H. I. Schneer, pp. 238–250. New York: Hoeber.

Mahler, M. S. (1952). On child psychosis and schizophrenia: autistic and symbiotic infantile psychoses. *Psychoanalytic Study of the Child* 7: 286–305.

——(1953). Autism and symbiosis, two extreme disturbances in identity. *International Journal of Psycho-Analysis* 39: 77–83.

——(1963). Thoughts about development and individuation. *Psychoanalytic Study of the Child* 18: 307–324.

——(1965a). On early infantile psychosis: the symbiotic and autistic syndromes. *Journal of the American Academy of Child Psychiatry* 4: 544–568.

——(1965b). On the significance of the normal separation-individuation phase: with reference to research in symbiotic child psychosis. In *Drives, Affects, Behavior,* vol. 2, ed. M. Schur, pp. 161–169. New York: International Universities Press.

——(1967). On human symbiosis and the vicissitudes of individuation: an overview of human symbiosis and individuation. *Journal of the American Psychoanalytic Association* 15: 740–763.

——(1968). On human symbiosis and the vicissitudes of individuation. *Infantile Psychosis,* vol. 1, pp. 7–31. New York: International Universities Press.

——(1971). A study of the separation-individuation process and its possible application to borderline phenomena in the psychoanalytic situation. *Psychoanalytic Study of the Child* 26: 403–424.

——(1972). On the first three subphases of the separation-individuation process. *International Journal of Psycho-Analysis* 53: 333–338.

Mahler, M. S., and Furer, M. (1963). Certain aspects of the separation-individuation phase. *Psychoanalytic Quarterly* 32: 1–14.

Mahler, M. S., Furer, M., and Settlage, C. F. (1959). Severe emotional disturbances in childhood: psychosis. In *American Handbook of Psychiatry*, vol. I, ed. S. Arieti, pp. 816–839. New York: Basic Books.

Mahler, M. S., and Gosliner, B. J. (1955). On symbiotic child psychosis: genetic, dynamic, and restitutive aspects. *Psychoanalytic Study of the Child* 10: 195–212.

Mahler, M. S., and Kaplan, L. (1977). Developmental aspects in the assessment of narcissistic and so-called borderline personalities. In *Borderline Personality Disorders: The Concept, the Syndrome, the Patient*, ed. P. Hartocollis, pp. 71–85. New York: International Universities Press.

Mahler, M. S., and LaPerriere, K. (1965). Mother-child interaction during separation-individuation. *Psychoanalytic Quarterly* 34: 483–498.

Mahler, M. S., and McDevitt, J. B. (1968). Observations on adaptation and defence *in statu nascendi*: developmental precursors in the first two years of life. *Psychoanalytic Quarterly* 37: 1–21.

Mahler, M. S., Pine, F., and Bergman, A. (1970). The mother's reaction to her toddler's drive for individuation. In *Parenthood: Its Psychology and Psychopathology*, ed. E. J. Anthony and T. Benedek. Boston: Little, Brown.

————(1975). *The Psychological Birth of the Human Infant: Symbiosis and Individuation*. New York: Basic Books.

Mahler, M. S., and Rabinovitch, R. (1956). The effects of marital conflict on child development. In *Neurotic Interaction in Marriage*, ed. V. W. Eisenstein, pp. 44–56. New York: Basic Books.

Mahler, M. S., Ross, J. R., Jr., and DeFries, Z. (1949). Clinical studies in benign and malignant cases of childhood psychosis (schizophrenic-like). *American Journal of Orthopsychiatry* 19: 295–305.

Main, T. F. (1946). The hospital as a therapeutic institution. *Bulletin of the Menninger Clinic* 10: 66–70.

Mandelbaum, A. (1959). Selection and preparation for residential treatment: the work with parents. Paper read at the American Orthopsychiatric Association Workshop, San Francisco, April.

————(1977). The family treatment of the borderline patient. In *Borderline Personality Disorders: The Concept, the Syndrome, the Patient*, ed. P. Hartocollis, pp. 423–438. New York: International Universities Press.

Masterson, J. F. (1967a). *The Psychiatric Dilemma of Adolescence*. Boston: Little, Brown.

————(1967b). The symptomatic adolescent five years later: he didn't grow out of it. *American Journal of Psychiatry* 123: 1338–1345.

————(1968). The psychiatric significance of adolescent turmoil. *American Journal of Psychiatry* 124: 1549–1554.

————(1971a). Diagnosis and treatment of the borderline syndrome in adolescents. *Confrontations Psychiatriques* 7: 125–155.

————(1971b). Treatment of the adolescent with borderline syndrome: a problem in separation-individuation. *Bulletin of the Menninger Clinic* 35: 5–18.

————(1972a). Intensive psychotherapy of the adolescent with a borderline syndrome. Buenos Aires: *Cuadernos de la Asociacion Argentina de Psiquiatria y Psicologia de la Infancia y de la Adolescencia* 3: 15–50.

————(1972b). *Treatment of the Borderline Adolescent: A Developmental Approach.* New York: Wiley-Interscience.

————(1973). The borderline adolescent. In *Adolescent Psychiatry, Vol. 2: Developmental and Clinical Studies,* ed. S. C. Feinstein and P. L. Giovacchini, pp. 240–268. New York: Basic Books.

————(1974). Intensive psychotherapy of the adolescent with a borderline syndrome. In *American Handbook of Psychiatry,* vol. 2, 2nd ed., ed. S. Arieti, pp. 250–263. New York: Basic Books.

————(1975). The splitting mechanism of the borderline adolescent: developmental and clinical aspects. In *Borderline States in Psychiatry,* ed. J. E. Mack, pp. 93–101. New York: Grune and Stratton.

————(1976). *Psychotherapy of the Borderline Adult: A Developmental Approach.* New York: Brunner/Mazel.

Masterson, J. F., Tucker, K., and Berk, G. (1963). Psychopathology in adolescence. IV. Clinical and dynamic characteristics. *American Journal of Psychiatry* 120: 357–366.

————(1966). The symptomatic adolescent: delineation of psychiatric syndromes. *Comprehensive Psychiatry* 7: 166–174.

Masterson, J. F., and Washburne, A. (1966). The symptomatic adolescent: psychiatric illness or adolescent turmoil? *American Journal of Psychiatry* 122: 1240–1248.

Maxwell, A. (1950). The inter-related movement of parent and child in residential treatment. *Quarterly Journal of Child Behavior* 2: 185–193.

McCord, W., McCord, J., and Verden, P. (1962). Family relationships and sexual deviance in lower-class adolescents. *International Journal of Social Psychiatry* 8: 165–179.

Meissner, W. W. (1961). Some indications of the sources of anxiety in adolescent boys. *Journal of Genetic Psychology* 99: 65–73.

————(1965). Parental interaction of the adolescent boy. *Journal of Genetic Psychology* 107: 225–233.

Mendelson, M. (1960). *Psychoanalytic Concepts of Depression.* Springfield, Illinois: Thomas.

Menninger, K. A. (1958). *Theory of Psychoanalytic Technique.* New York: Basic Books.

Menninger, K. A., Mayman, M., and Pruyser, P. W. (1963). *The Vital Balance.* New York: Viking.

Menninger, W. C. (1936a). Individuation in the prescription of nursing care of the psychiatric patient. *Journal of the American Medical Association* 106: 756–761.

————(1936b). Psychiatric hospital treatment designed to meet unconscious needs. *American Journal of Psychiatry* 93: 347–360.

————(1937). Psychoanalytic principles applied to the treatment of hospitalized patients. *Bulletin of the Menninger Clinic* 1: 35–43.

————(1939). Psychoanalytic principles in psychiatric hospital therapy. *Southern Medical Journal* 32: 348–354.

Miller, D. H. (1957). The treatment of adolescents in an adult hospital. *Bulletin of the Menninger Clinic* 21: 189–198.

Misbach, L. (1948). Psychoanalysis and theories of learning. *Psychological Review* 55: 143–156.

Mishler, E., and Waxler, N. (1966). Family interaction processes and schizophrenia. *International Journal of Psychiatry* 2: 375–413.

————(1968). *Family Processes and Schizophrenia.* New York: Jason Aronson.

Money-Kyrle, R. E. (1966). Melanie Klein and Kleinian psychoanalytic theory. In *American Handbook of Psychiatry,* vol. 3, ed. S. Arieti, pp. 225–229. New York: Basic Books.

Morrow, J. T., et al. (1972). The educational component of residential treatment centers. In *From Chaos to Order: A Collective View of the Residential Treatment of Children,* pp. 46–83. New York: Child Welfare League of America.

Mowrer, O. H. (1963a). *The New Group Therapy.* Princeton: Van Nostrand.

————(1963b). Payment or repayment? The problem of private practice. *American Psychologist* 18: 577–580.

Nelson, M. C., ed. (1977). *The Narcissistic Condition: A Fact of Our Lives and Times.* New York: Human Sciences Press.

Noshpitz, J. D. (1962). Notes on the theory of residential treatment. *Journal of the American Academy of Child Psychiatry* 1: 284–296.

Offer, D. (1967). Normal adolescents: interview strategy and selected results. *Archives of General Psychiatry* 17: 285–290.

Offer, D., Sabshin, M., and Marcus, D. (1965). Clinical evaluation of normal adolescents. *American Journal of Psychiatry* 121: 864–872.

Ornstein, P. H. (1974). On narcissism: beyond the introduction, highlights of Heinz Kohut's contributions to the psychoanalytic treatment of narcissistic personality disorders. *Annual of Psychoanalysis* 2: 127–149.

Parens, H., and Saul, L. J. (1971). *Dependency in Man: A Psychoanalytic Study.* New York: International Universities Press.

Paulsen, A. A. (1957). School phobia workshop, 1955. *American Journal of Orthopsychiatry* 27: 286–309.

Pearson, G. H. J. (1954). *Psychoanalysis and the Education of the Child.* New York: Norton.

Peck, H. B., Rabinovitch, R. D., and Cramer, J. B. (1949). A treatment for parents of schizophrenic children. *American Journal of Orthopsychiatry* 19: 592–598.

Piaget, J. (1954). *The Construction of Reality in the Child.* New York: Basic Books.

———(1957). *Logic and Psychology.* New York: Basic Books.

Potter, H. W. (1934a). A service for children in a psychiatric hospital. *Psychiatric Quarterly* 8(1): 16–33.

———(1934b). The treatment of problem children in a psychiatric hospital. *American Journal of Psychiatry* 91(4): 869–880.

Pruyser, P. W. (1977). The seamy side of current religious beliefs. *Bulletin of the Menninger Clinic* 41(4): 329–348.

Rado, S. (1928). The problem of melancholia. *International Journal of Psycho-Analysis* 9: 420–438.

———(1956). *Psychoanalysis of Behavior: Collected Papers,* vol. 1. New York: Grune and Stratton.

———(1962). *Psychoanalysis of Behavior: Collected Papers,* vol. 2. New York: Grune and Stratton.

Rank, B. (1949). Adaptation of the psychoanalytic technique for the treatment of young children with atypical development. *American Journal of Orthopsychiatry* 19: 130–139.

———(1955). Intensive study and treatment of pre-school children who show marked personality deviations or "atypical development" and their parents. In *Emotional Problems of Early Childhood,* ed. G. Caplan, pp. 491–501. New York: Basic Books.

Redl, F., and Wineman, D. (1951). *Children Who Hate*. Glencoe, Illinois: Free Press.

————(1952). *Controls from Within*. Glencoe, Illinois: Free Press.

Reid, J. H., and Hagan, H. R. (1952). *Residential Treatment of Emotionally Disturbed Children*. New York: Child Welfare League of America.

Reiser, D. E. (1963). Psychosis of infancy and early childhood, as manifested by children with atypical development. *New England Journal of Medicine* 259: 790–798, 844–850.

Rheingold, J. C. (1964). *The Fear of Being a Woman: A Theory of Maternal Destructiveness*. New York: Grune and Stratton.

Ribble, M. A. (1943). *The Rights of Infants*. New York: Columbia University Press.

Rimland, B. (1964). *Infantile Autism*. New York: Appleton-Century-Crofts.

Rinsley, D. B. (1962a). Basic fears a child brings to the classroom. *Kansas Teacher* 70: 21–23.

————(1962b). A contribution to the theory of ego and self. *Psychiatric Quarterly* 36: 96–120.

————(1963). Thioridazine in the treatment of hospitalized adolescents. *American Journal of Psychiatry* 120: 73–74.

————(1968a). Economic aspects of object relations. *International Journal of Psycho-Analysis* 49: 38–48.

————(1968b). Extended experience with thioridazine in the treatment of hospitalized adolescents. *Diseases of the Nervous System* 29: 36–37.

————(1971a). The adolescent inpatient: patterns of depersonification. *Psychiatric Quarterly* 45(1): 3–22.

————(1971b). Theory and practice of intensive residential treatment of adolescents (revised). In *Adolescent Psychiatry,* vol. 1: *Developmental and Clinical Studies,* ed. S. C. Feinstein, P. Giovacchini, and A. A. Miller. New York: Basic Books.

————(1972). Group psychotherapy within the wider residential context. In *Adolescents Grow in Groups: Experiences in Adolescent Group Psychotherapy,* ed. I. H. Berkovitz, pp. 233–242, New York: Brunner/Mazel.

————(1974). Residential treatment of adolescents. In *American Handbook of Psychiatry,* vol. 2, 2nd ed., ed. S. Arieti, pp. 353–366. New York: Basic Books.

————(1977). An object-relations view of borderline personality. In *Borderline Personality Disorders: The Concept, the Syndrome, the*

Patient, ed. P. Hartocollis, pp. 47–70. New York: International Universities Press.

———(1978a). Borderline psychopathology: a review of aetiology, dynamics and treatment. *International Review of Psychoanalysis* 5(1): 45–54.

———(1978b). Juvenile delinquency: a review of the past and a look at the future. *Bulletin of the Menninger Clinic* 42(3): 252–260.

———(1979). Fairbairn's object-relations theory: a reconsideration in terms of newer knowledge. *Bulletin of the Menninger Clinic* 43(6): 489–514.

———(1980). Principles of therapeutic milieu with children. In *Emotional Disorders in Children and Adolescents: Medical and Psychological Approaches to Treatment,* ed. G. P. Sholevar et al. New York: SP Medical and Scientific Books.

Robinson, J. F., et al. (1957). *Psychiatric Inpatient Treatment of Children.* Washington, D.C.: American Psychiatric Association.

Rodnick, E. H., and Goldstein, M. J. (1974). A research strategy for studying risk for schizophrenia during adolescence and early childhood. In *Children at Psychiatric Risk,* ed. E. J. Anthony and C. Koupernik, pp. 507–526. New York: Wiley.

Roy, R. S. (1967). The changing adolescent. In *Adolescence: Care and Counseling,* ed. G. L. Usdin, pp. 16–30. Philadelphia: Lippincott.

Ruesch, J. (1957). *Disturbed Communication.* New York: Norton.

Ruesch, J., and Bateson, B. (1951). *Communication, the Social Matrix of Psychiatry.* New York: Norton.

Ryan, J. H. (1962). The therapeutic value of the closed ward. *Journal of Nervous and Mental Diseases* 134: 256–262.

Sarason, S. B., Davidson, K., and Blatt, B. (1962). *The Preparation of Teachers: An Unstudied Problem in Education.* New York: Wiley.

Scheerer, M., Rothman, E., and Goldstein, K. (1958). A case of idiot savant: an experimental study of personality organization. *Psychological Monographs,* no. 57, pp. 3–290.

Schmideberg, M. (1948). Parents as children. *Psychiatric Quarterly Supplement,* part 2, 22: 207–218.

Schmiedeck, R. A. (1961). A treatment program for adolescents on an adult ward. *Bulletin of the Menninger Clinic* 25: 241–248.

Schugart, G. (1957). Casework with parents of psychotic children. *Social Casework* 38: 8–15.

Schwartz, G., and Merten, D. (1967). The language of adolescence: an anthropological approach to the youth culture. *American Journal of Sociology* 72: 453–468.

Schwartz, M. S. (1957). What is a therapeutic milieu? In *The Patient and the Mental Hospital,* ed. M. Greenblatt, D. J. Levinson, and R. H. Williams, pp. 130-144. Glencoe, Illinois: Free Press.

Shapiro, E. R. et al. (1975). The influence of family experience on borderline personality development. *International Review of Psychoanalysis* 2(4): 399-411.

Simmel, E. (1929). Psycho-analytic treatment in a sanitarium. *International Journal of Psycho-Analysis* 10: 70-89.

Singer, M. T., and Wynne, L. C. (1965a). Thought disorder and family relations of schizophrenics, III: Methodology using projective techniques. *Archives of General Psychiatry* 12(2): 186-200.

———(1965b). Thought disorder and family relations of schizophrenics, IV: Results and implications. *Archives of General Psychiatry* 12(2): 201-212.

Sperling, M. (1950). Children's interpretation and reaction to the unconscious of their mothers. *International Journal of Psycho-Analysis* 31: 1-6.

———(1952). Psychotherapeutic techniques in psychosomatic medicine. In *Specialized Techniques in Psychotherapy,* ed. G. Bychowski and J. Despert, pp. 279-301. New York: Basic Books.

———(1955). On appersonation. *International Journal of Psycho-Analysis* 25: 128-132.

———(1967). School phobias: classification, dynamics, and treatment. *Psychoanalytic Study of the Child* 22: 375-401.

———(1970). The clinical effects of parental neurosis on the child. In *Parenthood: Its Psychology and Psychopathology,* ed. E. J. Anthony and T. Benedek, pp. 539-569. Boston: Little, Brown.

Spiegel, L. A. (1951). A review of contributions to a psychoanalytic theory of adolescence. *Psychoanalytic Study of the Child* 6: 375-393.

Spiegel, R. (1959). Specific problems of communication in psychiatric conditions. In *American Handbook of Psychiatry,* vol. 1, ed. S. Arieti, pp. 909-949. New York: Basic Books.

Spitz, R. A. (1945). Hospitalism: an inquiry into the genesis of psychiatric conditions of early childhood. *Psychoanalytic Study of the Child* 1: 53-74.

———(1946). Hospitalism: a follow-up report. *Psychoanalytic Study of the Child* 2: 113-117.

———(1955). The primal cavity: a contribution to the genesis of perception and its role for psychoanalytic theory. *Psychoanalytic Study of the Child* 10: 215-240.

————(1957). *No and Yes: On the Genesis of Human Communication.* New York: International Universities Press.

————(1959). *A Genetic Field Theory of Ego Formation.* New York: International Universities Press.

————(1971). *The First Year of Life: A Psychoanalytic Study of Normal and Deviant Development of Object Relations.* New York: International Universities Press.

Spitz, R. A., and Wolf, K. M. (1946). Anaclitic depression: an inquiry into the genesis of psychiatric conditions of early childhood. II. *Psychoanalytic Study of the Child* 2: 313–342.

Stanton, A., and Schwartz, M. S. (1954). *The Mental Hospital.* New York: Basic Books.

Stragnell, G. (1922). Psychopathological disturbances from the avoidance of parental responsibility. *New York Medical Journal and Medical Records,* September 6.

Szasz, T. S. (1961). *The Myth of Mental Illness.* New York: Hoeber-Harper.

————(1965). *The Ethics of Psychoanalysis: The Theory and Method of Autonomous Psychotherapy.* New York: Basic Books.

Szurek, S. A. et al., eds. (1971). *Inpatient Care for the Psychotic Child* (Langley Porter Child Psychiatry Series, vol. 5). Palo Alto: Science and Behavior Books.

Terr, L. C. (1970). A family study of child abuse. *American Journal of Psychiatry* 127: 665–671.

Toolan, J. M., and Nicklin, G. (1959). Open door policy on an adolescent service in a psychiatric hospital. *American Journal of Psychiatry* 115: 790–792.

Toussieng, P. W. (1969). Teachers and differences. *American Journal of Orthopsychiatry* 39: 730–734.

Voth, H. M. (1974). *The Castrated Family.* Kansas City, Kan.: Sheed, Andrews and McMeel.

Wardle, C. J. (1974). Residential care of children with conduct disorders. In *The Residential Psychiatric Treatment of Children,* ed. P. A. Barker, pp. 48–104. New York: Wiley.

Warren, W. (1952). Inpatient treatment of adolescents with psychological illness. *Lancet* 262: 147–150.

Weil, A. P. (1953a). Certain severe disturbances of ego development in childhood. *Psychoanalytic Study of the Child* 8: 271–287.

————(1953b). Clinical data and dynamic considerations in certain cases of childhood schizophrenia. *American Journal of Orthopsychiatry* 23: 518–529.

————(1970). The basic core. *Psychoanalytic Study of the Child* 25: 442–460.

Weiner, I. B. (1971). The generation gap: fact and fancy. *Adolescence* 6: 155–166.

Werner, H. (1948). *Comparative Psychology of Mental Development.* New York: Follett Science Editions.

Werry, J. S., ed. (1978). *Pediatric Psychopharmacology: The Use of Behavior Modifying Drugs in Children.* New York: Brunner/Mazel.

White, J. H. (1977). *Pediatric Psychopharmacology: A Practical Guide to Clinical Application.* Baltimore: Williams and Wilkins.

Winnicott, D. W. (1949). Mind and its relation to the psychesoma. In *Collected Papers: Through Paediatrics to Psycho-Analysis,* pp. 243–254. New York: Basic Books, 1958.

————(1951). Transitional objects and transitional phenomena. In *Collected Papers: Through Paediatrics to Psycho-Analysis,* pp. 229–242. New York: Basic Books, 1958.

————(1960). Ego distortion in terms of true and false self. In *The Maturational Processes and the Facilitating Environment: Studies in the Theory of Emotional Development,* pp. 140–152. New York: International Universities Press, 1965.

Woodward, K. L., and Mark, R. (1978). The new narcissism. *Newsweek Magazine,* January 30, pp. 70–72.

Wynne, L. C. (1961). The study of intrafamilial alignments and splits in exploratory family therapy. In *Exploring the Base of Family Therapy,* ed. N. W. Ackerman et al., pp. 95–115. New York: Family Service Association of America.

————(1972). Communication disorders and the quest for relatedness in the families of schizophrenics. In *Progress in Group and Family Therapy,* ed. C. J. Sager and H. S. Kaplan, pp. 595–615. New York: Brunner/Mazel.

Wynne, L. C., and Singer, M. T. (1963a). Thought disorder and family relations of schizophrenics, I: Research strategy. *Archives of General Psychiatry* 9(3): 191–198.

————(1963b). Thought disorder and family relations of schizophrenics, II: A classification of forms of thinking. *Archives of General Psychiatry* 9(3): 199–206.

Zentner, E. B., and Aponte, H. (1970). The amorphous family nexus: a basis for diagnosis. *Psychiatric Quarterly* 44: 91–113.

Zilboorg, G., and Henry, G. W. (1941). *A History of Medical Psychology.* New York: Norton.

Source Notes

Chapter 1 originally appeared in the *Bulletin of the Menninger Clinic* 25(1961): 249–263. Reprinted by permission.

Chapter 2 originally appeared in the *Archives of General Psychiatry* 7(1962): 286–294. Copyright © 1962, the American Medical Association. Reprinted by permission.

Chapter 3 was first presented at the 119th Annual Meeting of the American Psychiatric Association, St. Louis, May 1963, and is reprinted by permission from the *Archives of General Psychiatry* 9(1963): 489–496. Copyright © 1963, American Medical Association.

Chapter 4 originally appeared in *Adolescence* 2(1967): 83–95. Reprinted by permission.

Chapter 5 originally appeared in *Psychiatric Quarterly* 39(1965): 405–429. Reprinted by permission.

Chapter 6 originally appeared in *Psychiatric Quarterly* 41(1967): 134–143. Reprinted by permission. It was presented at the workshop on adolescent psychiatry at the twentieth anniversary meeting of the Menninger Foundation, April 2, 1966.

Chapter 7 originally appeared in *Psychiatric Quarterly* 42(1968): 611–638. Reprinted by permission. Slightly revised from a lecture delivered at the Institute of the Pennsylvania Hospital, October 14, 1968, and published as a monograph by Roche Laboratories.

Chapter 8 first appeared, under the title "Special Education for Adolescents in Residential Psychiatric Treatment," in *Adolescent Psychiatry,* Volume 3: *Developmental and Clinical Studies,* edited by Sherman C. Feinstein and Peter C. Giovacchini, copyright © 1974 by American Society for Adolescent Psychiatry, Basic Books, Inc., Publishers, New York. Reprinted by permission. It was presented at the Symposium on Educating the Emotionally Disturbed, cosponsored by the Topeka State Hospital, Menninger Foundation, and the University of Kansas at Topeka, February 20, 1970.

Chapter 9 first appeared, under the title "Residential Treatment of Adolescents," in *American Handbook of Psychiatry,* second edition, Volume 3: *Child and Adolescent Psychiatry, Sociocultural and Community Psychiatry,* Silvano Arieti, Editor-in-Chief, Gerald Caplan, Editor, copyright © 1974 by Basic Books, Inc., Publishers, New York. Reprinted by permission.

Chapter 10 originally appeared in *Psychiatric Quarterly* 45(1971): 3–22. Reprinted by permission.

Chapter 11 originally appeared in *Psychiatric Quarterly* 46(1972): 159–186. Reprinted by permission.

Chapter 12 originally appeared in the *International Journal of Psycho-Analysis* 56(1975): 163–177. Reprinted by permission.

Chapter 13 appears here for the first time.

Chapter 14 originally appeared in the *Bulletin of the Menninger Clinic* 44(1980): 127–134. Reprinted by permission. A shortened version of a paper presented at the Workshop on Borderline and Narcissistic Disorders co-sponsored by the Menninger Foundation and Smith, Kline and French Laboratories, Vail, Colorado, May, 1979.

Chapter 15 originally appeared in the *Bulletin of the Menninger Clinic* 44(1980): 147–170. Reprinted by permission. Presented at the Workshop on Borderline and Narcissistic Disorders co-sponsored by the Menninger Foundation and Smith, Kline and French Laboratories, Vail, Colorado, May, 1979.

Index

superego introject, 109, 129n.
symbiotic adolescents, 143–144, 162–165
symbiotic phase, 287–288
symbiotic psychosis, 95, 101
of adolescence, 228–230
symbiotic syndromes, 230–236
symptomatic remission, 55–56
Szasz, T., 41, 47, 56, 107
Szurek, S. A., 5, 20n., 60, 166, 193, 199, 304, 312

teacher
countertransference responses of, 158
residential, 145, 153, 157–159
transference to, 138–139, 158
Terr, L. C., 190
tests
and grades, 155–156
for newly admitted adolescent inpatient, 152
Thematic Apperception Test, 152
therapeutic alliance, 258, 259
therapy, group and family, 177–178
thought disorder syndrome, 231
Toussieng, P. W., 141, 159n.
transference
of adolescents, 59–60
avoidance of, 51n.
borderline, 257–258
to classmates, 139
erotic, 26
in hospital milieu, 68
parental, 70
to teacher, 138–139
to treatment figures, 106–109
transference cures, 103
transference splitting, 13–15, 95,
110, 116, 169
treatability of adolescent, 71–74
treatment
basic goals of, 174–176
definitive phase of, 24, 50, 97–98, 121–127, 172–173
resistance phase of, 23–24, 50, 94–97, 114–121, 168–172
resolution phase of, 173–174
treatment milieus
"open type," 51n.
therapeutic and otherwise, 44
vegetable soup, 49–50, 91n.
Tucker, K., 231
Tuke, W., 67
"turmoil school" of adolescence, 213–218

unseparated personalities, 230

vanderSchraaf, A. H., 310
Verden, P., 199
Voth, H. M., 296

Waggoner, R. W., 177
Wardle, C. J., 311
Washburne, A., 217, 230
Waxler, N., 130n., 166, 211n.
weak ego, 104–110
Wechsler Intelligence Scale for Children, 143, 152, 162, 163
Wechsler Similarities Subtest, 238n.
Weil, A. P., 211n., 244
Weiner, I. B., 141, 143, 163
Werble, B., 310
Werner, H., 135
Werry, J. S., 316
Westley, W. A., 217
White, J. H., 316
Wide Range Achievement Test, 152

Treatment of the

SEVERELY

DISTURBED

Adolescent

Donald B. Rinsley, M. D.

Treatment of the Severely Disturbed Adolescent presents a point of view that breathes new hope for correcting the psychopathology of developmental failure and for achieving separation-individuation through intensive psychotherapy.

Eminently qualified to write about adolescent patients, Donald Rinsley brings clarity of thought and extensive theoretical and clinical experience to the task. The volume gains in thoroughness and usefulness by his presenting a psychoanalytic object-relations understanding not only of troubled adolescents, but of their families and treatment as well.

His discussion of disturbed adolescents and their families reveals clearly the vital contributions that good early object relations make to normal ego development. The longitudinal defects in object relations that typify these adolescents, their failure to resolve infantile object-dependency through normal separation-individuation, and their consequent inability to achieve autonomy of the self become the foci for an intensive and carefully articulated program directed at treatment of structural ego defects and functional ego regression.

This volume presents clear evidence that the adolescent borderline patient has a full capacity for internalization once what James Masterson calls abandonment depression has been worked through. Rinsley explains how the borderline adolescent deals with whole-objects as if they were part-objects, and then shows how the

(continued on back flap)